ALL ROADS LEAD
TO POWER

STUDIES IN GOVERNMENT
AND PUBLIC POLICY

ALL ROADS LEAD TO POWER

Appointed and Elected Paths to Public Office for US Women

Kaitlin N. Sidorsky

University Press of Kansas

Published by the University Press of Kansas (Lawrence, Kansas 66045), which was organized by the Kansas Board of Regents and is operated and funded by Emporia State University, Fort Hays State University, Kansas State University, Pittsburg State University, the University of Kansas, and Wichita State University.

Library of Congress Cataloging-in-Publication Data

Names: Sidorsky, Kaitlin N., author.
Title: All roads lead to power : the appointed and elected paths to public office for US women / Kaitlin N. Sidorsky.
Description: Lawrence : University Press of Kansas, 2019. | Series: Studies in government and public policy | Includes bibliographical references and index.
Identifiers: LCCN 2018059048
  ISBN 9780700627868 (cloth)
  ISBN 9780700636143 (paperback)
  ISBN 9780700627875 (ebook)
Subjects: LCSH: Women—Political activity—United States—States. | Women public officers—United States—States. | Women political candidates—United States—States. | BISAC: SOCIAL SCIENCE / Women's Studies. | POLITICAL SCIENCE / Government / National. | POLITICAL SCIENCE / Government / State & Provincial.
Classification: LCC HQ1236.5.U6 S556 2019 | DDC 320.082/0973—dc23 LC record available at https://lccn.loc.gov/2018059048.

British Library Cataloguing-in-Publication Data is available.

Printed in the United States of America

10 9 8 7 6 5 4 3 2 1

The paper used in this publication is acid free and meets the minimum requirements of the American National Standard for Permanence of Paper for Printed Library Materials Z39.48-1992.

CONTENTS

TABLES

FIGURES

PREFACE

In October of 2012, in the midst of my prospectus year in my graduate program, I knew that I wanted to write a dissertation in the field of women and politics. I was particularly intrigued by the work on women's recruitment and ambition but was not quite sure which direction my project would take. It was a presidential election year, and like many people, I was closely watching the race between President Barack Obama and former Massachusetts governor Mitt Romney. Little did I know that during the second debate on October 16, not far from my hometown on Long Island, Romney would say something that would become the inspiration for my dissertation and this book. Moderator Candy Crowley asked both Obama and Romney, "In what new ways do you intend to rectify the inequalities in the workplace, specifically regarding females making only 72 percent of what their male counterparts earn?" Obama, who answered first, would speak of the Lily Ledbetter Fair Pay Act, the first piece of legislation he signed into law as president of the United States. Romney started off by saying how important this issue was and how he personally dealt with this issue as governor of Massachusetts. As he was filling his cabinet, he noticed that all of the applicants were men. He questioned his staff, who said that these were all the people who had the qualifications necessary to fill the cabinet positions. This was not a satisfactory answer for Romney, so "we took concerted effort to go out and find women who had backgrounds that could be qualified to become members of our cabinet. I went to a number of women's groups and said: 'Can you help us find folks?' and they brought us whole binders full of women" (Commission on Presidential Debates 2012).

The initial reaction of many (and the later reaction of late-night hosts) was to laugh at the idea of binders full of women. And although I, too, found the phrase humorous, I was also intrigued. Here was a former state executive speaking about women in appointments. He was speaking about the inequalities in the appointment world in the same way we hear about inequalities in elected office. Yet, when I found that 35.1 percent of state-level appointments were filled by women—a number far higher than the numbers of women in any level of elected office—I was confused. Although far from parity, these were some of the highest numbers of women serving in any level of US government. Who were these women? How did they reach their positions? Were they ambitious for any further public offices? I knew I had found my project.

This book would never have been possible without the participation of appointed and elected officials across the United States. For some it was a quick fifteen-minute survey; for others it was more than two hours in a phone interview. Each one of them inspired and motivated me to tell his or her story, which revealed important contributions to the political process. Most people will never know that the medical professional they seek, the waterways they visit and use, and the utilities they pay are regulated by appointed officials who dedicate their time, energy, and expertise—often without compensation—to make their profession and the lives of their kindred citizens better and safer. I am honored to be able to share their contributions with the hope that other scholars will study these less visible public servants in future research. I thank the appointed and elected officials for their service and their participation in this project.

I am lucky that I still love the topics covered in this book as much as I did when I was first formulating the idea for this project in graduate school. Like all books, this project did not become the book in your hands in a vacuum. I had an incredible amount of support from mentors, colleagues, friends, and family. First, I would like to thank Wendy Schiller, my dissertation advisor, mentor, coauthor, and friend, who has helped make me the scholar I am today. Her support, wonderful feedback, and mentorship can never be appreciated enough. She is the scholar I strive to be every day. I would also like to thank the other two members of my dissertation committee, Susan Moffitt and James Morone, who provided excellent feedback and support when I completed the bulk of the work in this book as my dissertation. They always pushed me to think bigger and to see my project on the bookshelf of my field. For their dedication to my project from the beginning, they cannot be thanked enough.

I had wonderful friends and colleagues in graduate school and beyond who not only provided feedback on my work but also were there to provide their support. Thank you to Matthew Hodgetts, Aaron Weinstein, Colin Johnson, and Kelly Smith. I have had a wonderful experience working with the University Press of Kansas—from my editor, David Congdon, who was just as interested and invested in my project as I was, to the reviewers who provided insightful and encouraging feedback to strengthen the manuscript. I would also like to thank Kelly Chrisman Jacques for guiding me through the editing process of this book as well as Melanie Stafford for her thoughtful copyediting.

I must also thank my family. I am blessed to have parents who not only believed I could be whatever I wanted to be but also supported me in whatever way they possibly could to make my dreams a reality. From a young age, I was a person who always had questions; not once did my parents turn down an opportunity to answer them. Cathy and Gary Sidorsky had the patience to answer thousands of questions—patience I think led directly to my career and this project. Thank you, Mom and Dad, for your love and support. Finally, I want to thank my husband, Ryan Williams. Ryan has read and edited every word I have written related to this project. He has listened when I tried to explain to him what I was trying to argue and has always believed in my work. You make me a better scholar and a better person, Ryan—I love the life we have built together. This book is dedicated to you.

1. Reconceptualizing Women and Public Service

> I thought about the family that finally got a shot at their lifelong dream to launch a new restaurant—and it went belly-up. The young and very tired woman who described how she finally managed to leave her abusive ex-husband, but now she was alone with a pack of small children and a pile of bills. The elderly couple who had cashed out everything they owned and then went into debt to bail out their son and put him through rehab again and again. Two days later, I called Mike and said yes.
> —*Elizabeth Warren*

Although Elizabeth Warren is best known as a US senator from Massachusetts, her first foray into politics was not through elected office but through political appointment. Despite the fact that she was highly accomplished as a full professor at Harvard and one of the leading experts on bankruptcy and the law, by 1995 the extent of her political involvement was voting. Unbeknownst to Warren, her political life was about to change. Congress passed the Bankruptcy Reform Act of 1994, which included the creation of the National Bankruptcy Review Commission (NBRC) to do four things: study bankruptcy law, get the opinions of those involved with the bankruptcy system, "evaluate the advisability of proposals with respect to such issues, and prepare a report to be submitted to the President, Congress, and the Chief Justice" by 1997 (National Bankruptcy Review Commission 1997). Former Oklahoma congressman Mike Synar was appointed by President Bill Clinton to chair the commission. He was a classmate of Warren's in high school, and in 1995 he invited Warren to become a part of the commission. She said no. "I was deep in my research, and I thought the way I could make a difference was by writing books and doing more research about who was filing for bankruptcy and what had gone wrong in their lives. I didn't know anything about Washington, but the bits I picked up from the press made it sound pretty awful" (Warren 2014, 49). Synar was able to convince Warren to meet him for lunch to discuss it before she made her final decision.

At the end of that meeting, he told her to "think about the families the new commission would affect, the people who file for bankruptcy every year. Here's an opportunity for you to make a real difference" (Warren 2014, 49).

As the epigraph above shows, Synar's plea worked. Warren joined the commission, stayed on the commission when Synar died of cancer the following year, and helped to write a report that would protect the families who had filed for bankruptcy. Unfortunately, the experience was challenging—it became clear that the banks had the power, especially when they drafted their own version of a reform bill that would make it much harder for families to get bankruptcy relief. Despite Warren's disgust with politics, her passion to protect families stuck with her from that initial meeting with Synar. This passion made her more outspoken on the issue and got her a meeting with Senator Ted Kennedy, where she effectively argued against the bank-backed bankruptcy reform bill. Warren secured not only his support but his willingness to lead the fight against the bill in the Senate. Despite the support of Kennedy and numerous other senators and organizations, the bank-backed bill passed a few years later and would be a reminder to Warren how high the stakes are in the political arena.

Warren's story is illustrative of those of thousands of women across the United States who publicly serve via appointment, many of whom will never be on a ballot, and like Warren after her service on the NBRC are "sick of politics" (Warren 2014, 53). Similarly, most of these women get to their appointments through professional expertise or personal interest just as Warren did. They accept these appointments to help others, help their families, and make a difference. Most importantly, these women pursue these appointments for an ambition unrelated to the political career ladder—yet an important ambition all the same. This ambition is both personal and professional, but to many of these appointees it is absolutely not political.

In some ways, Warren's story is different from those of the women in this book because she decided to take the plunge and run for office. The women holding state-level appointments are more like Elaine Chao, a career bureaucrat who has never put her name on a ballot. Chao's resume is long and spans both the private and public sectors—and most importantly, began before her marriage to Senator Mitch McConnell (R-KY).

After a few years in the banking industry, Chao felt she needed a change and became a White House fellow in 1983. She then served under Presidents Ronald Reagan and George H. W. Bush on the Federal Maritime Commission, became the US deputy secretary of the US Department of Transportation in 1989, and was appointed director of the Peace Corps in 1991. Chao moved back to the private sector as president of the United Way during the Clinton administration and married Senator McConnell in 1993. Starting in 2001, Chao led the Department of Labor for the entirety of President George W. Bush's two terms in office (US Department of Transportation 2017). Most recently she added another position to her resume—secretary of transportation. When asked why she decided to return to public service, Chao said:

> Well, number one I'm an immigrant of this country and I have tremendous gratitude to this country for the opportunities that it has given to my parents and to me. We've always believed in public service— my parents have been great philanthropists who've always believed in giving back. So when this opportunity arose and I had the chance to contribute back to society and to America it was a decision that I did not want to look back on with regret. I feel that my experience can really help the president. (China Global Television Network America 2017)

Chao's reasons for becoming a public servant echo both Warren and the women studied in this book. Both exhibit a unique kind of ambition: a political ambition centered on personal and professional reasons for going into politics. This ambition leads them down a path to power almost completely overlooked by political science scholars: political appointment. Although Chao is unique in that she is married to the Senate majority leader at the time of this writing, her start in politics came before this marriage and was similar to how many women enter politics through appointments.

This book conceptualizes what it means to study political ambition and political participation. Through surveys and interviews of women and men in appointed state-level executive branch positions, I find evidence that women are participating in politics much more than scholars have acknowledged. These women are serving on advisory and policy-making commissions and have made it into the top tier of state political appointments. Most importantly, these women believe they are taking part in politics *without being political* because to many of them, politics is partisan, nasty, and an arena in which things do not get done. For these women, however, appointed positions are less divisive and speak to issues and professions that directly affect their lives. So why have women and politics scholars failed to study these women?

I argue in this book that women in appointments—particularly low-level appointments—are overlooked because scholars have used a specific definition of politics nearly *exclusively based upon electoral and party politics.* Elected officials and those most likely to become elected officials have been extensively surveyed about their backgrounds, recruitment, and ambitions for elected office—but elected office only. They are not asked about recruitment or ambition for appointed office, and they are often not asked about any appointed positions they have held. Yet appointed officials do incredibly important work, and in these appointments the highest number of women in politics can be found across the country (Figure 1.1). In 2007, women made up more than 35 percent of the top political appointments across the fifty states (Center for Women in Government and Civil Society 2008), giving them considerable access to and influence over the policies governors' administrations pursue and the regulations necessary for implementing laws. About 10–15 percent more women serve in appointed positions than in state legislatures or in Congress.

Political scientists have ignored studying political appointments as part of the pipeline to public service for other reasons as well. First, data on these individuals are scarce. Only a handful of surveys have targeted appointed officials, some of which are outdated or combine appointee and civil servant responses (Center for American Women in Politics 1983; Kelly et al. 1991; Swinerton 1968). Second, states and especially local governments do a poor job of tracking these appointments. In some states it is simply difficult to find all of the boards and commissions, and in states where the boards and commissions are more identifiable, the actual officeholders (and their contact information) can be challenging to locate. Finally, political scientists have neglected to study these appointments because it is not always clear what they actually contribute to the political process. It is easy to overlook advisory boards in lieu of state legislatures because it is obvious that state legislatures exist to create and pass laws. Although advisory boards might not have statutory author-

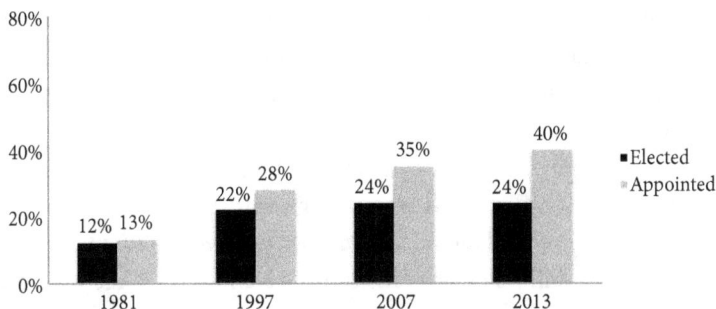

Figure 1.1 Female Representation in State Appointed and Elected Office Over Time

Source: Elected data from the Center for American Women and Politics, Rutgers University. Appointed data from the Center for Women in Government and Civil Society, State University of New York, Albany.

ity, they do have influence over lawmakers, and more importantly they signal to constituents issues state-level elected officials feel compelled to influence. In short, the existence of advisory boards, and the more powerful regulatory boards, tells citizens what is important to the state, from standards in professional licensing to expertise on health issues and diseases.

Although this book focuses exclusively on executive branch appointments and state legislative seats, it is important to note that both elected and appointed positions exist in the judicial branch at the state level. I do not focus on the judiciary for several reasons. The first reason concerns data. Compiling data on appointed positions across twenty states in four departments is challenging, and for practical reasons, I limited this research to executive branch positions. However, more substantively important is the unique nature of elected and appointed judgeships at the state level. Although it is an understudied area, the pathway to becoming a judge is insular: judges who want to progress up the judicial hierarchy usually set their sights on a federal appointment, which is beyond the scope of this book. If we want to understand ambition to become a judge, we study lawyers, who are not officeholders (Jensen and Martinek 2009; Williams 2008).[1] Finally, there is substantial overlap, as I will show in

1. Both the Jensen and Martinek (2009) and Williams (2008) studies found that lawyers who were women had more ambition to become judges than similarly situated men.

the subsequent chapters, between those serving in appointed and elected positions that does not extend to the judicial branch. Excluding judges provides for a more focused analysis of the pathways to power for individuals in state government.

Throughout this book, I will answer three questions that expand our understanding of women's interactions with the political world. First, *what kinds of individuals hold political appointments at all levels of state government?* Although several studies have looked at the backgrounds of state appointees, almost all of them focus on high-level appointees: department secretaries, undersecretaries, and commissioners. This is not representative because most appointees serve on the hundreds of low-level boards and commissions in each state. It is important to study these people and their political backgrounds to understand this arena of policy making, which is all but completely ignored.

Second, this book will examine *why these appointees seek out and/ or accept their appointments.* This requires understanding not only the external forces of recruitment in getting these appointees into their positions but also their internal motivations for wanting to serve in a department or on a board or commission. It is crucial that we answer this question because it can explain why many of the same women who have insisted they would never run for elected office have an ambition to serve via political appointment. These women are highly educated (more than 60 percent have a postgraduate degree) and have many of the connections necessary to run for elected office but adamantly refuse to do so. What is different about the politics of appointments versus the politics of elected office that makes this decision so clear for many of these women?

Finally, I will try to illustrate *what kind of ambition women in state political appointments exhibit.* Do they have ambition for higher appointed public office, or do they have ambition for elected office? What affects appointees' political ambitions versus elected officials' political ambitions? Understanding appointees' political ambitions is an important piece in understanding how they view politics and how they view their political and nonpolitical careers. By asking these appointees about their ambitions, I am able to show how many of the *women see themselves as nonpolitical public servants.*

To explore these core questions, I will be using surveys and interviews of both elected and appointed officials throughout this book. I include an analysis of the elected officials to provide direct comparisons between these two groups of public officials and to set a baseline for how appointees might respond to questions about motivation, recruitment, and ambition. Surprisingly, appointee results often do not mirror what has already been found by those studying people in elected office. Appointees often think about politics—and their interactions with politics through their positions—differently than do elected officials. The comparisons throughout this book will underscore my central argument that power in politics and women's ambition lies beyond elected office. A condensed overview of previous research on individuals in elected versus appointed office follows.

THE APPOINTED PATH

Thousands of men and women across the United States have gained access to public service via political appointment through their own professions and connections. Although an appointment to a board or commission that meets only four or five times a year might seem insignificant compared with election to a year-round legislature, often these appointees keep the wheels of state government turning. Additionally, these appointments can provide the opportunity for individuals to publicly serve without the pressure and competition that defines electoral politics. In fact, this book shows that appointees nearly always believe "politics" means partisan and electoral.

Political appointees exert influence across a broad range of issues. Thousands of women and men work throughout the departments and agencies of states as commissioners, department heads, agency leaders, and board and commission members.[2] In 2008, the Center for Women in Government and Civil Society (CWGCS) at the University of Albany placed the number of women in high political appointments at 35 percent. The study was limited to women who served as gubernatorial advisors, agency leaders, and cabinet secretaries, overlooking the hundreds of

2. Appointees in a bureaucracy have the ability to shape policy through rules and regulations and to have a large influence on the success of a particular program or law. They can "counteract inertia, ensure an influx of new ideas, and keep government in touch with a variety of interest groups and constituencies" (Bok 2003, 271).

board and commission positions many women held. Prior to this study, only one other study delved into the women in the appointment world, when in 1981 the Center for American Women in Politics (CAWP) at Rutgers completed an in-depth analysis of state appointees' backgrounds, prior experience, recruitment, and political ambition. At the time, there were only 126 women appointed to 987 cabinet-level positions across the fifty states (Center for American Women in Politics 1983).

Although the CAWP study found many similarities in the backgrounds of the men and women politically appointed at the state level, its authors also discovered notable differences, as did subsequent studies performed by other scholars. Unlike female elected officials, female political appointees were younger than their male counterparts (Bowling et al. 2006; Bullard and Wright 1993; Center for American Women in Politics 1983). Female appointees were less likely to be married, less likely to have children, and more likely to be living with their partners in long-term committed relationships, potentially suggesting that such women were completely avoiding the traditional dilemma of work and family instead of tackling it head on (M. Newman 1994, 280).

Since the 1970s, women appointees have been consistently more likely to identify as Democrats when compared with men appointees (Bowling et al. 2006; Center for American Women in Politics 1983). The CAWP study also found that although women had less experience in elected office prior to their appointments than men did, they had similar job histories to those of men appointees. Carroll (1984) was able to show that governors held women to higher standards than they did men when it came to their qualifications for appointed office, but no study since has investigated if this is still a common practice among governors looking to recruit women into their cabinets or administrations.[3]

The most useful part of the CAWP study is that it asked the political appointees their opinions. At that time, female appointees were more likely than male appointees to have put greater effort into obtaining their appointments but were less likely than appointees overall to think their qualifications were a significant reason for their appointment (Center for American Women in Politics 1983). Appointed women were far less likely

3. Women appointed by Democratic governors had more experience with campaign service (i.e., volunteering to work for a campaign) and were more likely to have held appointed positions at the federal level prior to their state appointment.

to believe that a woman would be more likely to receive an appointment than a man with equal qualifications.

The CAWP study did not stop at prior history and current appointment. It also delved into future political aspirations. Appointed women were more likely than men to accept a gubernatorial appointment in the future and were more likely than appointees overall to seek another appointed position or elective office (Center for American Women in Politics 1983). Appointed women were also more likely to pursue appointed versus elected office. More than 54 percent of female appointees—as compared with the main sample of 41 percent—aspired to appointed office, whereas 46 percent of women appointees as compared with 43 percent of the main sample aspired to elected office (Center for American Women in Politics 1983, 74). Unfortunately, this 1981 study was the most recent glimpse of the political aspirations of appointed women in state government until this book. After more than thirty years, this book attempts to fill these large holes in our understanding of this type of participation in government.

Glass Walls and Ceilings

Much of the more recent work on political appointments has focused on the abilities of women and minorities to move up and across bureaucratic departments. Studies tracking the raw numbers of political appointments at the state level have noted gains by women and minorities in different departments and agencies. In the 1970s, 52 percent of men and 29 percent of women appointed obtained office via a policy path.[4] Also in the 1970s, governors appointed 37 percent of men and 26 percent of women. Fast-forward twenty years to the 1990s, and the picture was different. The 23 percent gap that separated the policy pathway to appointment for men and women shrank to only 4 percent, with 45 percent of men and 41 percent of women taking the policy pathway to top administrative office. The 11 percent gap separating men and women appointed by governors (instead of taking a policy pathway to appointment) had not only decreased but flipped entirely. By the 1990s women had become

4. The authors defined a policy appointment as an appointment to a board or commission or as a department head, in contrast with a gubernatorial appointment, which could occur with or without legislative consent (Bowling et al. 2006).

more likely to be appointed by a governor at 40 percent versus men at 36 percent (Bowling et al. 2006, 829).

Yet even thirty years ago, there was evidence that women were making gains in gender-specific areas, such as public welfare, employment departments, and security agencies. One finding has held true from some of the earliest studies of bureaucratic composition: the consistent sex segregation found among bureaucratic departments. Although sex segregation has decreased since these early studies, even the most recent scholarship on the composition of bureaucratic departments has found that women tend to dominate more "female-oriented" agencies and departments: health, welfare, and human services (Bowling et al. 2006). Glass walls are particularly significant when departments are broken down into distributive, redistributive, and regulatory schemas.

Glass walls are not a problem for redistributive departments such as health and human services, where women tend to congregate, but they are problematic for distributive and regulatory departments, particularly the regulatory agencies of law enforcement and fire protection. Women are more prevalent in redistributive agencies because they not only tend to be more women-friendly but also tend to be more supportive of affirmative action goals and thus more likely to hire those their departments are designed to serve. Lower-level positions in redistributive agencies are much more accessible for women because these agencies emphasize recruitment at the bottom and often use this pool of lower-level workers for internal promotion as opposed to seeking executives from outside of the agency (Reid, Miller, and Kerr 2004). Regulatory agencies and distributive agencies tend to consist mostly of men, especially regulatory agencies because they tend to be hierarchical and in male-dominated areas such as law enforcement and corrections. As Reid and colleagues say, regulatory agencies "have developed a host of ways to keep women (and people of color) out of their ranks" (Reid, Miller, and Kerr 2004). Lastly, distributive agencies such as highway and park departments and certain sectors of environmental departments employ larger numbers of subject specialists, and "their employees operate in cultures that may emphasize professional norms over formal, legal procedures and due process" (Reid, Miller, and Kerr 2004, 381). Sex segregation is common in distributive agencies, and unfortunately, some agencies—such as police departments—have both hard walls and hard ceilings (Kelly et al. 1991; Reid, Miller, and Kerr 2003; Sneed 2007).

The most recent studies of political appointees prior to this one are from 2007. The Women's Campaign Forum (WCF) and the Center for Women in Government and Civil Society (CWGCS) continued to confirm the presence of glass walls.[5] The WCF reported that women held a mere 31 percent of cabinet-level appointments, whereas the CWGCS reported a slightly higher percentage of 35.1 percent (Center for Women in Government and Civil Society 2008; Women's Campaign Forum 2008).

The WCF reported that tourism, education, and human resources were the three departments with the highest percentages of women appointed at the cabinet level, and the CWGCS reported that health, labor/human resources, and public welfare/employment security had the highest percentages of women as department heads across the fifty states (Center for Women in Government and Civil Society 2008, 4; Women's Campaign Forum 2008, 9). For both studies, the public safety/military departments had among the lowest numbers of women appointments, along with fire protection and corrections departments. Although gains have been made, glass walls are still a real and troubling problem for many women interested in moving between certain departments at the state level. These barriers not only affect the total number of women in state-level appointed office but might also decrease active representation of women appointees in particular departments and agencies at the state level. Unfortunately, lateral movement for political appointment is not the only limited option for women at the state level; upward movement can be just as restricted by the presence of glass ceilings.

Additional evidence showed that the women in these agencies were still at a lower status than the men were (Cayer and Sigelman 1980). The glass ceiling is particularly hard to crack in distributive and regulatory agencies at the state level, and although progress has been made in these

5. The CWGCS study included appointees that directed boards, commissions, and authorities. It did not specify if there were limited response rates from appointments at that level, and it did not provide a breakdown by type of policy leader. Because the study reported a total of only 1,834 appointees, it must have included a limited number of board/commission/authority members; normally states have more than a hundred boards and commissions.

agencies (Bowling et al. 2006, 823), pay for women and minorities tends to be significantly lower than for men in these arenas (Reid, Miller, and Kerr 2004, 397; Riccucci 2009, 379). Evidence has also been found of women circumventing the glass ceiling by seeking higher appointment in newer agencies and departments rather than fighting their way up the ladder in one specific agency (Bowling et al. 2006, 825).

Susan J. Carroll used the Center for American Women in Politics (1983) state cabinet appointee dataset to test the hypothesis that female state cabinet members would be more strictly held to the standards governors had set for political appointees. Looking at three indicators—credentials and experience, social background, and loyalty to the governor/party—Carroll (1984) found that appointed women were more likely to come from elite backgrounds than were appointees overall, credentials were more important for younger appointed women than for older appointed women, and older women exhibited more party loyalty than did younger women. Even though the study is more than thirty years old, Carroll pointed to specific ways in which women hit the glass ceiling that might still be relevant for women today. In sum, to study women in appointed office is to study women in light of specific barriers beyond their control. Although useful in understanding the status of women in appointments overall, it typically masked the decisions these women made in terms of public service and their own careers. This book will place the appointees at the center of the analysis to understand gender representation at the state level.

THE ELECTORAL PATH

The literature on women in elected office is much more robust. However, scholars have noted a concerning pattern within these offices: low, if any, women's representation. For example, only 23.7 percent of Congress members are women, only recently did a major party nominate a female candidate for the presidency, and only two women have run as major party vice presidential candidates (Center for American Women in Politics 2018a). According to the CAWP, only 28.6 percent of state legislators are women, with the rare state—such as Nevada—reaching gender parity (50.8 percent women). Most states lag far behind, especially Louisiana and Mississippi, which each have less than 15 percent of women elected to their legislatures (Center for American Women in Politics 2018b). Elected positions in the executive office at the state level are even less gender balanced. Only nine states have a woman governor (18 percent), and nearly half of all the states have never had a woman executive elected to office (Center for American Women in Politics 2018a).[6]

In their book *More Women Can Run,* Susan Carroll and Kira Sanbonmatsu (2013) compared the characteristics of the men and women serving in state legislatures in 1981 to the men and women in state legislatures in 2008. They found similarities and differences to the women who were legislators more than thirty years ago, with several surprising similarities. For example, they found that the gender gap in the occupational backgrounds of men and women state legislators had remained the same. Specifically, female state legislators in 1981 and 2008 were more likely than male state legislators to come from education and health fields, both of which tend to be dominated by women. Gaps in educational attainment between male and female state legislators have also persisted, with male legislators more likely to have a law degree (Carroll and Sanbonmatsu 2013).

In general, studies of the pathway to elected office fall into one of three categories: studies of institutional barriers, discrimination/stereotypes, and political ambition. Each study has added to our understanding of why and how women get on the elected office pathway, although none has considered how these variables affect the appointed office pathway. Below is a short explanation of reasons by category that women do not pursue elected office.

Institutional Barriers

Specific institutional barriers, such as the ways electoral districts and electoral rules affect the likelihood of women being elected to office, have been studied in detail. For example, we know that winner-takes-all elections in large, rural, Republican districts depress the numbers of women elected to office (Rule 1990; Welch 2008). More often than not, the states or districts that are more accepting of women in politics are liberal and

6. Twenty states have never elected a female governor (Center for American Women in Politics 2018a).

diverse. More diverse constituencies, measured in higher percentages of blacks, Latinos, and foreign-born residents, have been associated with more women in public office, along with women and minorities paving the way for others by holding elected office (Burrell 1994; MacManus and Bullock 1994; Palmer and Simon 2006). Unsurprisingly, women in state legislatures tend to be Democrats as opposed to Republicans and are more likely to be Latina or African American than Caucasian (Epstein, Niemi, and Powell 2005; Fox and Oxley 2003; Sanbonmatsu 2004; Thomas 1994).

Women are more likely to run for state legislature in states with a larger pool of professional women (e.g., lawyers) or where the legislature is less professional (Arceneaux 2001; Carroll 1994; Hogan 2001; Norrander and Wilcox 2005; Sanbonmatsu 2004; Welch 2008). Although some believed the institution of term limits would open more spots for women in state legislatures (Reed and Schansberg 1995; Thompson and Moncrief 1993), this has proven incorrect for two reasons. First, term limits eject well-established, qualified women incumbents. Second, the ambition gap between men and women qualified to run for office often results in women counting themselves out of the electoral arena before they have even tried running for office (Lawless 2012; Lawless and Fox 2005, 2010; Sanbonmatsu 2004).

Political parties also have a significant impact on the number of women running for office. More often than not, the party establishment within a state is described as a "good old boys' network," and party officials often doubt the viability of female candidates despite evidence to the contrary (Niven 1998; Sanbonmatsu 2004).[7] Women are more likely to run for office when party officials recruit and endorse them in primary elections, most likely because their lower self-perception of their qualifications—particularly when it comes to fund-raising—can be boosted considerably when the party establishment sufficiently supports them (Darcy and Schramm 1977; Flammang 1985; Norrander and Wilcox 2005; Volgy, Schwartz, and Gottlieb 1986). Crowder-Meyer (2010, 2013) found that recruitment by organizations for local political office can be the most important factor in getting women into public office. Although Sanbonmatsu (2004) and Lawless and Fox (2010) found that women

7. See Niven (2006) for instances in which women have been dissuaded from running for office.

are less likely to be recruited, Fulton and colleagues (2006) did not find gender differences in state legislator recruitment for the US House, and Preece, Stoddard, and Fisher (2016) found that despite similar levels of recruitment, politically active women are less responsive to it than are politically active men.[8]

Women and Stereotypes

The foregoing summary of the institutional barriers for women running for elected office demonstrates how it can be more difficult for women than for men to be candidates for elected public office. However, the literature has also asked if gender is a factor when it comes to actually voting for a woman, and the answer is not always clear. Gender is not always a salient factor when voting for a female candidate. In fact, Kathleen Dolan (2004) emphasized in *Voting for Women* that "candidate sex, and the gendered considerations it can raise, has a more complex and nuanced impact on voters," especially through the lens of political parties (154). Female Democrats were more often evaluated on the basis of their sex or their ideology than were female Republicans, and female Democrats were perceived as more liberal than their male counterparts (K. Dolan 2004). This led Dolan to conclude that the amount of gendered information highly influences whether their sex will be significant when constituents evaluate candidates and explains why gender is not always relevant in the voting booth (K. Dolan 2004).[9] Dolan (2014) revisits the question of gendered stereotypes in *When Does Gender Matter?* and finds that gender stereotypes are not nearly as strong as they once were and that instead "traditional political influences" shape voter choices for Congress members and governors (187).[10]

8. The kind of encouragement might matter as well. Pruysers and Blais (2018a) found that online impersonal encouragement did not increase political ambition. A second study also found that the source of recruitment matters (Pruysers and Blais 2018b).

9. See Rosenthal (1995) along with Epstein, Niemi, and Powell (2005) on when women and groups are more likely to support female candidates.

10. Cassese and Holman (2017) studied negative campaigning and found that women candidates are more likely to be affected when they are attacked on traits associated with their gender.

The political culture or ideology of a state also affects the number of women in elected office. States with voters less accepting of women in politics have fewer women in their state legislatures (Arceneaux 2001; Hill 1981; Nechemias 1987; Rule 1981, 1990; Sanbonmatsu 2002; Windett 2011), and states with traditional southern culture (Oxley and Fox 2004) tend to reduce the number of women in the state legislature (Diamond 1977; Nechemias 1987; Rule 1990; Windett 2011).

Despite all the barriers scholars of women and politics have discovered, one of the most promising findings is that women are just as likely to win bids for the state legislature as men are, showing just how far the country has come in its willingness to elect women as representatives in government (Burrell 1994; Darcy and Schramm 1977; Darcy, Welch, and Clark 1994; Ekstrand and Eckert 1981; J. Newman 1994; Sanbonmatsu 2004). However, this does not resolve the real problems of lower ambitions among women in the electorate and the good old boys' club of the political parties.

The Ambition Factor

The third perspective on women's representation concerns women's ambitions for public office.[11] Scholars have argued that there are different kinds of ambition: progressive (those who want to move up the career ladder), static (those who want to keep their current office), and discrete (those who do not seek reelection). Researchers have also argued that ambition can change over the course of an individual's life because it is affected by one's changing environment (Black 1972; Fox and Lawless 2011).[12]

A multitude of factors influence progressive ambition, not the least of which is whether officeholders are risk takers, the prestige of their current office, and how staunch their potential competition is (Rohde 1979). Risk calculation when it comes to progressive ambition is not gender specific. Barbara Palmer and Dennis Simon (2003) found that "careerist women in the [US] House are strategic when deciding whether to take advantage of an opportunity to run for the Senate. This decision to run

11. See Joseph Schlesinger's (1966) definitive *Ambition and Politics* for a more general study of political ambition.

12. Herrick and Moore (1993) have studied intra-institutional ambition.

for higher office incorporates the probability of winning, the value of the office, and the costs of running" (127).

Robert A. Bernstein (1986) argued that after people get older, their level of ambition decreases. By the mid-1980s, research on women and politics had already demonstrated that women tended to be older when they first entered politics, with childbearing and childrearing the two major reasons for the delay (Carroll 1985a, 1985b; Diamond 1977; Dolan and Ford 1997; Kirkpatrick 1974). Bernstein (1986) found evidence that not only were younger candidates most likely to win primaries but also that women were increasingly facing younger, more ambitious men.[13] However, childrearing does not solely affect women when it comes to their political ambitions. Both men and women reported family-related conflict regarding holding office or thinking about running for office, but men reported higher levels of conflict than did women (Sapiro 1982). Sapiro argued that women tended to forgo politically ambitious opportunities until they could devote their energy to them without losing time with their families; hence the consistent finding that female politicians tended to be older than male politicians. Men, however, were not as likely to pass up an opportunity for reasons relating to their family lives and instead had to deal with—and might still have to—the heightened amount of conflict when they pursued an ambitious career in addition to family responsibilities (Sapiro 1982).

Much of the early work on political ambitions focused on those of people who were already elected officials or party activists (Carroll 1985b; Costantini 1990; Maestas 2000). More recently, Jennifer Lawless and Richard Fox (2005, 2010) suggest that the reason more women do not run for elected office is lower levels of ambition among those most likely to run for elected office. Using the Citizen Political Ambition Study, a pool of 3,800 of those most likely to run for office, they found that socialization to traditional gender roles did not make or break a woman's decision to run for office, but it does make that decision more complicated. Party gatekeepers also play an integral role in encouraging women to run for political office (Lawless and Fox 2005, 2010). Lawless and Fox's biggest contribution, however, is their finding on the differences between men

13. Moore (2005) discovered that the local context matters for the effects of race and conservative religious beliefs on women's ambitions for political office and that experiencing sexual discrimination increased women's ambition for public office.

and women's ambitions to run for political office. Put simply, women think they are less qualified and are taking themselves out of the political game before they have even begun.

Fox and Lawless (2011) have also demonstrated that political ambition is not static but dynamic. In two iterations of their Citizen Political Ambition Study, they found that political ambition rises and falls based on a variety of factors, including changes in political efficacy, recruitment patterns, and family life. Although political ambition might be dynamic, one thing is true of the gender gap between men and women: it has its roots in the perceptual differences men and women have about their own qualifications for elected office (Fox and Lawless 2011).[14] Thankfully, not all women fall victim to the same doubts about their qualifications for elected office.[15]

Carroll and Sanbonmatsu (2013) challenge the single model of candidate emergence. They argue for a relationally embedded model of candidacy. Within a relationally embedded model of candidacy,

> women's decision making about office holding is more likely to be influenced by the beliefs and reactions, both real and perceived, of other people and to involve considerations of how candidacy and office holding would affect the lives of others with whom the potential candidate has close relationships. The candidacy decision-making process takes place in the context of a network of relations and is deeply influenced by relational considerations. (45)

This argument does not assume that politically interested people will become officeholders or that current officeholders are ambitious for higher office. Instead, "ambition and candidacy may arise simultaneously," for example, as a result of recruitment (Carroll and Sanbonmatsu 2013, 44).

---

14. Ambition not only affects the political careers of men and women but also affects the kinds of politicians they will become. Cherie Maestas (2000) found that ambitious men and women in professional state legislatures have been more responsive to constituent concerns and more motivated to meet their constituents' needs because they need their constituents' support when seeking higher office (665).

15. Using anecdotal evidence, Angela Frederick (2013) found that women of color actually had more ambition for public office than white women did. Women officeholders are also more likely to see themselves as vulnerable to losing an election (Bledsoe and Herring 1990).

Unfortunately, discussion of political ambition in the realm of the bureaucracy, particularly among appointees, is scant. A study from the 1960s found that state executives who were younger, still in their first term, and more involved with their party were the most ambitious (Swinerton 1968; see also Moore 2005). Studies have looked at the political backgrounds of men and women in the upper echelons of political appointments, but their ambitions have not been studied, let alone those of low-level political appointees.[16]

The lack of discussion about appointed officials' ambition brings up many questions—notably whether elected office was ever of interest to political appointees, why elected officials might have opted out of the appointment route, and what role recruitment might play in ambition for political appointment. We do know that women appointed in bureaucracies tend to be younger than male appointees *and* female elected officials. They are also less likely to be married and have children than are male appointees (Center for American Women in Politics 1983). But why is this the case? Does this mean that political appointments are more conducive to raising children while having a political career, as opposed to raising children first, then entering political office, as elected women most often do? Or does it mean that appointments are less conducive to women's family concerns than elected office is? For either explanation, it is important to understand why appointments can help or hinder women's home lives. We need to be able to compare across elected and appointed positions to better understand all the obstacles women face in public office, not just in the world of electoral politics.

Studying these appointees might also help us better understand the candidate emergence process. If candidate emergence is relationally embedded, as Carroll and Sanbonmatsu (2013) argue, and women are more affected by their opinions of themselves and how office holding would affect their lives, then understanding how the prospects of appointed versus elected office might shape a woman's interest in pursuing such an office is crucial to understanding candidate emergence. Because attaining appointed and elected positions often entails different characteristics—first and foremost that of how to obtain the office—a study comparing

16. See Jerry Mitchell (1997), "Representative in Government Boards and Commissions," for a rare study of low-level appointees. No advisory boards were included in this study, however.

elected with appointed positions takes into consideration what such offices might require of emerging candidates and how women might differ from men in their opinions of those factors.

CHAPTER OUTLINE

This book seeks to detail where women hold public office and specifically to understand how women view and interact with the political world broadly defined as public service beyond the confines of electoral office. To answer these questions, I use data and interviews from an original survey of state-level appointed and elected officials. Chapter 2 presents these data by comparing elected and appointed officials on three categories: their demographics, family life, and political participation. Our lack of understanding of those who hold appointed offices—high and low level alike—suggests that we do not consider political appointments important public offices that women can hold as compared with elected offices. Discovering who holds appointed versus elected positions at the state level is another road to understanding why they hold these offices and if women should consider appointments a viable alternative to elected office holding.

In Chapter 3, I analyze whether women in appointments are recruited for public office in the same ways women are recruited for elected office and compare their differences in motivations for appointed office (Chapter 4). If we want to understand whether women prefer political appointments instead of elected office, and if political appointments are a viable pathway through the pipeline of elected and appointed office for women, then we have to understand how women obtain these appointments and what their motivations are in seeking them.

We also need to understand how each type of officeholder might consider moving up the career ladder. Put simply, how do appointed positions fit into the hierarchy of politics—are they a separate ladder or are they just another rung on the same one? Through analysis of appointed officials' progressive ambitions (Chapter 5), I go from understanding how women initially achieve appointed office to whether women in appointed office are ambitious for future public office. In Chapter 6, I continue this analysis by studying appointees' specific interest in elected office.

Chapter 7 examines elected officials at the state level. In this chapter I compile the findings on elected officials' recruitment, motivations for public service, and ambitions for higher office and appointed office. This chapter provides an excellent foil to Chapters 3–6 and highlights the unique appeal of appointed office for women in state-level politics.

Chapter 8 concludes the book by presenting a comprehensive picture of women and their decisions to enter political office. Throughout the analysis, I find that women in appointed positions have a distinct definition of what it means to be political, and often it does not refer to their own positions even when they are officials in a governor's cabinet. These findings suggest a disavowal of politics that goes much deeper than any research has encountered before. Moreover, my research suggests a pathway through which more women could be persuaded to enter the political arena: through targeted recruitment to appointments closely related to a woman's personal or professional life and perceived as nonpolitical. The main reason more women might be recruited to or pursue appointments instead of running for elected office is because they do not see such appointments as political. This is relevant because it suggests women have a unique definition of politics that exerts noticeable effects on their interest in office holding.

In order to truly understand the status of women in politics and the political career choices they make, appointed positions must be studied to the same depth as elected positions. This means delving beyond appearances to understand the full breadth and depth of political appointments, from the lowest boards and commissions to cabinet secretary positions. My research demonstrates that when we exclude questions of past and potential future appointment for elected officials from surveys, we are missing important aspects of the political careers of women and thereby limiting our capacity to effect change in the status of women in state politics. Nearly one-third of the public officials in my sample held an appointment prior to their current position. Men and women who hold high-level appointed *and* elected positions have often started at the board and commission level. Sanbonmatsu, Carroll, and Walsh (2009), for example, found that 38 percent of women state representatives had served on a local or county board or commission as their first office. If we do not ask about prior political appointment or interest in future political appointment, we are pretending that part of women's political life does not exist, when in fact it might have been the origin of future electoral engagement just as it was for Elizabeth Warren. Or it might be the start of a long career in the bureaucracy as it was for Elaine Chao. In the next chapter, I begin the journey with an overview of the appointed and elected positions studied in this book and the backgrounds of the individuals who serve in these positions.

2. The Men and Women in Elected and Appointed Office at the State Level

> I've been involved in politics . . . kind of retail politics, since I was in high school. And I've always participated in campaigning, kind of grassroots kind of thing. . . . I've always been interested in politics.
> —*Donna Abramson, board and commission member*

Donna Abramson has had a lifelong interest in politics.[1] This enthusiasm has fueled an ambition for elected and appointed office. She had sought three appointments at both the local and state level prior to one on an Iowa commission. Her first appointment was to the Iowa Great Places Advisory Board, which chooses finalists to become a "great place" in the state. This program seeks to "create bold thought, innovation, and entrepreneurship at the local and regional level in Iowa" (Iowa Boards and Commissions 2018). She left that board after receiving a call from the governor appointing her to her current board. She intends to leave this board after her five-year term ends. She particularly wants to run for elected office and has been saying she wants to run for years, but "it's depressing how little the people closest to me support the idea. My husband and my parents all don't support me in that regard." When asked why she has put off running for elected office, she talks about her personal goals:

> I've always wanted to run for office, ever since I can remember, but there are things in my life that led me to believe I wasn't ready; if that's true or not I'm not sure. But I wanted to get my kids raised first, and I wanted to be financially stable and have some community experiences before I ran, and I know that those aren't requirements per se, but I just felt like it would make me a better official, so that's what I decided to do.

Abramson captures the views of unique personal and political lives of appointees at the state level. The literature on women and politics gives us a good indication about the kinds of women most likely to run

1. All names were changed to protect the privacy of the individuals in this study.

for elected office (Burrell 1994; K. Dolan 2008; Lawless and Fox 2005), and at times can even suggest the types of women who will seek or be sought out for political appointment (Riccucci and Saidel 2001). Yet little is known about the whole spectrum of political appointments at the state level, encompassing the lowest-level boards and commissions all the way to the highest-level cabinet secretary. The last comprehensive study of female appointees at the state level was more than thirty years ago, by the Center for American Women and Politics (1983). What kind of people hold state political appointments? What are the backgrounds, family lives, and political activities of these individuals? And how do the backgrounds of political appointees at the board and commission level, who have never been surveyed, match up with those of higher-level appointed or elected political officials?

This chapter is an introduction to the original data collected in my State Political Pathways Survey, completed by more than 1,500 elected and appointed officials in the fall of 2013. The overview will detail the kinds of men and women appointed and elected to various levels in state government and will help point us in the right direction for further analysis in the following chapters. The analysis in this chapter is broken up into three major parts, starting with the basic demographics of the appointed and elected officials who took part in the survey; then moving on to the appointees' and elected officials' family lives (including their marital status and whether they have children); and ending on the public officials' political involvement, including their party identification and political activities. Before embarking on the introduction to those who hold state-level office, here is an overview of the methodology followed by a description of these state-level positions.

STUDYING WOMEN IN PUBLIC OFFICE AT THE STATE LEVEL

This project used a combination of an online survey and follow-up phone interviews. The survey, located in Appendix A, consisted of approximately fifty-five to sixty-five questions. It is rare to see a survey that targets both elected and appointed officials. Among those surveys that do, few do so with any kind of precision. Some target elected officials at the state level, but appointed officials at the federal level (Carroll 1989). Others do not differentiate between appointed officials and those in the civil service (Bullard and Wright 1993; Reid, Miller, and Kerr 2003). This is also an issue with the few surveys that have analyzed bureaucratic officials. Many of these studies do not differentiate between career civil service and appointed positions, and almost all completely bypass lower-level political appointees to ask only high-level ones at both the state and federal levels about their opinions and experiences (Brehm and Gates 1999; J. Dolan 2000a, 2000b; Reid, Miller, and Kerr 2003).

My survey was administered online to elected and appointed officials using Qualtrics.[2] I collected the contact information of the elected and appointed officials from a number of places, including state websites, professional association websites, educational institutions, and the 2013 *Book of States Directory III,* which contains the contact information of selected directors of administrative agencies. Nearly all of the elected officials' contact information could be accessed on the Internet, but many of the appointed officials' contact information, particularly those on low-level boards and commissions, could not be obtained this way. However, because there is such a large number of political appointees at the lower level, I was able to gather a sufficient number of email addresses via the Internet alone. In many cases there were biographies of the board members or they were a part of professional licensing boards, which helped narrow how I could search for them.

In total, 2,829 state legislators were contacted to complete the survey, and 3,587 political appointees were contacted.[3] Making a 14.4 percent response rate, 407 state legislators responded, and constituting a 31.5 percent response rate, 1,129 political appointees responded. The overall response rate was 24 percent (see Table 2.1). Elected officials and political appointees had separate surveys customized to their specific offices. Many of the questions between the two surveys were the same, which allowed for direct comparisons when necessary.

2. Appointees came from four types of departments: commerce, environment, natural resources, and health, covering each of Lowi's (1972) bureaucratic offices: distributive, redistributive, and regulatory.

3. I gathered 12,544 appointee names from 1,314 boards and commissions and 60 state agencies and departments. Of the names I collected, I found emails for 3,587 of them.

Table 2.1 Survey Response Rates

Position	Total Contacted	Completed Survey	Response Rate
Appointed:	3,587	1,130	31.5%
High appointed	494	157	31.7%
Boards/commissions	3,093	972	31.4%
Elected:	2,829	407	14.4%
Senate	757	90	11.9%
House	2,072	317	15.3%
Total	6,416	1,536	23.9%

The survey covered four areas:

- Prior political history
- Current position opinions
- Future political ambitions
- Demographics

More than 46 percent of respondents said they were willing to take part in a follow-up phone interview. The interview script (located in Appendix B) expands on the data obtained from the survey. Many of the interview questions specifically asked what it was like to be a public official in their state and sought a deeper understanding of their personal and professional backgrounds. I interviewed twenty-one public officials at the state level, all female. Of those, seventeen were appointed and four were elected. Interviews averaged approximately thirty-five minutes and were conducted via telephone. A more detailed breakdown of the number and gender of the interviewees can be found in Appendix B. Below is an overview of the responsibilities of each of the officeholders included in the study.

ELECTED AND APPOINTED POSITIONS AT THE STATE LEVEL

The State Legislature

One of the first entry points for individuals interested in state-level elected office is through election to their state legislature. Every state except Nebraska has an upper and a lower chamber, with most states referring to the lower one as the house of representatives and the upper one as the senate (Council of State Governments 2014).[4] States have qualifications for election similar to those of the US Congress. Every state legislature has a minimum age. This can vary from as low as age eighteen (required by eighteen lower and thirteen upper chambers) to as high as age thirty (Council of State Governments 2014).[5] A majority of the states require legislators to be US citizens, and most require legislators to be state and district residents for a certain period before running for election. Each state legislature has its own calendar for being in session, with thirty-two meeting every year, four every odd year, and eleven for two subsequent years.[6] Additionally, each legislature meets for a certain number of months of their legislative year. Massachusetts, for example, meets year-round, whereas Arkansas meets from January to March.

The state legislatures also have different levels of professionalism. Citizen legislatures are considered part time, hybrid legislatures somewhere between part and full time, and professional legislatures full time. Representatives in professional legislatures have large staffs and a living wage. They usually meet throughout the year, though not always, as in California (National Conference of State Legislatures 2014). The National Conference of State Legislatures (NCSL) describes legislators in hybrid legislatures as "spend[ing] more than two-thirds of a full-time job being legislators. Although their income from legislative work is greater than that in the [citizen legislature] states, it's usually not enough to allow them to make a living without having other sources of income" (2014). Twenty-six state legislatures in the United States are hybrid. In comparison, the fourteen citizen legislatures provide little to no staff, pay low, and do not meet throughout the year or even every year. To put into context the salaries of professional, hybrid, and citizen legislatures, a California (professional) state legislator's salary in 2018 was $107,241; an Indiana (hybrid) state legislator's salary was $25,945, and a Rhode Island (citizen) state legislator's salary was $15,630. However, the salary alone does

4. Nebraska refers to its one-chamber legislative branch as the *legislature*. California, Nevada, New Jersey, New York, and Wisconsin refer to their lower chamber as the *assembly* or *general assembly*. Maryland, Virginia, and West Virginia call their lower chamber the *house of delegates*.

5. No lower chambers have an age requirement as high as thirty, but five upper chambers do. Most lower chambers have two-year terms (Alabama has four-year terms) and upper chambers have a mix of two- and four-year terms. Fifteen states have term limits.

6. Maine and North Carolina have different schedules from those outlined. See Council of State Governments (2014) for more information.

not indicate the professionalism of a legislature; for example, Alaska is a professional legislature but provides a salary of only $50,400, and New Jersey is a hybrid legislature that provides a salary of $49,000 (Mahoney 2018).

The state legislators who participated in the State Political Pathways Survey came from all three types of legislatures. More than 40 percent were from citizen legislatures, 46 percent were from hybrid legislatures, and 12 percent were from professional legislatures. There were no major differences in the sex of the legislators based on whether the legislatures in which they served were citizen, hybrid, or professional. For each kind of legislature, the average percentage of men was approximately 70 percent.

The state legislatures are responsible for passing state laws, approving state budgets, and at times (depending on the state) approving gubernatorial appointees. Through service on committees within each chamber, state legislators have the opportunity to propose laws and mark up bills referred to those committees. After a bill comes out of committee onto the floor, each representative has the responsibility to vote on the bill. Therefore, legislators spend much of their time researching both for bills they want to propose and bills they review, writing the budget, handling constituent concerns, and meeting with citizens groups and donors in their districts (Squire and Moncrief 2015). One woman said this about her responsibilities as a state senator:

> All of the bills—your moral obligation, not your legal obligation, is to
> participate in the hearing and try your best to understand them so when
> they get to the floor you can try to amend them, or speak to them, or vote
> knowledgeably; in reality, it's not possible to really understand everything
> you vote on, and I have voted on lots of things that I haven't read all the
> way through, including the budget, 600 pages. And lots of things are
> sort of meaningless to me, so that's part of it, but then what you do is you
> have to have people whose opinions you respect, or disrespect, and kind
> of rely on them.

Another senator focused on constituent service when relaying her duties as a state senator:

> I also think that it's my responsibility as the state elected official to
> remain engaged with all of my constituents, and all of my government

units—local government units as well as all of my not-for-profits—to
understand and to advocate for them, to understand what their problems
are, what their issues are, and to advocate on their behalf. So that we can
address them, correct them, obtain additional financial aid for them
if that's what the issue is, and then that's true also for your constituents,
is to provide excellent constituent service with regard to their dealing
with the state.

Individuals in the state legislatures must balance both the demands of
their roles within the legislature and the demands of their constituents.
Undeniably, serving as a legislator in state government has unique challenges and responsibilities.

High-Level Political Appointees

Many different positions within state government can be considered
higher-level political appointments, from deputy directors within state
agencies all the way up to cabinet secretaries. Most of the responsibilities
associated with these appointments are specific not only to the level of
the position but also an area of government (such as health, commerce,
or environment). A few examples from high-level appointees of their
responsibilities enable us to understand their positions better.

A high-level appointee from a natural resources department said
about her responsibilities:

> I am responsible for the trust lands that were given to the state at
> statehood for education purposes, and so we currently have about right
> around, 750,000 acres of uplands that are owned by the state for the
> common school fund. . . . I am responsible for implementing the state's
> removal-fill laws for removing material or putting material into state
> owned waterways, waters of the state. I'm responsible for implementing
> the Unclaimed Property Act, which is an act that requires people, entities
> that have money that's not claimed by individuals to report it to the state,
> and we hold it in trust until the rightful owners can be found. . . . I'm also
> the head of the state portion of the national estuarine research reserve.

In comparison, a deputy commissioner from a health department had
the following duties in her appointment: "I am responsible for oversight
for about seven divisions within our department, I co-lead kind of high-

level statewide public efforts, I would say, or initiatives. I represent the department, along with the commissioner, sometimes replace the commissioner, sometimes independent of the commissioner. I assist with major budget decisions. And I help set direction; I would say I help set priorities and strategic direction." A commissioner in a commerce department listed her work requirements as:

> I do everything from human resources and restructure the department to make it more efficient and make sure people's skills match the job duties. I've led major pieces of outreach and education to improve our designations, and then last year did—last couple of years—updated those statutorily and provided more incentives. We've also done [this] because we had tropical storm Irene; our agency was very involved in response and recovery, and now long-term resiliency efforts, and now we've got several—we've worked with EPA on grants and we've got an EPA grant now as well. So it's pretty varied.

These individuals also supervised various other people. The high-level appointee from the department of natural resources mentioned above supervised 105 individuals, and the appointee from the health department oversaw about 300 people. The appointee from the commerce department directed around 50 staff members. In general, high-level appointees are responsible for setting the direction of their agencies, with those in the highest appointments particularly focusing on this aspect of their job as well as reporting directly to the governor.[7] High-level appointees are also in charge of implementing the laws the state legislature has passed through the creation of state regulations, and they work with the state legislature and federal government to attain more funding for their programs. Thus, a department-level appointee's responsibilities can be different from those of appointees to boards and commissions within each state.

7. Only 60 percent of the high-level appointees in the sample were appointed by the governor. In other cases, 20 percent were appointed by a cabinet secretary, 8 percent were appointed by someone within their department, 5 percent were appointed by the state legislature, and 6 percent were appointed by some other official.

Boards and Commissions

Like those in high-level department appointments, the responsibilities and degree of influence of appointees to boards and commissions can vary widely. Generally, boards and commissions can be separated into three categories: regulatory, advisory, and policy making. Most boards and commissions in the state government are either advisory or regulatory, with a few powerful policy-making boards and commissions as well.

The Illinois Nature Preserves Commission is an example of a natural resources board with a relatively wide scope of authority. The commission has nine members who must be recommended by the director of the Natural History Survey and the State Museum to be appointed by the governor. Members serve three-year terms and meet three or four times a year, although they can meet more often if necessary. The commission's purpose is to protect and set policy for the land within the Illinois Nature Preserves System. This gives the commission the authority to protect lands currently within the system and preserve the lands by overseeing a staff of biologists. No lands currently in the system can be taken under the power of eminent domain without the approval of the commission, governor, and other invested public owners (Illinois Department of Natural Resources 2014). Boards and commissions such as the Illinois Nature Preserves Commission are both policy makers and regulators within their respective jurisdictions. The Iowa Alcoholic Beverages Commission is another policy-making board at the state level, and according to one board member they do the following:

> We review quite a bit of policy; for example, right now powdered alcohol is becoming popular in some other areas of the country, and we're working right now with state legislators to prohibitively ban powdered alcohol in the state of Iowa, and I have a feeling that will probably pass this year. So we work with legislators to draft legislation, we recommend certain products be not listed in the first place, or be listed if they are controversial; for example, Four Loko was one of those, it was kind of a Kool-Aid, it looked like Kool-Aid, but it was very powerful—one can of Four Loko had the equivalent of four cans of beer's worth of alcohol in it, and kids were just drinking it and dropping like flies, so we decided to ban that in the state of Iowa; so we worked with the legislators and the FDA to do that.

As a regulatory board, the Illinois Real Estate Administration and Disciplinary Board (IREADB) has only regulatory power over the licensing of real estate agents within the state.[8] Members are appointed to four-year terms with a maximum of three terms. There are ten members on the commission, including the director of the Department of Financial and Professional Regulation (DFPR), who serves as the nonvoting chair. Six members must be employed and licensed real estate brokers for at least ten years, and the remaining three members are public members who cannot be real estate brokers, married to realtors, or have any ownership or interest in the real estate brokerage business. The meetings for the IREADB consist mostly of reviewing disciplinary cases and deciding the fines, penalties, and possible revocation of real estate licenses. The board meets monthly, and all members are appointed by the governor except the chair (Illinois Office of Executive Appointments 2014).

A woman from another regulatory board, the Engineers and Professional Land Surveying Board, said the following about her responsibilities as a member:

> We are responsible for responding to any complaints of professional
> engineers and land surveyors as far as competence or ethics . . . and
> making sure our statute is up to date and guarded as far as being what
> is in the best interests of the health and life and safety of the people of
> our state, and having our rule comply with the statute, and again be[ing]
> up to date with current technology, as well as reviewing applicants and
> screening applicants to make sure that they meet our state statutes and
> rules in order to be licensed within our state, again to protect the public.

The final example is the Illinois Advisory Board for Services for Persons Who Are Deaf and Blind (IABDB), a purely advisory board. The IABDB was created in 1975 and "provides advice to the State Superintendent of Education, the Governor, and the General Assembly on all matters pertaining to policy concerning persons who are deaf/blind, including the implementation of legislation enacted on their behalf"

8. For a history on the development of professional licensing boards, see Carman (1958), Gross (1984), and Shimberg (1982). Saundra Schneider (1986) studied professional licensing boards in Missouri and found that those with larger constituencies and larger budgets were more likely to take disciplinary action. Public representation on the boards had no effect on their decision making.

(Illinois Advisory Board for Services for Persons Who Are Deaf and Blind 2014). The board consists of eleven members, three of whom are appointed by the governor and the others appointed either by the Department of Human Services, the Department of Children and Family Services, or the Illinois State Board of Education.

The board must have one person who is at least sixty years old, one consumer who is deaf or blind, and one parent of a person who is deaf or blind. The board must meet at least four times a year but no more than twelve times a year, and the term length is three years. This board can act as a voice for the deaf and blind communities and make recommendations on their behalf, but it cannot make any regulations regarding services for individuals who are deaf or blind or implement any policies on behalf of those populations.

An Advisory Water Planning Council member gave this explanation about her responsibilities:

> The responsibilities are pretty much: we have monthly meetings, so to attend the meetings, provide input to what the water planning council is doing, which is developing—they are looking at developing a comprehensive water plan for the state of Connecticut, so the advisory group is providing technical expertise and information to the water planning council; as part of that I've been chairing, actually co-chairing, a drought management team that's looking at updating our drought management plan. That would be approved by the water planning council, so that's kind of the responsibility. So it's really, it's a lot of technical work.

In my sample, more than 80 percent of the board and commission members were appointed by governors, although a handful of members were appointed by higher-level appointees, leadership of the state legislatures, or outside organizations. More than 34 percent of the appointees served on advisory boards, 52 percent on regulatory boards, and 14 percent on policy-making boards. Close to 70 percent of board and commission appointments are part time, and nearly 60 percent are term limited.[9] The kinds of individuals appointed to boards can also vary. For

9. This number might actually be significantly higher. More than 20 percent of the low-level appointees said they did not know if their appointment was full time or part time. These boards and commissions vary with regard to compensation for their members. For example, 28 percent of board and commission members received

example, regulatory boards such as the IREADB must have members from the profession on the board, whereas other regulatory boards need individuals from the profession and a few public board members. These public board members are not intended to be affiliated with the mission of the board in any way and are meant to represent the interests of the public. More than 50 percent of the board and commission members who participated in my State Political Pathways Survey were public members.[10]

As seen from the previous discussion, board and commission members can have varied responsibilities and roles on behalf of their states. This discussion also shows the countless different ways individuals can get involved in state-level government, from the legislative body to the governor's cabinet and even the boards and commissions that meet only two times a year. Now that we have a sense of what these positions entail, we can move on to who fills these positions in state-level government.

THE MEN AND WOMEN OF THE STATE POLITICAL PATHWAYS SURVEY

Demographics

The last comprehensive survey of political appointees revealed that women made up 13 percent of governors' cabinets—126 women out of 987 total cabinet members (Center for American Women in Politics 1983). A few patterns emerged from that survey, notably that the female appointed officials at the state level averaged four and a half years younger than appointees overall (Center for American Women in Politics 1983) and were still behind men in being appointed to higher levels (Center for Women in Government and Civil Society 2008). Unlike appointees, elected women were often older than elected men, but they trended even further behind men in sheer numbers because of lower ambitions (Law-

---

no compensation for their involvement on their board. Just more than 6 percent received a salary, and 30 percent were compensated on a per-diem basis. Similarly, 57 percent received compensation for travel expenses.

10. In the survey, I asked respondents if they were public members of their boards and commissions. Not all states or board websites clarify whether an appointee is a specialist in the field, is a public member, or fulfills some other kind of role.

less 2012; Lawless and Fox 2005, 2010) and institutional barriers (Palmer and Simon 2006; Rule 1990; Welch 2008). Although the backgrounds of the men and women previously elected to office at the state level have been known, the same cannot be said of state appointees, which my State Political Pathways Survey helps to rectify. Table 2.2 provides the basic demographic summary statistics for appointed and elected officials.

Table 2.2 is broken down by total appointees and total elected officials and then further divided into two kinds of offices within each area: board and commission appointments versus higher-level appointments, and state representatives versus state senators. I conducted a difference-of-means test between all appointees and all elected officials, and those that are statistically significant are noted in the total appointees column.

The main variable of interest here is gender. We can see that women are, unsurprisingly, underrepresented at all levels. Approximately 40 percent of the appointees surveyed were women, and approximately 30 percent of the elected officials surveyed were women. Gender difference between appointed and elected officials at the state level is a significant factor. The CAWP reports that approximately 25.4 percent of state legislative seats are held by women, and the last census of political appointees—which included only high-level appointees and board and commission chairs—placed the number of appointments held at the state level by women at 35.1 percent, making my findings consistent (Center for American Women in Politics 2013; Center for Women in Government and Civil Society 2008).

The survey results are also exceedingly white in both elected and appointed office, with small percentages of African Americans, Asian Americans, Latino/as, Native Americans, and other races and ethnicities. African American was the only race out of the six listed that was statistically different between elected and appointed positions, showing African Americans as more likely to hold elected office than be in appointed positions at the state level. The low numbers of nonwhites in appointed positions was not surprising. The last survey of political appointees revealed that 84 percent of policy leaders, including department and agency heads, leaders of commissions, and top policy advisors, were white. In fact, between 1997 and 2007, the percentage of nonwhites holding appointed office across all fifty states increased by a scant 2 percent (Center for Women in Government and Civil Society 2008; Women's

Table 2.2 Demographics of Elected and Appointed Officials at the State Level

	Appointed Total	Boards and Commissions	High Appointees	Elected Total	State Reps.	State Senators
Gender						
Male	59.73%	59.77%	59.87%	70.52%	69.10%	75.56%
Female	40.27%**	40.23%	40.13%	29.48%	30.90%	24.44%
Race						
White	92.38%	92.09%	94.12%	89.19%	87.07%	96.67%
Black	2.27%**	2.22%	2.61%	4.91%	5.99%	1.11%
Hispanic	1.09%	1.16%	< 1.00%	1.97%	2.52%	0.00%
Other	4.26%	4.54%	2.61%	3.93%	4.42%	2.22%
Age						
20–40	9.38%*	8.85%	12.74%	13.02%	14.20%	8.89%
41–60	57.70%**	56.38%	65.61%	44.96%	46.64%	38.89%
Over 60	32.92%**	34.77%	21.66%	42.01%	39.12%	52.22%
Family Income						
Under $50,000	3.81%**	4.42%	0.00%	7.62%	8.20%	5.56%
$50,000–$100,000	23.98%**	26.13%	10.83%	40.29%	41.64%	35.56%
Over $100,000	70.29%**	67.15%	88.82%	48.95%	46.80%	56.47%
Education						
Some high school	0.00%	0.00%	0.00%	< 1.00%	< 1.00%	0.00%
High school graduate	< 1.00%	1.04%	0.00%	2.49%	2.24%	3.33%
Some college	5.56%	6.25%	1.29%	6.72%	8.01%	2.22%
Associate's degree	2.60%	2.71%	1.94%	3.73%	3.21%	5.56%
BA or BS degree	19.71%**	20.21%	16.13%	27.61%	26.60%	31.11%
Some grad school	9.14%	8.44%	13.55%	9.45%	10.90%	4.44%
Completed grad school	62.10%**	61.35%	67.10%	49.75%	48.72%	53.33%
N	1,130	972	157	407	317	90

Note: Levels of significance in difference of means and chi-square tests comparing all appointees with all elected officials in the sample. Where frequencies were less than five, Fischer's exact test was used instead of chi-square. ** $p < 0.01$, * $p < 0.05$, + $p < 0.10$.

Campaign Forum 2008). Although my sample has a slightly higher percentage of whites compared with the CWGCS study, my sample also included members of boards and commissions, not just those who led boards and commissions. When comparing appointed men with appointed women and elected men with elected women, race was not statistically significant.

One interesting facet of the appointment versus electoral pathways is the difference in age between the sexes, as seen in Figures 2.1 and 2.2.

Although elected women were slightly older than elected men (Carroll and Sanbonmatsu 2013; Dubeck 1976; Kirkpatrick 1974; Lee 1976; Werner 1966), appointed women were actually younger than appointed men. For some time now political scholars have known that elected women are generally older than elected men because many felt the need to raise their children before beginning their political careers (Carroll 1985b; Diamond 1977; Dolan and Ford 1997). Does this mean that appointed office is more conducive to raising children while having a political career? Or does it mean that appointed office is actually not friendly at all to women who want children, meaning that it attracts women not interested in having children?

The average age for the sample of elected and appointed officials overall was 55.6 years old. Appointed women were the youngest group in

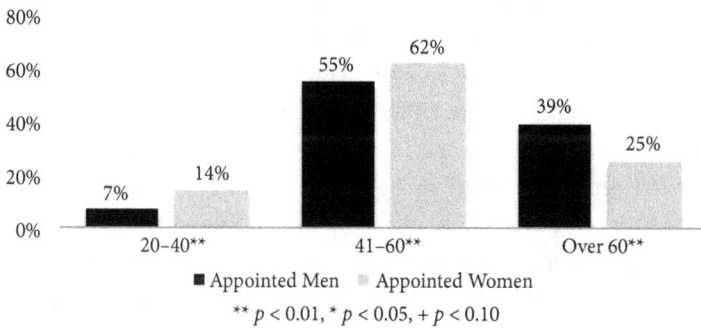

Figure 2.1 Gender and Age of State Appointees

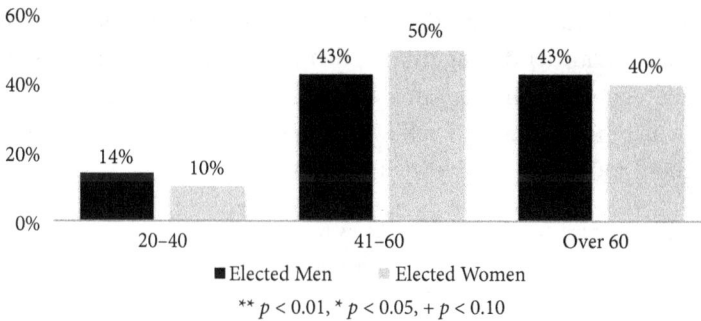

Figure 2.2 Gender and Age of State Legislators

my sample, with an average age of 52.8, versus appointed men at 56.9.[11] Age was highly significant between appointed and elected officials as well as between male and female political appointees (see Table 2.2 and Figure 2.1). Appointees overall were marginally younger than elected officials at the state level: elected officials averaged 56.4, and appointees averaged 55.3. High-level appointees were the youngest out of any type of officeholder, with an average age of 52.4. Age held a statistically significant difference between appointed and elected officials in all three age categories, with the noticeable trend of appointees being younger than their elected counterparts.

What can these age differences indicate about gender dynamics at the state level? First, they demonstrate that the difference in age between appointed men and women at the state level has persisted since the early 1980s. Second, they show some of the first signs of the gender gap in age for elected officials decreasing because few of the categories for age had statistically significant differences between elected men and women. Third, they could be driving the lower interest in high political office and elected office by appointed women, which I discuss in Chapter 5.

Younger women in the childbearing or childrearing stages of their lives might not be interested in pursuing further political offices, but high-level appointments in state government might be more compatible with that time in their lives. In fact, political interest might come with age for appointees, as one board member from the state of Washington explained in the survey. She stated, "I got interested in politics late in life, after fifty. So there is hope for the disinterested young today. I never felt put down because I was a minority woman while in politics." In Chapter 7, predicting political ambition, I control for age and having children to assess their relative effects on future political ambitions.

Finally, I asked the participants in my sample two socioeconomic questions to further distinguish the demographic portion of the survey. Overall, appointees in the sample were highly educated and had high family incomes. More than half of the appointees had completed graduate school and had incomes over $100,000. The elected officials were a bit

11. The average age of the other offices were as follows: female elected officials 56.75; male elected officials 56.2; state senators 59.7; female state senators 60; male state senators 59.6; state representatives 55.4; female state representatives 56.1; male state representatives 55.1; low-level appointees 55.7; female low-level appointees 53.1; male low-level appointees 57.5.

more varied in terms of income and education. Whereas state senators boasted high family incomes and high percentages of graduate school completion, state representatives had lower family incomes and graduate school completion rates, although their income and education levels were still high compared with those of the general population.[12]

Family income was a highly significant difference between appointees and elected officials ($p < 0.01$) and was also more significantly different between the sexes for appointees than for elected officials (Figures 2.3 and 2.4). Elected women were only slightly behind elected men in

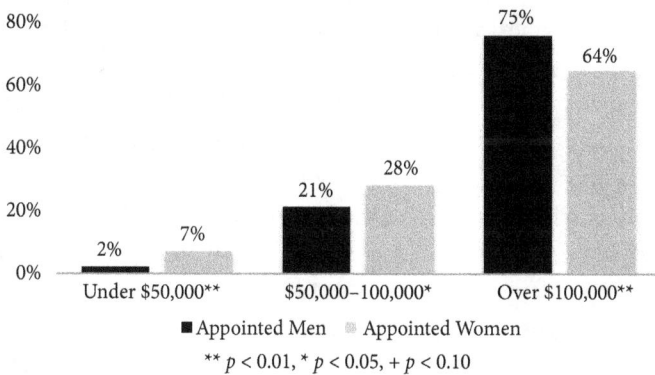

Figure 2.3 Gender and Family Income of State Appointees

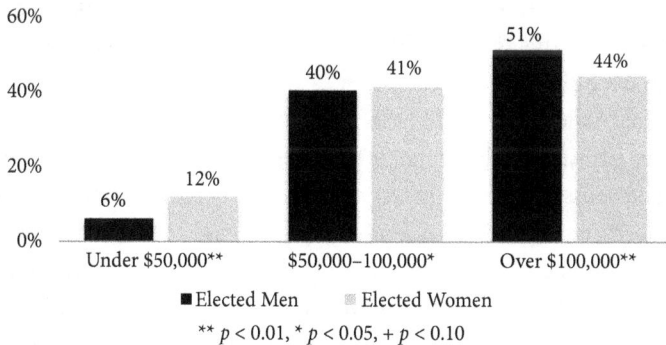

Figure 2.4 Gender and Family Income of State Legislators

12. According to the US Census Bureau (2013), only 28.5 percent of the US population aged twenty-five and older had achieved a bachelor's or higher degree between 2008 and 2012. More than 90 percent of the appointees alone had achieved a bachelor's or higher degree in my sample—an astounding 62 percent gap.

terms of family income, but appointed women were noticeably behind appointed men when it came to family income even though they were statistically significantly more educated than men appointees. There was an 11 percent gender gap in family income for those making over $100,000 alone. One explanation for this gender gap in income might be the persistently lower pay scale for women working in government at the state level (Bowling et al. 2006).

Family Life

The Center for American Women in Politics (1983) study of cabinet-level leaders in state government found that "women appointees were much less likely than appointees overall to be married[, and] women were more than three times as likely to have never been married and almost twice as likely to be divorced or separated as appointees overall" (10). The lower likelihood of being married and the higher likelihood of being divorced or separated were also associated with higher incidences of women appointees having fewer children or not having children at all. Table 2.3 contains the responses to questions regarding family life. Statistical differences were found between elected and appointed officials overall, but most of the statistically significant difference was between the sexes in each respective office. Although appointed and elected officials were equally likely not to have children, appointees were more likely to have children under the age of eighteen, whereas elected officials were more likely to have children over eighteen.

Elected officials having higher incidences of children over eighteen might be a result of the slight age gap between elected and appointed officials discussed earlier. On average, elected officials were a year older than appointed officials. The gender gap in the age of these officials' children is more likely a function of the higher incidences of children under eighteen belonging to high-level appointees. High-level appointees were three years younger than low-level appointees, seven years younger than state senators, and three years younger than state representatives. Younger children of those in high-level appointed office might also be indicative of a feasible work/life balance elected women perceive as not being available to them. In part this might be true for elected women in citizen or hybrid state legislatures who most likely have to hold another

Table 2.3 Family Life of State Elected and Appointed Officials

	Appointed Total	Boards and Commissions	High Appointees	Elected Total	State Reps.	State Senators
Marital Status						
Single	6.74%	6.79%	6.49%	7.69%	8.57%	4.55%
Long-term relationship	3.60%	3.66%	3.25%	3.47%	3.49%	3.41%
Married	81.56%	80.88%	85.71%	80.40%	79.68%	82.95%
Other	8.10%	8.67%	4.55%	8.43%	8.25%	9.09%
Children						
No children	17.00%	17.40%	14.65%	17.94%	18.61%	15.56%
Children under eighteen	24.80%*	23.46%	33.12%	19.80%	20.06%	18.90%
Children over eighteen	62.12%*	63.27%	54.78%	67.81%	66.25%	73.33%
Parent Suggestion						
Frequently	2.36%	2.33%	2.60%	3.56%	3.29%	4.49%
Occasionally	13.45%	12.59%	18.83%	15.78%	16.45%	13.48%
Seldom	15.27%	15.45%	14.29%	13.23%	12.83%	14.61%
Never	68.91%	69.63%	64.29%	67.43%	67.43%	67.42%
N	1,129	157	972	407	317	90

Note: Levels of significance in difference of means and chi-square tests comparing all appointees with all elected officials in the sample. Where frequencies were less than five, Fischer's exact test was used instead of chi-square. *Other* marital status includes widowed, separated, and divorced. *Parental suggestion* asks if as a child their parent ever encouraged them to run for elected office or seek political appointment. ** $p < 0.01$, * $p < 0.05$, + $p < 0.10$

job to support their families. Those in full-time appointments typically had only that one position, and most of the low-level boards and commissions met infrequently enough that having a career outside of that appointment was feasible.

Most of the elected and appointed officials who participated in my sample were married, although state representatives had higher incidences of being single than any other group, at 8 percent. High-level appointees had the highest percentage of children under eighteen, at 29 percent, whereas state senators had the highest percentage of children over eighteen, at 73 percent. There was only a 3 percent difference among those in the four offices when it came to having no children.

Although the non-gender-divided demographics above do not show much variation in terms of marital status, differences emerge when we break up the data by sex (Figures 2.5 and 2.6). More than 6 percent more women appointees identified as single compared with men appointees, a statistically significant difference at the $p < 0.01$ level. These women were also more than 12 percent less likely to identify as married, which is a similar finding to that regarding women elected officials, who were also less likely to identify as being married. Being in long-term relationships represented a statistically significant difference between men and women appointees, just as it had been a more common status for women more than twenty years ago in a study of appointed officials (M. A. Newman 1994). Women appointees were more likely to be in a committed relationship by approximately 3 percentage points. In fact, the numbers

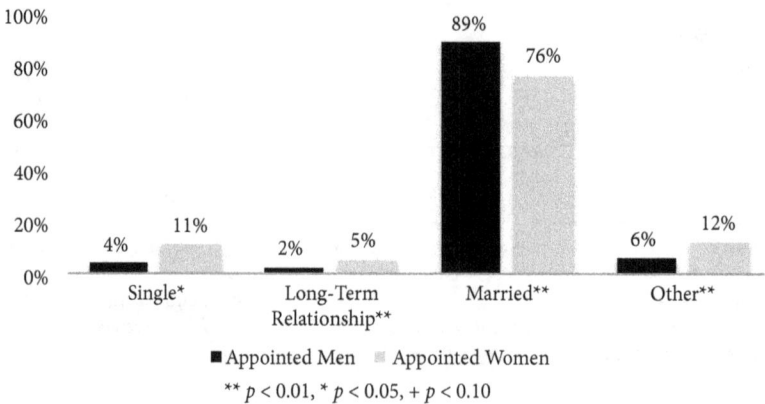

Appointed Men   Appointed Women
** $p < 0.01$, * $p < 0.05$, + $p < 0.10$

Figure 2.5 Gender and Marital Status of State Appointees

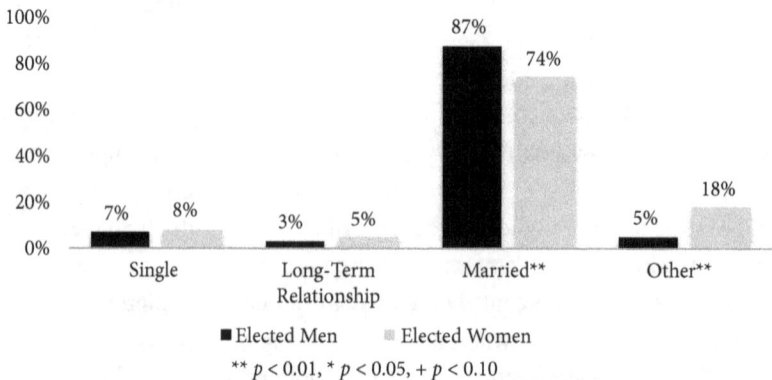

Elected Men   Elected Women
** $p < 0.01$, * $p < 0.05$, + $p < 0.10$

Figure 2.6 Gender and Marital Status of State Legislators

of men and women in committed relationships were remarkably similar to those identified in Newman's 1994 study.

Finally, another area of significant gender differences emerges regarding the number of children of the appointees and elected officials. In general, appointees were more likely than elected officials to have children under eighteen. However, beyond this, women appointees were much more likely than men appointees to have no children at all (Figure 2.7). When they did have children, they were more likely to have younger children, which might have been related to the younger ages of appointed women than those of appointed men. These gender dynamics did not carry over to elected officials. There was little to no difference in the number of children among elected men and women (Figure 2.8).

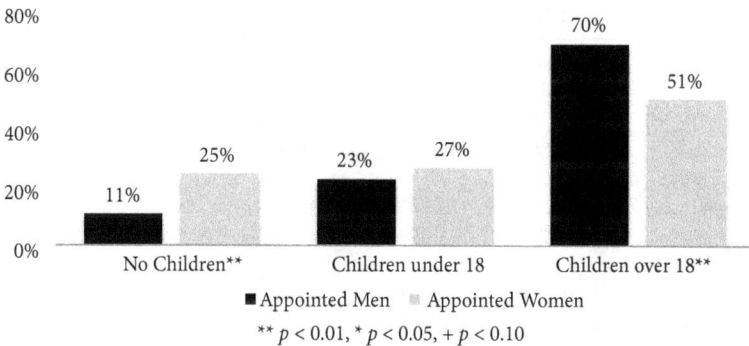

Figure 2.7 Children and Gender of State Appointees

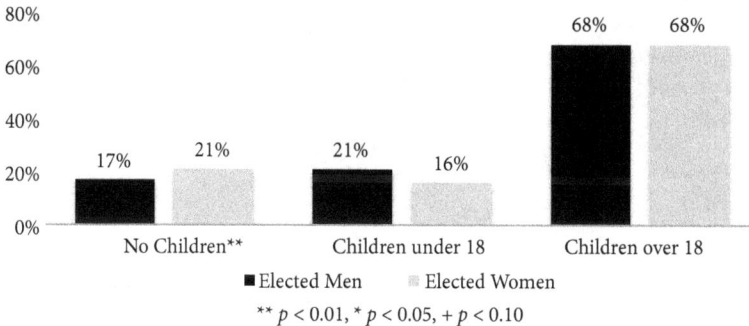

Figure 2.8 Children and Gender of State Legislators

Political Involvement

We'll discuss two areas regarding political involvement: party identification and political activities (Table 2.4). One of the most interesting patterns from the survey is the response to the party identification question, in response to which appointees were much more likely than elected officials to label themselves as Independents, including Independent leaning Democrat or Republican. Few elected officials identified as Independents at all, with most identifying strongly as Democrats or Republicans.

Party also continued to be significantly different by gender in each office, particularly in appointed office. Men were more likely to label them-

Table 2.4 Political Involvement of State Elected and Appointed Officials

	Appointed Total	Boards and Commissions	High Appointees	Elected Total	State Reps.	State Senators
Party						
Strong Democrat	17.25%**	17.30%	17.11%	25.81%	27.16%	21.11%
Democrat	18.25%	18.24%	18.42%	20.35%	21.09%	17.78%
Independent, leaning Democrat	16.80%**	16.88%	16.45%	4.47%	4.47%	4.44%
Independent	11.20%**	10.90%	13.16%	0.74%	< 1%	0%
Independent, leaning Republican	14.72%**	15.09%	12.50%	4.47%	4.47%	4.44%
Republican	16.17%**	15.62%	19.08%	21.84%	2.36%	20%
Strong Republican	5.60%**	5.97%	3.29%	22.33%	19.49%	32.22%
Political Activity						
Volunteered/worked for a candidate	51.15%**	50.62%	54.78%	83.78%	82.65%	87.78%
Attended city council/ school board meeting	80.09%**	80.14%	80.25%	93.61%	93.06%	95.56%
Attended political party meeting/event	54.69%**	54.12%	58.60%	88.70%	88.01%	91.11%
Observed/attended state legislative committee meeting	71.68%**	69.86%	83.44%	78.87%	76.66%	86.67%
Served on board of nonprofit or foundation	75.04%+	76.34%	67.52%	79.61%	77.29%	87.78%
N	1,129	972	157	407	317	90

Note: Levels of significance in difference of means and chi-square tests comparing all appointees to all elected officials in the sample. Where frequencies were less than five, Fischer's exact test was used instead of chi-square. ** $p < 0.01$, * $p < 0.05$, + $p < 0.10$.

selves Republicans compared with appointed women, who were much more likely to label themselves Democrats (significant at the $p < 0.01$ level; see Figure 2.9). This might be a result of the slightly higher rates of appointment of women by Democratic governors as opposed to appointment of men, found in both a 2001 study (Riccucci and Saidel 2001) and my survey.[13] Figure 2.10 puts the party differences in perspective, demonstrating how wide the gulf is in party identification between elected and appointed officials. Barely any elected officials see themselves as

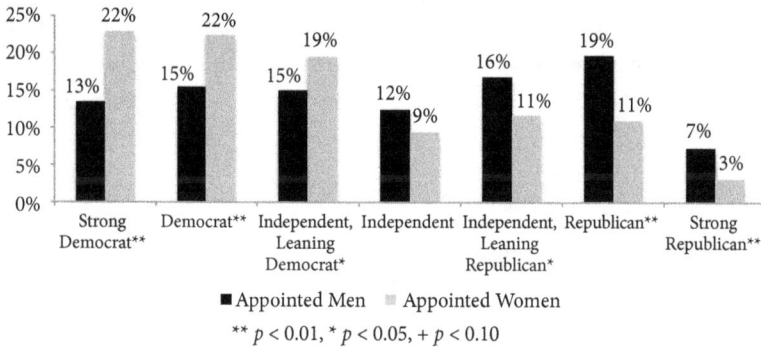

** $p < 0.01$, * $p < 0.05$, + $p < 0.10$

Figure 2.9 Gender and Party ID of State Appointees

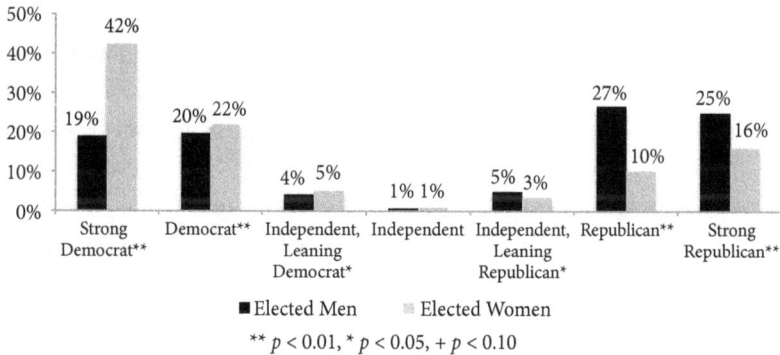

** $p < 0.01$, * $p < 0.05$, + $p < 0.10$

Figure 2.10 Gender and Party ID of State Legislators

13. Of those appointed by governors, 59 percent of the women were appointed by a Democratic governor compared with 56 percent of the men appointed by a Democratic governor. On the other side of the aisle, 44 percent of the men were appointed by a Republican governor, and 41 percent of the women were appointed by a Republican governor.

Independents, even one leaning toward either party. This is consistent with research on polarization within the United States (Bafumi and Shapiro 2009; Fiorina and Abrams 2008; Levendusky 2009). It is interesting, however, that this polarization has not seemed to seep into the executive branch of state governments. Upon further investigation, there is little party difference when I separate the data into higher- and lower-level appointees, indicating that even those appointees exposed to partisan politics—and most likely appointed because of partisan politics—were not nearly as polarized as were their elected counterparts.

When we move to political activities, we see that elected officials were significantly more likely to have taken part in all the political activity options provided in the survey. This was particularly true for attending a political party meeting, convention, or event; elected officials were more than 30 percent more likely to have taken part in these activities than were appointees. Another significant difference between appointees and elected officials was volunteering or working for a candidate, which again elected officials did much more often than appointed officials did.[14]

IN THEIR OWN WORDS: PUBLIC OFFICIALS ON THEIR POLITICAL AND PERSONAL LIVES

Before the results of this survey, there was little understanding of who served on state boards and commissions or how gender played a role in recruitment and ambition patterns for political appointments in general. Few scholars have comprehensively studied state-level appointees and few have ever gone beyond predicting what affects the number of women and minorities, such as governor gender or party (Riccucci and Saidel 2001), to discover their full political histories, trajectories, and opinions.

The last major study to take a census of the number of women and minorities in political appointments at the state level did not capture the full spectrum of political appointments because it studied only high-level appointments such as cabinet secretary and director of a state agency (Center for Women in Government and Civil Society 2008). Although

14. The question on political activities was, "Besides during your political career, have you ever . . . " to try to discover political activities unrelated to their positions.

the study was comprehensive by including all fifty states, more studies should attempt to examine all political appointments because lower-level appointments can act as a stepping-stone to higher office. The next level of statistical analysis of my data sheds more light on how recruitment affects patterns of achieving public office, with Chapter 5 illuminating how recruitment and self-perceived qualifications affect interest in future office holding.

A few interesting findings have already emerged from this preliminary analysis of the survey. In appointments overall, women continue to be younger than men, but now we know this is also true for those women on the low-level boards and commissions, who tend to be younger by more than four years than are men appointed to the same level. The fact that in my sample female higher-level appointees were the youngest out of any type of officeholder is particularly interesting when paired with the finding that higher-level female appointees were the most likely not to have children at all as well as the most likely to have children under eighteen if they did have children.

There appears to be a deep split for higher-level women appointees between having children and pursuing their political careers. This is not to say that women at the board and commission level do not understand the difficulties of having children and pursuing public office. One woman from a landscape architect board had this to say regarding children:

> While I feel public service is important, I know people have very different reasons for pursuing appointed and elected positions. I am divorced and have no children, which affords me ample time to serve; however, I honestly would do a lot less if I had a family. I am fortunate to have the time, flexibility (level in my career/firm), and willingness to serve. I believe I have a lot to contribute, and I have never thought my opinion didn't matter.

However, also interesting is that two male appointees on commerce boards mentioned conflicts between their interest in running for office and affording the costs of child care. One male economic development advisory board member said he was "not seeking additional elected or appointed positions because they do not help with child care, which is too expensive to pay for and serve in low-paying elected positions." The second male, who served on an economic development board, stated:

I have always liked being politically active and involved in public policy at local, state, and federal levels. I can't afford to take a cut in pay to run for office with five children. I had senators and Congressmen both ask me to run for state and federal offices. I was within a day of making the decision when I was thirty-five to run for attorney general of our state but backed off when I was getting married the same year and didn't want to put a statewide election on top of our first months married.

Having children is seen as a serious barrier by some appointees with the ambition to make the leap from appointment to elected office. However, having children was also a key reason for some of the appointees to get involved in politics in some way, even though many did not view their position as political. One woman on an advisory board from Illinois said:

My appointment really has nothing to do with politics. It was an advisory board for a specific special needs population. I requested appointment when I was asked by an affiliated organization representative. I wanted to give back to the population that had given to us and make sure that I had a say in my daughter's life, since she is part of the population/community that the board is involved in. I would have loved to have gotten a degree in political science or law and possibly ran for an office but went a different route.

A large portion of those who left comments in the open-ended section of the survey also believed their positions were not political, even though the boards and commissions on which they served were funded and endorsed by their state governments. Although many of these positions, particularly those on professional licensing boards, have varying degrees of influence on state government, most of these appointments affect the regulations the state supports.

Part of the reason these individuals did not like to think of their positions as political might have been because of the considerable number of respondents who viewed politics in a negative light. Many individuals expressed disappointment and outright disgust at current politics in the United States. Comments such as, "The federal government is sclerotic and unresponsive in most agencies" (male commerce director), and "I am generally disgusted by politics and want to have nothing to do with it. I serve on my profession's board because we are a small profession and my children are older and so I have more time for it than many of my colleagues" (female on a naturopathic medicine board) were a common theme among the 307 individuals who expanded upon their survey answers. These comments were not limited to low-level appointees. House representatives, senators, and high-level appointees also expressed disappointment with the current state of politics, which might have been a contributing factor for those not interested in climbing the career ladder, even when they were uniquely positioned to do so. This disgust about politics—specifically differences in how women view the political arena—will crop up repeatedly throughout the rest of the book.

A final area of interest when comparing the history of appointees and elected officials at the state level are differences in their political backgrounds. Looking back to Table 2.4, we see statistically significant differences between appointees and elected officials for each of the political involvement variables. Elected officials were more likely to have taken part in the traditional political activities, such as volunteering for a candidate or attending city council or school board meetings. This remains true even when I break up the data by high- and low-level appointees, senators, and representatives.

When we turn to what the public officials said about their political backgrounds in their own words, we see that many of them seemed to have stumbled into politics. A male state senator said, "At the age of 26 I was recruited by two neighbors who were both former legislators to seek election to the Montana Legislature. I did it even though it was a burden to take the time while continuing my chosen career as a self-employed farmer." A female house representative whose father had been an appointee in the Richard Nixon/Gerald Ford and Ronald Reagan/George H. W. Bush administrations said something similar: "I ran because I was asked. It had never crossed my mind to run before."

Similar sentiments were also common among the appointees. One appointee on a regional advisory board in Utah had a lengthy political background in elected office but admitted he had never intended to get involved in politics:

> I have run for county council, city council, and state legislature
> representative twice. I currently serve on our city planning commission
> and on an advisory council for our Division of Wildlife Resources.

I never intended to become politically active in the sense of actively seeking office. I have been active in political party activities, community councils, and advisory councils for federal decision-making processes. I ran a strong campaign for county council and lost by a very small margin. I am active in conservation issues and favor liberal politics in a very conservative state and in an even more conservative community. I do not expect to make huge changes in the near future but believe efforts must be continuous and lasting to eventually succeed.

Yet other appointees and elected officials took active steps to get involved in politics and exhibited signs of political interest as children. A woman on an accounting board was asked to sit on a professional state licensing board after her initial interest in a local circuit court judgeship. She was not successful in that bid, but it had put her on the governor's radar for appointment. This positive experience changed her mind about future elected office. She explained, "I had never thought much of running for office, but I was surprised at the positive experience in my interview with members of the governor's office (both white men) and thought that perhaps someday I might run for some political office." One house representative said he "started as a small child helping with getting the voting place ready for election. It was a one-room schoolhouse that happened to be on our land. Dad and I would go and he'd build a fire while I washed the last elections vote count off the board. Probably was ten when I attended my first political convention."

The open-answer question on my survey uncovers some interesting patterns in the opinions of the appointees and elected officials who participated. Two of the most consistent patterns to emerge among appointees are dissatisfaction with politics and the belief that their positions were not political. Although only a fraction of the participants expanded upon their survey answers in the open-ended question, it is interesting that these patterns have emerged for several reasons. First, Lawless (2012) has uncovered the effects of political cynicism on political ambition, and they do not bode well for interest in political office. Those who became more cynical about politics were much more likely to lose all of their ambition to run for office. Additionally, research has shown that millennials do not see politics as the way to get things done, even when they are uniquely qualified to participate in them (Lawless and Fox 2015; Shames 2017). It is not surprising, then, to see that few political appointees were interested in future elected office (see Chapter 6).

Second, dissatisfaction with politics and the belief that the political appointee's position was not political are related. Many of these individuals had low time commitments to these boards and commissions, and many expressed how honored they were to serve on their board or commission with people they admired and respected. From this perspective, political appointments, especially at the lower levels, might be uniquely protected from the cynicism present in electoral politics, making political appointments a viable and perhaps even a positive option for those seeking to serve specific communities (such as their professional community) or become involved in politics in some way. We can definitely learn from the respondents' answers that each appointment and election is unique, but the officeholders had similar struggles, such as dissatisfaction with politics or trying to balance family life with political ambitions, that crossed gender and party lines. How these experiences differed depending upon whether an individual was a man or a woman is further elucidated in the following chapters.

CONCLUSION

In this chapter, I have presented the descriptive results of my survey, which contacted appointed and elected officeholders at the state level, and I have made a concerted effort to expand upon prior studies of political appointment and visualize the world of boards and commissions. We are now better situated to understand the differences in the backgrounds—both politically and personally—between elected and appointed officials as well as between men and women. This allows us to use these differences as a jumping-off point for upcoming analyses regarding political recruitment, motivation for office holding, and future political ambitions. The variables of gender, age, family income, having children, and belonging to a party will be particularly important to include because they held some of the largest differences between elected and appointed officials. Many of these variables become even more significant when comparing men and women within appointed and elected office, and many of the comments from the officials themselves support the gender dynamics occurring within each type of office.

One high-level appointee from the South expressed her confusion, because of the values her family instilled in her, with the way gender works in politics:

> I grew up in a family where sexism did not exist. I was raised to believe that I could do anything that I set my mind to do. Also, failure was not an option. If something did not work, then I was always encouraged to dust myself off and try again until I succeeded. I think that is the most challenging area for us to address now in today's political arena; it is almost as if we as a nation have gone back in time. I am honored to be one of the few female CIOs in the nation, but I also do not differentiate my role from a male CIO.

How gender was perceived by the elected and appointed officials and how it was acted upon within each arena are important components to understanding how women fared in both positions. The next chapter will tackle some of the other questions that need to be answered, including the issues of recruitment and motivations to hold political appointment.

3. You Should Be Appointed
Political Recruitment for State-Level Appointed Officials

> So I do not think of it as getting involved in politics; I've been involved in public health, and the position that I was put into in 2011 happened to be an appointed position.
>
> —*Jennifer Clifton, commissioner of health department*

Jennifer Clifton was first appointed as the deputy commissioner of her state's Department of Health in 2011. In her role as deputy commissioner, she was responsible for 300 state employees. She co-led "high-level state-wide public efforts [and] represent[ed] the department, along with the commissioner." She also assisted with the budget as well as helping set the priorities for the department as a whole. When asked about how she obtained her position, she spoke about how she was recruited by the department commissioner to accept the appointment. This same commissioner also encouraged her to accept a position on her local school board. Despite her high-level appointment and school board position, Clifton was very clear that she just "happened" to be in politics. She said her position "was only political because the position happens to be appointed, but my goal is not politics."

Clifton's experience of recruitment demonstrates the role political elites in appointed positions have in getting more women into public service. Political recruitment, both for those first entering politics and for those poised to run for higher office, is an essential part of who gets into politics. It is also important for understanding who stays in power and why some people are consistently excluded from the political arena.

To fully understand why women land in certain kinds of public offices versus others, we need to examine the external forces that help women see themselves as viable candidates and the internal forces that push these women to actively seek public office or—at the very least—be willing to see themselves as future officeholders. In this chapter I argue that political recruitment studies need to be expanded to include political appointments because, although recruitment might look similar for the elected and appointed realms, the calculus behind actively responding to the recruitment is different. For starters, appointees usually accept their appointments for specific reasons: their career, the limitations of a disease that affects themselves or a family member, or an interest in a specific area. Second, many governors' offices or state departments have an office whose sole job is to search for and approve appointments. Because most state-level appointments are to low-level boards and commissions, many people are recruited to fill an open slot. Furthermore, some states, such as Iowa, mandate gender parity on these boards and commissions, which means women can be targeted to fill these positions in ways they cannot for elected positions. Finally, the nature of elected office—being competitive, visible, and potentially partisan—is different from that of appointments, which discourages many women from ever running for office. Chapters 5 and 6 will use recruitment as an explanatory variable to understand whether recruitment influences appointee political ambition. This chapter will focus on differences in recruitment for appointees, arguing that an elected, appointed, or party official can ask a woman to seek an appointed office in the same way he or she can ask a woman to run for elected office.

Second, I argue that recruitment is more complex than simply asking someone to run for elected office or accept a political appointment. A few scholars in the field have already begun to realize this by separating out recruitment by party (Carroll and Sanbonmatsu 2013) and by breaking it down by kinds of recruiters (Lawless and Fox 2010). However, more study is needed in these areas in two ways. First, we need to further unravel whether recruitment is different for elected versus appointed officials, starting with the people recruiting them. Second, we need to understand what appointees versus elected officials are being recruited for and whether appointees really are overlooked as viable candidates for elected office, despite being highly educated and often politically involved. The analysis will show that gender affects recruitment for appointees differently than it affects that for elected officials.

In many ways, the results are not surprising because Lawless and Fox (2010) and Sanbonmatsu (2006) established that women are less likely to be recruited for elected office. My results show that appointed women are similarly disadvantaged. In other ways, the following analysis is unexpected because many more women hold appointed office than they do elected office. Knowing that women are more likely to be in appointed versus elected office, yet are less likely to be recruited for appointed positions, suggests women appointees are self-motivated to seek and hold these positions in a way women elected officials are not. Put simply, recruitment might be much more important to get women to run for elected office than to seek political appointments. I argue throughout the remaining chapters that this phenomenon is connected to a visceral, negative opinion of electoral politics that in turn shapes appointees' definition of politics and pushes them toward the less "political" appointment world. In this chapter I focus specifically on the recruitment of appointed officials. As a comparison, I address the recruitment of elected officials in Chapter 7.

POLITICAL RECRUITMENT AND THE CONNECTION TO INTERNAL MOTIVATIONS TO HOLD PUBLIC OFFICE

Many women who participated in my State Political Pathways Survey discussed specific motivations in accepting their appointment or considering running for office. Many would say it was purely because of their careers, as a woman from an environmental health board in Oregon expressed: "The motivation to serve on a board in my state is related to my career. I am not at all interested in politics." For others it is a personal endeavor, such as for Stephanie Hicks, a woman on a historic trails commission who said the following:

> I was willing to become involved with this because I do have interests in the historic trails and was working on a book that involved historic trails. [I went to] Baker's City, where the Bureau of Land Management's big museum is, and there were some things there that I didn't feel were historically correct and discovered very quickly that my only hope of having any influence on that was to be a part of a political body. An advisory council for historic trails was the most logical place to get involved with the hope of making some changes.

Uncovering the motivations of appointed women for holding public office might also help us understand why other women do not consider public office a viable option.

Many of the women who participated in my survey simultaneously expressed that they were not actually on political bodies and that they harbored no interest in running for public office or seeking a more "political" appointment. For example, Lauren Connelly, a commissioner for a department for seniors, described herself as an "accidental commissioner," said she had to be asked three times to take the position, and only accepted the third time after the governor told her he could appoint someone to the position who would get all the credit for her work or she could just take the position and get the credit for her own work. Connelly was incredibly wary of politics. She said, "To me having to play the game is not always in the interest of the people we serve."

Two other appointees who took part in follow-up interviews expressed similar sentiments. Meredith Kincaid, a woman appointed to a council on disabilities, had this to say:

> Well, it's interesting because really when you call it politics, I don't. What I do—I feel like is educate and advocate. But a lot of people feel like that's part of the political scene, of course. I actually got involved because I'm a parent of a child with disabilities. And so my advocacy really grew from there, and I continued to look around and see all the need that existed and really try to see what more we can do as a society to improve the outcomes for this population. And so that's where my involvement came from, and so I guess in that sense I've been involved from the very beginning, from 1990.

Finally, Cindy Covens, an appointee to a pollution prevention board of directors, said the following when asked about her political background:

> I am not involved in politics. I was appointed as a public service, as a public representative to the board of a company that uses some public money. So our state funds this company that I am on the board. It's a pollution prevention center; they work with companies to prevent them, to help them clean up or not pollute or that kind of thing, and so a lot of state money goes into that company every year, and they need a public representative; that's my only involvement.

These women (and the many others who also expressed similar opinions) had very specific motivations for accepting their appointments, and they had nothing to do with political ambition for public office. On the one hand, this sentiment raises the question of what about the political arena makes these women so vehemently opposed to being a part of it. On the other hand, it illuminates a potential pathway to getting more women interested in public office. It might not only be recruitment but recruitment for specific positions closely related to women's careers, personal lives, or interests that matters. All three of these women were recruited for their positions, but there is a strong underlying sense that they accepted these positions only because they were closely related to issues, constituencies, or work in which they were already deeply involved. In other words, these women were recruited for the only positions intriguing to them. There is a strong possibility that if they were recruited for any other position, they would have turned it down because it did not line up with their nonpolitical interests and motivations. It could also be that if these women were recruited for more "political" positions, they would have said no. I think the fact that they do not see these positions as political is crucial to why they accepted the positions.

Covens said she was recruited for another office—an elected office—and turned it down because she had no interest in holding that kind of office. Understanding internal and external forces on ambition for public office is crucial if we want to know why some women make it onto the political stage and others do not; it is perhaps even more important that we elucidate the link between the two, so as to realize the full range of reasons and motivations to publicly serve. This chapter will help us understand the external force of recruitment on public office holding, and Chapter 4 will continue with that analysis through the study of internal motivations to seek political appointment.

THE STUDY OF POLITICAL RECRUITMENT

Our understanding of the effects of political recruitment on women's interest in elected office is somewhat limited. For instance, we know that states with strong party networks can act as gatekeepers to public office for women (Sanbonmatsu 2006), and we know that women are less likely to be recruited for elected office than men are (Fox and Lawless 2010). Recent reports have also shown that political recruitment was a key reason for most women who held state legislative seats to seek their positions (Sanbonmatsu, Carroll, and Walsh 2009). However, elected office is not the only kind of public office for which women can be recruited. So far, no study has asked men or women if they have been recruited for appointed office or if appointed officials have recruited them for elected office. How does political recruitment function within the appointment arena?

The process of how one becomes appointed to state-level boards and commissions, and even some high appointments, is not well known. For instance, not many people know that for nearly all boards and commissions, individuals have to go through an application process. Although many individuals will receive prompting to apply for the openings on boards and commissions, others, such as those considering elected office, think about applying for the appointments on their own. This is how Donna Abramson, mentioned in Chapter 2, obtained her position: "I just applied for a board, and this is the one I got. I didn't actually apply for this particular board; they just had an opening on this board for a female Democrat, and so they asked me if I would like to serve, and I said sure."

Others might not be recruited for their appointments because the positions are statutory. For example, Darlene Vesko was appointed to the Commission for the Blind because someone from the National Federation of the Blind had to serve on the board. She was in a leadership position in the federation at the time and decided to be the one to take the appointment. Similarly, Wendy Jenkins was appointed to the Water Planning Advisory Council because she had a staff position in water planning management in municipal government.

In the Center for American Women in Politics (1983) study on political appointees, the amount of effort each woman put into seeking her appointment varied. A much lower percentage of women from the main sample reported having made no effort as well as needing to be convinced to accept their appointments. The highest percentage consisted of the women who reported "[I] made no effort but was receptive to the idea of serving" (41). More than 22 percent of the female appointees reported having made some effort to get their appointments, and more than 18 percent actively sought their appointments (Center for American Women in Politics 1983). The CAWP political appointee study is the only project to date to ask appointees about how they were appointed, but even from more than thirty-year-old data we see many ways women can achieve appointment—most notably on their own or by being recruited.

The high-level appointees in my sample also reported a mix of recruitment and individual action, with some saying they were asked and others saying they applied on their own. Riley Cunningham, director of a natural resources department, said that she was not recruited at all, and she simply applied for her position. Commerce commissioner Madison Williams said others put her name forth as a candidate for the position. She said:

> From what I understand is a lot of different people put in my name, so folks from the historic preservation world, the environmental world, legislators put my name forward, and I don't know the inner workings but they called me in, there was a group, four or five people that interviewed me, just saying that they were interviewing people and they weren't really sure for which position at that point. So they would just ask me questions about what my goals were, what my work had been. . . . [They] called and said they wanted me to come work for the organization.

For some of these appointments, high or low, recruitment is similar to that for elected office: someone approached them and asked them to apply for the appointment. There are also similar self-starting tendencies between some appointees and elected officials. They have an interest or see a need and want to take part in the political process, even when no one asks them to try for appointment. For both kinds of office, there is an interesting middle ground between no recruitment and active recruitment, and that is the suggestion to run for office or seek political appointment. This occurs when a colleague, family member, or even a political actor says something like, "I think you should run for office someday" or "You should seek a political appointment." This is not active recruitment for a specific office but more of a suggestion for someone to consider any political office in the future.

Where appointments and elected office diverge most significantly is in their respective nomination processes. Many appointees can simply be nominated for a position, like Stephanie Hicks, the historic trails council appointee quoted earlier who "got a call from the governor's office saying that my name had been submitted as a possible person to fill a vacancy on the council, and would I be interested, and I said yes." This is different from elected office and is something we should be aware of as we try to understand how women get appointed. My survey and interviews have also been able to demonstrate that women in political appointments can be actively recruited, just as women in elected office can, and that they can also exhibit self-starting tendencies when no one recruits them to seek appointed office.

It goes without question that accepting a political appointment and agreeing to run for public office are two substantially different ways to serve. Agreeing to run for elected office means exposing themselves and their families to public scrutiny with no guarantee that they will get their party's nomination, let alone win the seat in the general election. Seeking a political appointment, on the contrary, is a much more private endeavor. It means filling out an application for most low-level appointments and agreeing to some sort of interview for high-level appointments. High-level appointments in certain states could include more public scrutiny through legislative approval of executive appointments. However, generally, the exposure associated with seeking an appointment versus running for elected office is vastly different. Some might argue that this fundamentally changes the recruitment process because certain individuals—women specifically—might be less receptive to recruitment to elected office than recruitment to appointed office. However, I argue that studying recruitment as a separate phenomenon is important. It is important to understand whether recruitment actually makes a difference and that recruitment means nothing if it is not happening for women or for women in certain political positions. As Chapter 2 demonstrates, women in appointments are highly educated and politically involved. They should be prime targets for recruitment to other appointed and elected positions. In this chapter I will demonstrate that despite having many of the characteristics of those recruited, women appointees are still less likely to be recruited than are similarly situated men appointees. Chapter 7 will further show that appointed women are also less likely to be recruited than elected women are. I will use this recruitment variable in Chapters 5 and 6 to help explain political ambition for higher office and elected office among appointees.

Although it is important to consider the role appointers have in recruiting more women to appointments at the state level, I argue that this approach ignores a lot of the agency women have when considering whether to pursue or even accept political appointment. We can learn a considerable amount about the culture of a bureaucratic agency and what kinds of policies increase descriptive representation when researching appointers. However, by overlooking appointees' backgrounds and decisions about public service, we continue to disqualify appointed public service as part of the political pipeline. The men and women included in this book demonstrate that their work and political trajectories are important.

That being said, a substantial number of scholars has studied appointed office from the perspective of the appointer. In *A Government of Strangers* (1977), Hugh Heclo studied the recruitment of appointees in presidential administrations. Although the process varied from administration to administration, by Jimmy Carter's presidency it seemed the White House made an effort to neutrally gather names and rank candidates on their qualifications (Heclo 1977, 94). Of course there are other stakeholders in this process including Congress members, other appointees, the party organizations, and interest groups. The White House must juggle these stakeholders with who the administration feels is best qualified for the position. As Heclo (1977) succinctly stated, "What an outsider is unlikely to appreciate is that these personnel struggles have to do not only with a product but a process. The process of filling jobs is an important facet of political interaction because of its symbolic significance in the mutual calculations of political power" (98).

In *The In-and-Outers* (1987), James Pfiffner also studied the process of White House recruitment. He, like Heclo, noted the more professional nature of appointee recruitment, which works best when a president gives his or her full support to the individual in charge of personnel decisions. At times, this recruitment relies on networking, which can lead to active recruitment. Presidents such as Ronald Reagan further centralized the appointment process as a way to maintain political control over the bureaucracy (Michaels 1997). The Office of Presidential Personnel (OPP) must pay "close attention to the wishes of the individual president not merely to recruit the individuals the president personally knows and wants to appoint but also to seek out those individuals who share the president's values and have the skills, character, and experience to carry out his or her policy directives" (Pfiffner 2001, 51).

In her book *The President's Cabinet* (2002), Maryanne Borelli looked at the federal bureaucracy through the lens of gender. She argued that four variables affect a president's choice of cabinet secretary: indebtedness, symbolism, political relationships, and managerial needs (42). Borelli (2002) found that most of the female secretaries-designate were policy generalists as opposed to specialists or liaisons.[1] Being generalists means women are less likely to have "the political resources to act as independent powerbrokers" (54). Furthermore, these female nominees are often nominated for less visible and less powerful cabinet positions, such as secretary of the Department of Education. Borelli (2002) concludes from the presidential nominations that masculinity still matters. The story of cabinet recruitment is not only political but also gendered.

Although this overview of the literature on recruitment from the perspective of the appointer is based on federal appointments, it does point to the importance of understanding the political and managerial needs of an executive. Although the demands and needs of a presidential administration are larger, similar demands are placed on governors by their states. It is important to acknowledge that a governor's administration might make a more concerted effort to diversify regarding gender and race (part of the reason some state governments *are* more diverse), but I argue it is important to understand this process from the appointees' position as well. Asking appointees if they have been recruited reveals patterns of who is on the radar of recruiters as well as signaling what states, party leaders, and executives believe is important in their public officials. For example, if we find that women are less likely to be recruited (as I expect), this suggests that women are not in the same networks as similarly situated men to be recruited for state public office. It could also suggest that even if women are in these networks, they are simply not recruited as often as men are. For either outcome, studying recruitment from the perspective of appointees is an important endeavor. Finally, studying recruitment from appointees' perspective tells us when recruitment might work; studying appointers shows us only the success stories.

This external force of political recruitment is at the heart of the analysis in this chapter. The first half will uncover the differences in political

1. A pattern noted more than ten years earlier by Janet Martin (1989) in "The Recruitment of Women to Cabinet and Subcabinet Posts."

recruitment among appointed officials, focusing specifically on any gender differences. I will explore the differences in who is recruiting men versus women for appointment and for what kinds of offices they are recruiting. The second half will provide a statistical analysis of the recruiters and what kinds of appointees they are recruiting.

POLITICAL RECRUITMENT AS AN EXTERNAL MOTIVATION TO SERVE IN PUBLIC OFFICE

Chapter 2 provides the first indication of the differences between appointed and elected officials, even on the basic measures of demographics, family life, and political participation. The exclusion of appointed office from recruitment studies means we are missing alternative explanations or recruitment patterns for women at the state level. My data confirm this by showing that 52 percent of political appointees were recruited for appointed or elected office at some point in their careers.[2] Furthermore, Figure 3.1 reveals that the differences in recruitment depended on the gender of the individual and his or her level of office. For example, high-level appointed women were 8 percent more likely than high-level appointed men to have been recruited for public office, but this pattern was reversed for low-level appointees. At the board and commission level, men were 8 percent more likely to be recruited than

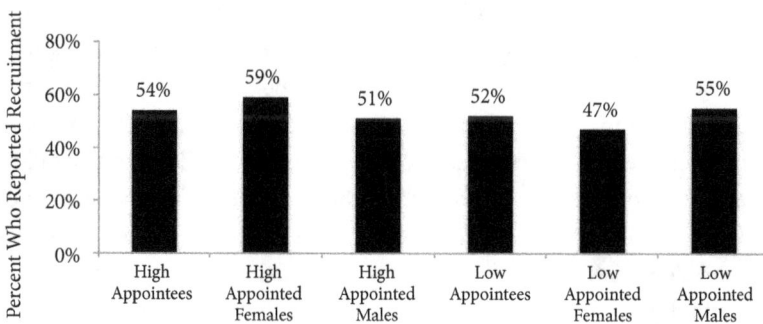

Figure 3.1 State Appointee Political Recruitment

2. This covers recruitment by elected, appointed, or party officials as well as recruitment by gubernatorial staff and women's organizations. It covers recruitment prior to their positions and since they attained their positions.

Appointed Office Recruitment

Elected Office Recruitment

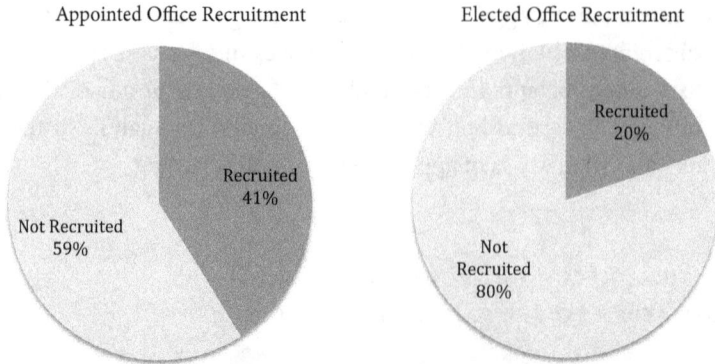

Figure 3.2 Female Appointees Recruited for Appointed versus Elected Office

were women ($p < 0.05$). It is also important to note that recruitment did not change substantially depending upon whether an individual was in a high-level state appointment or low-level state appointment.

Of the 455 appointed women in my sample, 90 of them had been recruited for elected office at some point in their careers, compared with 188 who had been recruited for appointed office (Figure 3.2). More than 64 percent of the 90 female appointees recruited for elected office ($n = 58$) had also been recruited for appointed office, and even more importantly, nearly 36 percent of the women never recruited for elected office were recruited for appointed office at some point. These results suggest that a sizeable portion of women's recruitment for appointed and elected office has taken place beyond the scope of every other recruitment study.

The previously exclusive focus on recruitment for elected office is not the only area in which recruitment studies fall short. How recruitment functions after an individual is in office, especially low-level public office, is also unknown. Many pundits and scholars lament the low number of women in public office, and one of the first statistics they inevitably discuss to demonstrate this is that only 23.7 percent of Congress is women (Center for American Women in Politics 2018a). However, few if any women wake up one morning and decide they want to run for Congress, let alone actually win a seat. Instead, many men and women set their sights lower, such as the school board, town council, or even state legislature, and then consider moving up the political ladder.

What we do not know is if that consideration is affected by recruitment to another office or even what this recruitment entails.[3] It is not clear whether women continue to be as disadvantaged after they hold office or if recruitment is as important when a woman has already won public office and is poised to climb the political career ladder. A third of the appointed women never recruited to elected office were recruited to appointed office; this proves we cannot assume that all recruitment is the same or that only recruitment to elected office matters.

A woman on a health board from Illinois is the perfect example of a woman who slipped through the cracks of prior recruitment studies. At the time of the study, she had never been recruited for elected office but was recruited for appointed office prior to her position and since her position by appointed officials and women's organizations. Another appointee, a public health commissioner at the time of the study, was recruited for both elected and appointed office prior to her position and continued to be recruited for both kinds of offices. The recruitment of a high-level state commissioner to both elected and appointed office definitively demonstrates the need to expand political recruitment studies outside of the electoral world.

Just who is recruiting state-level appointed officials? According to Table 3.1, the answer is different depending on the recruiter and whether the prospective appointee is a man or a woman. Appointed officials in general are more likely to have been recruited by appointed and elected officials. This makes sense because it is either appointed or elected officials who have powers of appointment. Women trail men in recruitment in almost every category except that of women's organizations.[4] The only major difference in recruitment patterns based upon the level of appointment is found in recruitment of high-level appointed officials: 41 percent of high-level appointees compared with 30 percent of low-level appointees reported appointed official recruitment ($p < 0.01$). For every kind of recruiter, high-level female appointees were more likely to be recruited

3. Or as Carroll and Sanbonmatsu (2013) have found, if women had never considered moving up the career ladder but recruitment prompted them to consider it.

4. This result might be biased in favor of only one kind of organization. Because I only asked if women's organizations recruited appointees/elected officials, I cannot report on differences on how other organizations might have recruited candidates.

than were men. Except for recruitment by a women's organization, the inverse was true for low-level female appointees; they were less likely to report recruitment than were their male counterparts. This suggests that high-level appointed women are a source for political recruiters but that low-level appointed women are not seen in the same way.

Table 3.1 provides the most general depiction of political recruitment at the state level. Table 3.2 shows us for which type of office appointees are being recruited. In general, most recruitment seemed to be for appointed office. About 45 percent of all appointees were recruited for appointed office versus 24 percent who were recruited for elected office. These percentages do not preclude recruitment for elected office, but as can be seen in the second to last row of the table, it was rare for an appointee to have been recruited for both types of offices. Male appointees were more likely to be recruited for either kind of office than were female appointees. There was not much variation in recruitment for elected versus appointed office between high-level men and women appointees (high-

Table 3.1 Political Recruitment by Recruiter

Recruiter	All Appointees	Appointed Men	Appointed Women
Elected official	30.53%	34.37%	24.84%**
Appointed official	31.15%	32.59%	29.01%
Party official	16.28%	18.67%	12.75%**
Governor's staff	24.87%	26.37%	22.64%
Women's organization	10.53%	5.93%	17.36%**
N	1,130	675	455

Note: Chi-2 tests were used to find the difference in means, with Fisher's exact test used when observations were less than or equal to five. $+ p < 0.10$, $* p < 0.05$, $** p < 0.01$.

Table 3.2 Recruitment for Elected versus Appointed Office

	All Appointees	Appointed Men	Appointed Women
Recruited for appointed office	44.60%	46.81%	41.32%+
Recruited for elected office	23.81%	26.52%	19.78%**
Recruited for both	16.37%	18.81%	12.75%*
N	1,130	675	455

Note: Chi-2 tests were used to find the difference in means, with Fisher's exact test used when observations were less than or equal to five. $+ p < 0.10$, $* p < 0.05$, $** p < 0.01$.

level appointed women were slightly more likely to be recruited, but the differences were not statistically significant). Low-level appointed men were 8 percent more likely than low-level appointed women to be recruited for elected office ($p < 0.01$) and were 6 percent more likely to be recruited for appointed office ($p < 0.05$).

We have covered general recruitment patterns, including who is recruiting appointed officials and for what kind of offices they are recruiting. I have already found major differences in the recruitment patterns of appointed men and women, mirroring much of the research on the recruitment of elected officials. The next section will test differences in recruitment through regression analysis.

Dependent Variables

Table 3.3 contains five models, each with a dependent variable predicting recruitment of political appointees. Models 1–4 predict recruitment by elected officials, appointed officials, party officials, and women's organizations, respectively. Model 5 predicts recruitment by all of these political actors in addition to recruitment by gubernatorial staff. Appointees are considered recruited by any of these gatekeepers if they responded affirmatively to the following question in the survey: "Regardless of whether or not you are interested in seeking elective office or higher political appointment, have any of the following individuals/groups ever recruited you to run or seek higher office since you obtained your current political appointment?" Therefore, this analysis regards political recruitment of current officeholders and not any recruitment they might have received prior to their position.[5] Approximately 29 percent of the appointees had been recruited since attaining their position; men were slightly more likely to be recruited than women were, and high-level appointees were 5 percent more likely to be recruited than low-level appointees were (neither difference was statistically significant). Each dependent variable is coded as 0 for no recruitment and 1 for recruitment. Table 3.4 contains the predicted probabilities from the analysis in Table 3.3. I duplicate this same analysis for the state legislators in Chapter 7.

5. Because there are only two outcomes for each dependent variable, not being recruited (0) and being recruited (1), I ran logistic regression with robust standard errors.

Table 3.3 Predicting State Appointee Recruitment by Recruiter

	Recruited by Elected Official	Recruited by Appointed Official	Recruited by Party Official	Recruited by Women's Organization	Recruited by Any Official
Demographics					
Female	−0.433* (0.219)	−0.096 (0.199)	−0.495+ (0.267)	1.260** (0.307)	−0.055 (0.171)
Age	−0.033** (0.011)	−0.031** (0.009)	−0.013 (0.012)	−0.004 (0.013)	−0.015+ (0.008)
Nonwhite	0.943** (0.306)	0.425 (0.287)	0.684+ (0.410)	0.671 (0.424)	0.788** (0.279)
Family income	0.052 (0.107)	0.128 (0.095)	0.340 (0.118)	−0.159 (0.136)	0.073 (0.082)
Education	0.103 (0.080)	0.043 (0.744)	−0.059 (0.094)	−0.076 (0.110)	0.038 (0.064)
Political Environment					
Republican	0.152 (0.279)	−0.168 (0.253)	0.609+ (0.382)	−0.590 (0.414)	0.086 (0.222)
Democrat	0.117 (0.230)	−0.243 (0.209)	0.519+ (0.304)	0.239 (0.315)	0.026 (0.182)
Political participation	4.002** (0.554)	2.244** (0.375)	4.965** (0.759)	3.353** (0.709)	2.555** (0.340)
Moralistic	−0.305 (0.294)	0.119 (0.246)	−0.481 (0.384)	−0.431 (0.420)	−0.070 (0.221)
Local political opportunity structure	0.0002 (0.0003)	−0.0001 (0.002)	0.0004 (0.0003)	0.0002 (0.0004)	0.0003 (0.0002)
State political opportunity structure	0.0001 (0.003)	0.0001 (0.003)	0.002 (0.004)	0.006 (0.004)	−0.0015 (0.0025)
Percent female state legislature 2012	0.004 (0.017)	0.023 (0.016)	0.021 (0.022)	−0.034 (0.027)	0.010 (0.015)
Percent female appointees 2007	−0.407 (1.494)	−0.774 (1.328)	0.460 (1.803)	−0.994 (2.032)	0.092 (1.166)
Current Office Characteristics					
Had mentor/sponsor	0.331 (0.221)	0.392* (0.197)	0.078 (0.274)	−0.155 (0.299)	0.222 (0.181)
Number of years in position	−0.026 (0.012)*	−0.025 (0.011)*	0.0009 (0.015)	−0.024 (0.018)	−0.363** (0.010)
High appointee	−0.509+ (0.299)	0.292 (0.244)	−0.235 (0.375)	0.303 (0.400)	−0.109 (0.228)
Held elected office	0.952** (0.249)	0.735** (0.229)	0.995** (0.273)	0.571+ (0.333)	0.830** (0.214)
Held appointed office	0.735** (0.216)	0.303 (0.200)	0.415 (0.256)	0.234 (0.282)	0.539** (0.174)
Compensation salary	0.284 (0.380)	0.378 (0.361)	0.252 (0.462)	0.054 (0.540)	0.574+ (0.304)
Constant	−3.940** (1.086)	−2.613** (0.887)	−6.700 (1.258)	−3.558** (1.338)	−2.949** (0.811)
N	999	999	999	999	999
Pseudo-R^2	0.2362	0.1170	0.2588	0.1847	0.1557

Note: Standard errors in parentheses. + $p < 0.10$, * $p < 0.05$, ** $p < 0.01$

Table 3.4 Predicted Probabilities for Appointee Recruitment

	Recruited by Elected Official	Recruited by Appointed Official	Recruited by Party Official	Recruited by Women's Organization	Recruited by Any Official
Female	-2.76%	—	-1.73%	+6.17%	—
Age	-5.12%	-5.53%	—	—	-4.67%
Nonwhite	+10.76%	—	+5.03%	—	+14.70%
Political participation	+19.90%	+11.67%	+15.87%	+5.87%	+22.52%
Republican	—	—	+4.13	—	—
Democrat	—	—	+1.96%	—	—
Had sponsor/mentor	—	+4.06%	—	—	—
High-level appointee	-2.99%	—	—	—	—
Held elected office	+10.84%	+8.86%	+7.35%	+2.09%	+15.36%
Held appointed office	+7.54%	—	—	—	+9.61%
Compensation salary	—	—	—	—	+10.38%
Number of years in position	-2.91%	-3.11%	—	—	-7.70%

Note: Democrat was set to 1. Sex, nonwhite, having a sponsor/mentor, Republican, high-level appointee, moralistic, held elected office, held appointed office, and compensation salary were set to 0. All other variables were set at their means.

Independent Variables

The independent variables can be broken down into four major categories: *sociodemographic* variables, such as sex, education, and race; *political characteristic* variables, such as party identification and political participation history; *characteristics of their current office* variables, such as whether it is term limited and the number of years the individual has been in the position; and *state-specific* variables, such as culture and political opportunity structure. Diverse variables can affect whether an individual gets recruited, and we already know from Lawless and Fox's (2010) study that political participation and gender are two major variables affecting political recruitment; individuals who participate more politically will be more likely to be recruited, and women are less likely to be recruited for elected office. We also know that women from different political parties will be recruited differently and that the Republican Party lags far behind the Democratic Party in its recruitment of women candidates (Sanbonmatsu, Carroll, and Walsh 2009).

In addition to the boosts certain sociodemographic variables might give to potential recruited individuals (such as those with more education and income being recruited more often), the characteristics of a state itself can also increase or decrease recruitment. States with moralistic political cultures might have higher instances of recruitment because public service is often seen as a noble duty (Elazar 1966), and states with large numbers of public offices (both at the state and local levels) might have more instances of recruitment because there are more positions to fill (this is represented by state and local political opportunity structure). Finally, characteristics of the office the appointed official holds, such as whether it is term limited, might affect recruitment. Individuals with term limits, for example, might be seen as viable candidates for a different office after they have completed their terms. My expectation for the role of sex is that appointed women are less likely to be recruited, particularly by traditional electoral gatekeepers such as elected and party officials. Because many of the appointed women in my study were similar to the women who did not hold office but were most likely to be recruited, I expect them to display similar recruitment patterns. I particularly expect this for women on boards and commissions, which provide less visible public service opportunities than do higher-level appointments.

The results from the analysis in Table 3.3 (predicted probabilities are located in Table 3.4) show mixed support for the effect of sex on recruitment. Appointed women were less likely to be recruited for appointed or elected office by elected and party officials, but they were not less likely to be recruited by appointed officials. They were 6 percent more likely to be recruited by women's organizations. Overall, women were not less likely to be recruited than men were, and when we look at individual recruiters, the effect was small. Female appointees were only 2–3 percent less likely than male appointees to report being recruited by elected or party officials. Political participation and having held elected office were two of the strongest predictors of recruitment by any gatekeeper and collectively by the gatekeepers. Being politically active increased reports of recruitment anywhere from 6 percent (recruitment by women's organizations) to as much as 23 percent (recruitment by any political actor). Having held elected office increased likelihood of recruitment by more than 15 percent. Interestingly, being nonwhite also had a relatively strong effect on recruitment, pointing to the importance of political gatekeepers of diversity in candidates for these positions.

Part of the reason appointees' sex might not have had an effect on collective political recruitment by gatekeepers is a result of the dispro-portional effect of women's organizations who, unsurprisingly, were predisposed to recruit women. Yet even when women's organizations are dropped from the analysis—therefore predicting recruitment from elected officials, appointed officials, party officials, and gubernatorial staff only—sex still does not become significant, and none of the other variables change significantly. However, the original models did not ac-count for the unique position of women in high-level appointments. I noted earlier that high-level appointed women were not only in more visible public offices but also they reported higher levels of recruitment by all of the recruiters. Table 3.5 presents the same statistical analysis from Model 5 of Table 3.3, predicting political recruitment from all gate-keepers excluding women's organizations. Additionally, this analysis includes an interaction for high-level appointed women—with some re-vealing results.

First, sex becomes significant: female appointees were almost 6 per-cent less likely to be recruited by elected, party, or appointed officials or gubernatorial staff. However, high-level appointed women were more than 18 percent more likely to be recruited by these gatekeepers than were low-level appointed women and all appointed men. What does this mean, and what are the implications? First, women in low-level appoint-ments—boards and commissions—were passed over at higher rates than were similarly situated men. In this way women in low-level appoint-ments were similar to the women in Lawless and Fox's (2010) study of in-dividuals who had never held elected office. Second, it shows that women can be attractive recruitment candidates to these gatekeepers after they have reached a certain level of office. What this means is that women might have to work harder (or achieve more) to receive the same kind of attention for higher-level appointment or elected office than do similarly situated men because the men in low-level appointments are more likely than are women in low-level appointments to be recruited. It could also be evidence of tokenism: few women are found at the upper echelons of state-level elected and appointed office, and when one has made it, she is seen as a good candidate for other offices.

Women in high-level appointments might also be more likely to be recruited because administrations who want to diversify see them as good candidates for other positions. Although I do not conduct the

Table 3.5 Gender and Level of Office Effect on Recruitment

	Recruited by Any Official Except Women's Organizations		Predicted Probability
Demographics			
Female	−0.419*	(0.192)	−5.53%
Age	−0.018*	(0.008)	−5.40%
Nonwhite	0.779**	(0.281)	+15.20%
Family income	0.036	(0.083)	—
Education	0.013	(0.065)	—
Political Environment			
Republican	0.166	(0.225)	—
Democrat	0.015	(0.186)	—
Political participation	2.566**	(0.350)	+22.76%
Moralistic			
Local political opportunity structure	0.0004*	(0.0002)	+6.75%
State political opportunity structure	−0.002	(0.003)	—
Percent female state legislature 2012	0.016	(0.015)	—
Percent female appointees 2007	−0.301	(1.196)	—
Current Office Characteristics			
Had mentor/sponsor	0.256	(0.183)	—
Number of years in position	−0.035**	(0.010)	−7.39%
High-level appointee	−0.220	(0.306)	—
Held elected office	0.821**	(0.213)	+15.52%
Held appointed office	0.499**	(0.177)	+9.00%
Compensation salary	0.665*	(0.302)	+12.16%
High female appointee	0.919*	(0.442)	+18.44%
Constant	−2.491**	(0.830)	—
N	999		
Pseudo-R^2	0.1625		

Note: For predicted probabilities Democrat was set to 1. Sex, nonwhite, having a sponsor/mentor, Republican, high-level appointee, moralistic, high female appointee, held elected office, held appointed office, and compensation salary were set to 0. All other variables were set at their means. $+ p < 0.10$, $* p < 0.05$, $** p < 0.01$.

same analysis here that Borrelli completed (2002), it is incumbent upon scholars of state executive office to understand the gendered nature of appointments. In particular, Borelli found that women were appointed to federal office as generalists to positions in which they did not have as much background and therefore had to rely on their male president for power and influence. From my interviews alone, this is not the case for high-level female state appointees. The women in these positions had considerable professional and educational background as well as connections with people in government who saw them as good prospects for their appointments. In short, female appointees at the state level might enjoy much more influence in their positions than do women in federal positions.

FOR WHAT ARE APPOINTEES BEING RECRUITED?

So far, my analysis in this chapter has revealed who recruits appointees. In that analysis, we saw that appointed women are less likely than men to be recruited—specifically for appointed or elected office—by elected and party officials. When taking into consideration all the recruiters, low-level appointed women on boards and commissions are less likely to be recruited, but after they reach a higher appointment level, they become more likely to be recruited by electoral and appointed gatekeepers.

There is still a final question that needs to be answered: Are appointed officials recruited differently for different kinds of office? More than 21 percent of the appointees had been recruited for appointed office since attaining their positions compared with 15 percent of appointees recruited for elected office.[6] Table 3.6 predicts political recruitment of appointees to elected versus appointed office, excluding recruitment by women's organizations and including a variable accounting for high-level female appointees. The results continue the trend from the earlier analysis: low-level appointed women are less likely to be recruited for elected and appointed office, and being a woman seems to be more detrimental in recruitment to appointed office. It is not quite clear why women in appointments are less likely to be recruited for appointed office than for elected office. It might be that female appointees are in specialized positions, such as positions on boards regarding certain diseases or disabilities, that do not have a clear relationship to other appointed offices in government. It might also be that recruitment overall is considerably less for appointed positions compared with that for elected office. This

6. Of men appointees, 22 percent were recruited for appointed office since attaining their position versus 20 percent of women appointees; 16 percent of men appointees and 12 percent of women appointees were recruited for elected office ($p < 0.10$).

Table 3.6 Predicting Recruitment for Appointed versus Elected Office: Appointed Officials

	Recruited for Elected Office Excluding Recruitment by a Women's Organization	Predicted Probability	Recruited for Appointed Office Excluding Recruitment by a Women's Organization	Predicted Probability
Demographics				
Female	-0.736 (0.261)**	-2.82%	-0.419 (0.192)*	-5.45%
Age	-0.033 (0.012)**	-3.50%	-0.018 (0.008)*	-5.46%
Nonwhite	0.739 (0.373)*	+6.17%	0.779 (0.281)**	+14.83%
Family income	0.0009 (0.110)	—	0.035 (0.083)	—
Education	-0.002 (0.086)	—	0.013 (0.065)	—
Political Environment				
Republican	-0.119 (0.292)	—	0.166 (0.225)	—
Democrat	-0.200 (0.261)	—	0.015 (0.188)	—
Political participation	4.733 (0.627)**	+17.44%	2.566 (0.350)**	+22.58%
Moralistic	-0.650 (0.334)+	-2.47%	-0.067 (0.226)	—
Local political opportunity structure	0.0001 (0.0003)	—	0.0004 (0.0002)*	+6.78%
State political opportunity structure	0.004 (0.003)	—	-0.002 (0.003)	—
Percent female state legislature 2012	0.002 (0.020)	—	0.016 (0.015)	—
Percent female appointees 2007	-0.392 (1.614)	—	-0.301 (1.196)	—
Current Office Characteristics				
Had sponsor or mentor	0.143 (0.242)	—	0.256 (0.184)	—
High-level appointee	-0.800 (0.411)+	-2.76%	0.220 (0.306)	—
Number of years in position	-0.020 (0.014)	—	-0.035 (0.010)**	-7.44%
Held elected office	1.250 (0.259)**	+11.63%	0.821 (0.213)**	+15.43%
Held appointed office	0.824 (0.233)**	+6.36%	0.499 (0.177)**	+8.67%
Compensation salary	0.112 (0.432)	—	0.665 (0.302)*	+12.64%
High-level appointee × female	1.136 (0.579)*	+11.42%	0.919 (0.442)*	+18.30%
constant	-3.833 (1.058)**	—	-2.491 (0.830)**	—
N	999		999	
Pseudo-R^2	0.2746		0.1625	

Note: For predicted probabilities Democrat was set to 1. Sex, nonwhite, having a sponsor/mentor, Republican, high-level appointee, moralistic, held elected office, held appointed office, high female appointee, and compensation salary were set to 0. All other variables were set at their means.
+ $p < 0.10$, * $p < 0.05$, ** $p < 0.01$.

is significant because there are many more women in appointed office than elected office at the state level, regardless of level of appointment. Political participation continues to matter in recruitment for both types of offices, as does having held prior elected or appointed office. A high-level female appointee is 11 percent more likely to be recruited for elected office and 18 percent more likely to be recruited for appointed office compared with all appointed men and low-level appointed women.

Nearly all of the same variables are significant when predicting recruitment for elected versus appointed office, with only a few exceptions. Being from a state with a moralistic culture or being a high-level appointee negatively affected recruitment to elected office, yet neither is significant when predicting appointed office recruitment. In contrast, a larger number of offices at the local level, as well as appointees being offered salaries, led to higher levels of recruitment. The other significant variables trend in the same direction for recruitment to appointed and elected office but to different degrees. For example, being nonwhite increased recruitment for elected office by 6 percent but increased recruitment for appointed office by almost 15 percent. Likewise, having held elected office or another appointed office had a larger effect on recruitment to appointed office than to elected office. Overall, these results suggest that many of the same variables predict recruitment to either type of office, with notable variations that scholars of recruitment should take into consideration.

CONCLUSION

Recruitment is an essential component to getting more women into elected and appointed office. This chapter began with the premise that we need to understand the external motivations for public service beyond elected office. As has already been established, thousands of individuals in the United States serve in appointed positions, and they are oftentimes overlooked in studies on public service. Through the analysis in this chapter we learned that more than half of appointees are recruited for public office, yet no one has asked them about this recruitment—who the recruiters are and for what kinds of candidates they are recruiting.

There are some limitations to my analysis in this chapter. For example, the analysis predicts recruitment since the appointees have attained their positions. This leaves out a significant amount of recruitment that happened prior to their positions and most importantly the recruitment that led them into their positions. Although we can see that still matters for recruitment of current officeholders, which in itself is significant, we still do not know how recruitment works for appointments initially. In short, this chapter is just the beginning step to understanding how recruitment functions for women in appointed office.

4. Why Hold Public Office?
Appointed Officials' Motivations to Hold Public Office

> So really the only reason—it took me, just to be honest, a good
> month probably to make a decision, mostly because I haven't had any
> aspirations to be in office, to be in state government even, to be honest.
> But I do have a passion for aging and I thought [of it] as ultimately as
> a good opportunity to really impact policies, funding, and other such
> things for aging programs and services.
> —*Suzanne Richards, director of an agency that serves seniors*

Suzanne Richards is quintessentially apolitical. When asked about her
involvement in politics she said, "This is the first time I've ever really
been involved in politics. . . . I have no affiliation, have had no affiliation
to any party, have not run any campaigns, have not been involved in any
campaigns." Richards does have a background in advocacy: she was the
director of public policy for an association that advocated on behalf of
nonprofits, a position for which she was recruited while she was a com-
munications director for a service provider for the senior population.
Her interest in those services came from personal experience, watching
her grandparents age. She explained:

> Watching them get supportive services at home, and then ultimately
> needing really that hands-on 24 [hour] home, really opened my eyes to
> the needs of older adults. There's a lot of loneliness, a lot of people that
> are in nursing homes that don't have family members anymore, and so
> that sparked my interest; it wasn't until I went to graduate school . . . and
> went into public administration, where they have a concentration in
> nonprofit management, and then you can pick your policy track, which I
> chose aging policy, and learned so much more about the world of aging
> and understood that it's not just nursing homes but that there's this
> whole other world, and so then I started realizing that I could actually
> potentially make a career out of working in [services for the] aging.

This dedication to a career in services for seniors made her consider taking the appointment when the governor's chief strategy officer approached her about a prospective appointment. She had worked with the strategy officer when they jointly ran a council, a partnership between nonprofit organizations and state government. Perhaps most relevant was how clearly Richards made it known to the governor and his staff that she was not interested in politics. She told the governor's chief of staff from the beginning that she was "not in this to be a spokesperson for the party; I'm in this because of what I think we need to do with aging." Richards is just one of many women who not only landed in state government by chance but also accepted her appointment only because she could keep it apolitical while advocating for a cause important to her.

In her role as director of her state's agency for senior services, Richards oversees about thirty people. The agency works with the state legislature on policy and funding and administers state and federal dollars for specific programs, such as Meals on Wheels. Notably (and in line with Richards's previous work for the nonprofit), she and her colleagues are meant to be advocates for the senior community, something she says "doesn't always jive with state government all that well." Within their agency, the long-term care ombudsperson, who goes into nursing homes and advocates for the residents, is the perfect example of their advocacy "because we act in the interests of the older adults, regardless of what the larger state policy may be. . . . That's probably what gives us the most distinct role from the rest of state government."

Chapter 3, through an analysis of political recruitment, uncovers differences in the external motivations of appointed officials to hold public office. However, another side to this story is the internal motivation side. What motivates individuals in state-level politics to actively seek or accept appointed office? As Susan J. Carroll and Kira Sanbonmatsu argue in their book *More Women Can Run* (2013), "Candidacy and ambition can, and often do, arise simultaneously" for female state legislators (125). Because many women do not follow the normal ambition patterns of climbing the political career ladder as men do, Carroll and Sanbonmatsu argue that expanding our conceptions of how to get more women into politics is imperative to increasing the number of women seeking and holding elected office. Put simply, it is necessary to understand what it is about politics, or the political environment, that makes some women say no to public office, even when they have the support and resources available to run for elected office or accept a political appointment.

In this chapter I explore the internal motivations of accepting political appointment. Most of this analysis will involve the responses of the appointees themselves, through detailed follow-up interviews, but it will also include the statistical analysis of the gender differences present in the motivations to hold public office derived from my State Political Pathways Survey.

INTERNAL MOTIVATIONS TO SERVE IN APPOINTED OFFICE AT THE STATE LEVEL

The gender dynamics in the motivation to seek elected office at the state level have been studied, but they have not been expanded to studies of appointed office since the Center for American Women in Politics (CAWP) study (1983). In the most recent study of the motivations for pursuing state-level elected office, Carroll and Sanbonmatsu (2013) uncovered different reasons for men and women to run based upon their party identification. Democratic and Republican women were more likely than Democratic and Republican men to say that public policy was an important reason for their decision to seek a seat in the state legislature (97). Carroll and Sanbonmatsu (2013) also found that female state legislators were more likely to say recruitment was a major factor in their decision to seek their office, whereas male state legislators were more likely to cite reasons such as a "desire to be involved in politics" or a "desire to change the way government works" (59).

The CAWP study of female appointees, however, found fewer differences between women and appointees overall when surveying the reasons women accepted their appointments. Although the study cited earlier findings that men tended to serve in public office for "self-serving considerations" and women tended to serve for "public-serving considerations," the results for appointees showed this was not necessarily their experience (Center for American Women in Politics 1983; see also Costantini and Craik 1972).

Fewer appointed women than appointees overall cited their career paths as a reason for accepting their appointments, and fewer appointed women cited personal reasons or the opportunity for public service as a reason for accepting their appointments (Center for American Women in Politics 1983). According to these studies, we might expect differing public service motivations based not only upon sex but also upon whether individuals were appointed or elected.

The analysis in Chapter 3 gives us a clear indication of how political recruitment functions for state-level appointed individuals. Political recruitment is only one force, an external force, that can affect whether an individual exhibits an interest in seeking or accepting a public office. Even after recruitment of them for public office, many women still decline to run. Chapter 5 reveals the gaps in progressive ambition among appointed officials, but we also need to understand why certain public officials decided to take the plunge. This will be done by analyzing differences in motivation between appointed men and women.

With my State Political Pathways Survey, I asked respondents why they decided to run for elected office or accept their political appointments. The follow-up interviews of the elected and appointed women expanded upon this question, providing insight into their motivations for running for the state legislature or accepting their appointments (see Chapter 7 for the results for the elected official sample). The beginning of Chapter 4 suggests what some of these motivations could be. Table 4.1 reveals whether appointed officials who participated in the State Political Pathways Survey follow the same motivations as did those in earlier studies.

Two motivations were particularly strong among appointees: interest in a policy area/issue and an opportunity for public service.[1] More than 72 percent of appointees said their interest in a policy area or issue was a reason they accepted their appointments. This motivation is particularly strong among low-level appointees: 74 percent of them compared with 63 percent of high-level appointees cited an interest in a policy area or issue as a reason for accepting their appointments ($p < 0.01$). Because many of the low-level appointees serve on boards and commissions that address specific diseases, professions, or constituencies, this gap is not surprising.

1. In the survey I asked the appointees, "Why did you accept your political appointment?"

Table 4.1 Motivations for Accepting Political Appointment

Motivation	All Appointees	High-Level Appointees	Low-Level Appointees
Interest in policy area or issues	72.65%	63.06%**	74.18%
Opportunity for public service	69.03%	70.70%	68.83%
Opportunity for broadening experience	52.21%	62.42%**	50.62%
Career advancement/reason related to career	30.44%	63.06%**	25.21%
Interest in state government	29.29%	49.04%**	26.13%
Opportunity to work with the governor in his/her administration	20.09%	54.55%**	14.20%
Support for governor's policies	16.02%	41.82%**	11.61%
Opportunity for future elected office	3.89%	3.82%	3.91%
N	1,129	157	972

Note: Chi-2 tests were used to find the difference in means. $^+ p < 0.10$, $^* p < 0.05$, $^{**} p < 0.01$.

The perfect example of a low-level appointee getting involved in a board through an issue is Cathy O'Connor, who served on an athletic trainers' board. While in graduate school, O'Connor noticed that many of the staff were involved in state and national organizations for the athletic training community, which "role modeled for me that it is important to be involved." This led her to pursue the presidency of her state's athletic trainers' society. Because she lived near her state capital, she had attended the state athletic trainers' board meetings, at which it became clear that some expertise on the education of athletic trainers was missing from the board discussions:

> There was a lot of controversy at the state level of . . . do you or do you not allow these students to participate that are high school students that have an interest? You kind of go back and forth if you want to garner interest in your profession, but you don't want to allow them to do too much because then why do you really need somebody who is licensed then if a high school student can do it? And should they be taping ankles of high school kids? So there was a lot of that discussion, and a lot of the board members didn't necessarily know the answers tied to accreditation and things like that. So I kind of took a step back and said, well I will probably help the board because I have that knowledge, so that's why I decided to step up and apply.

If O'Connor's expertise had not been missing at these meetings, the motivation to pursue her appointment might not have transpired.

Also unsurprising is the large gap between high- and low-level appointed officials in their response to citing career advancement as a major reason for accepting their appointments. Although 30 percent of all appointees said career advancement was a reason they accepted their appointments, more than 60 percent of high-level appointees said career advancement was a reason for accepting their appointment compared with only 25 percent of low-level appointees ($p < 0.01$). This makes sense because more than half of the high-level appointees had never held public office before and said in follow-up interviews that they did not consider their position political and/or did not take it for political reasons. Instead, many of these high-level appointees were not exhibiting what we consider political ambition but might actually have been expressing ambitions related to their career that just happened to involve holding public office.

Appointees' prior political histories seem to support this explanation. Although fewer than half of the high-level appointees had held elected or appointed office prior to their positions at the time of the study (37 percent of high-level appointees had held prior public office, 30 percent had held prior appointments, and 14 percent had held prior elected offices), high-level female appointees actually held prior office more often than high-level male appointees did. I asked respondents if they had ever sought or run for elected or appointed office, trying to measure intention/interest in public office holding that might have been missed by asking only about offices actually held. Overall, appointed men were about 3 percent more likely to say they had sought appointment prior to their position and about 10 percent more likely to have run for elected office than were appointed women. The gender gap in seeking appointment was similar for high-level appointed men and women, although the gender gap in running for elected office among high-level appointed officials decreased to less than 1 percent. Low-level appointed men were about 12 percent more likely to have run for elected office than were low-level appointed women.

Nearly 47 percent of high-level women and 37 percent of high-level men had held elected or appointed office before their positions (see Figure 4.1). The high-level women appointees, however, were much more

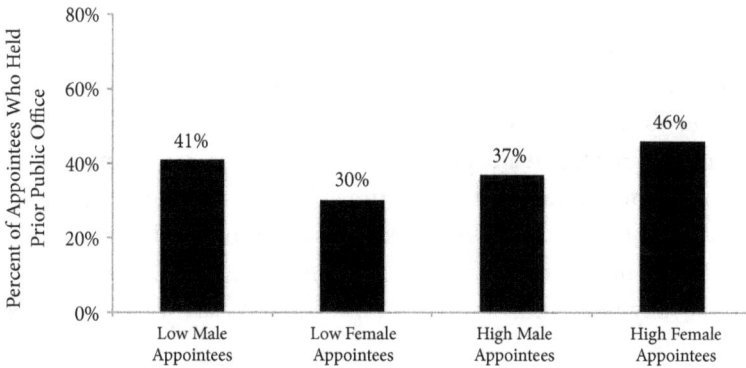

Figure 4.1   **Prior Public Officeholding**

likely to have held appointed office—especially as deputy directors and agency leaders—compared with elected office than were high-level appointed men. Because many of these women saw their appointments as part of their careers, it makes sense that they were more likely to have held appointed office and were more likely to have held offices leading up to their positions.[2]

Runner-up to interest in policy area/issues as a motivation for accepting appointments was an opportunity for public service. Twenty-eight appointees answered in the open-ended section of the motivation question that giving back, representing their profession/certain groups, and public service were main reasons for accepting their appointments. A high-level appointee from a health department said he accepted his appointment for the "opportunity to serve people and make a difference." Similarly, a health board member from Connecticut cited "advancing [a] health and social services agenda for people of color" as a reason she accepted/pursued her appointment. In short, public service was an important factor for both high- and low-level appointees at the state level in deciding to seek or accept their appointments.

2. None of the differences in holding appointed or elected office were statistically significant for high-level appointees after running difference-of-means tests. More than 40 percent of men and 30 percent of women appointed to boards and commissions had held prior public office ($p < 0.01$), 17 percent of low-level appointed men compared with 10 percent of low-level appointed women had held prior elected office ($p < 0.01$), and 31 percent of low-level appointed men compared with 24 percent of low-level appointed women had held prior appointments ($p < 0.05$).

A number of the high-level appointees expressed loyalty to other appointees or the department's mission as a reason for accepting their appointments. An assistant secretary in a commerce department explained that her "belief in my agency's secretary" was motivation for accepting her appointment, and a deputy commissioner in an environmental department cited "loyalty to my department" as a reason for accepting his appointment. Seven high-level appointees (four men and three women) cited either their dedication to the mission of their departments and/or their loyalty/interest in working with higher officials within those departments.

Even though we can find common ground between high- and low-level appointed officials on their motivations for pursuing or accepting their offices, we need to look beyond the limited survey answers to what many of these individuals said in the interviews or the open-ended parts of the survey. A political appointee's motivation for public office in wanting to publicly serve or having an interest in a policy area or issue does not mean he or she wants to be political. On the contrary, many of them explicitly said they did not want to be involved in politics.

Many of the women appointees touched upon reasons they disliked politics or felt their positions were not at all political. Among the women board and commission members was a seeming tension between those who believed their positions were quite political and those who thought their positions were not political at all. Two low-level appointed women said their positions were political; one was appointed to an alcoholic beverages commission and the other was Darlene Vesko, an appointee to a commission for the blind. The appointee on the alcoholic beverages commission said the following about the nature of her service:

> It's very political because the governor tends to control major policy decisions. I'll give you an example. We were tasked, about five years ago, with coming up with a different model for dram insurance, and dram insurance is the insurance that bars and restaurants pay to be able to serve alcohol, and not every state has dram insurance, but we do—and we have a high threshold for liability. Consequently, we came up with some guidelines that said bars and restaurants would have to have a half a million dollar deductible, or a half a million dollar liability minimum, and that was our recommendation after about two and a half

years of studying the issue, and the governor just completely tabled it; he didn't move on it, essentially he killed it, and it was very disappointing because we had spent a ton of time going all over the state hearing from everybody, and that was our recommendation, and he didn't like it, so it went nowhere. So that's just an example of how things get political.

Darlene Vesko, who served on the commission for the blind, had similar feelings:

I would say it's very political, dealing with some of the—well some of the members of the board are more political than others; some of that has to do with your degree of knowledge with the environment, but yeah, I would say it's a political position, absolutely. I mean I got to be responsible for interviewing and hiring the agency director; I don't know how much more political you can get than that.

These two appointees clearly addressed the political nature of some boards and commissions, which for the alcoholic beverages commission appointee meant opposition from the governor and for the second appointee meant choosing the leader of a state agency.

Other female appointees did not have a clear definition of *political* but nevertheless could see how their positions were "political" at times, such as Stephanie Hicks from the historic trails commission:

I guess I was going to ask you what your definition of political is, in the sense that they have the ability to make changes in things; if you consider that political, yes. If you consider them political in the sense of being liberal or conservative or that, I don't know that I would even though— however working in [my state] we've had a very liberal governor forever, so you kind of have to be a little bit careful in what you say and do, because you are appointed by the governor.

This female appointee suggested that the definition of political was subjective and that being political meant identifying with a political ideology. The subjective nature of defining politics was a consistent and central finding from my interviews of the appointees.

Four low-level female appointees challenged a broader conception of politics and thought their jobs were not explicitly political. Wendy Jenkins, who served on a water planning council, believed politics was tied to electoral office but did not actually define it. She said:

> I'm not an elected official. I'm on the water planning council advisory committee; the water planning council is made up of staff itself, and the water planning council advisory committee . . . is not political either; it's not made up of people who are political, it's made up of people who are appointed basically to it by the water planning council, which is made up of—so our Department of Environmental Protection, the head of the Environmental Protection, head of Agriculture, so I don't know how other people are answering the questions because no one that I know is an elected official on there.

For this appointee, politics meant elected office only. Interestingly, when asked whether she felt her council was political, she had this to say:

> It's not like you have to run for office or whatever, although I did say I wanted to be on this and basically asked the people to put my name in. In terms of political, all state organizations, doesn't matter, when you are in government, it has politics. It may not be partisan politics, may not be Democrat against Republican, but there is always politics involved, because it's always limited resources and that has to do with budgets. There's also the reality of let's say a recommendation comes out of the water planning council, to do something let's say with rates that have to do with the water utilities. Well, of course that may require legislation to get done, so there's always something political when you are dealing with the agencies, and I think one of the things you try to do is bring in—let's make it science based—let's make it resource based and try to leave the politics out of it, but the reality is that there's economics and politics in everything.

This appointee demonstrated a tension many of the female appointees expressed: working with the political while trying not to be political themselves. For some, all it took was simply changing the semantics around their positions. Cindy Covens was the perfect example of this. Covens was a low-level political appointee on a pollution prevention board of directors. Asked when she first got involved in "politics," she was emphatic that she was not a political person:

I am not, that may be something we've been mistaken from the, I am
not involved in politics. I was appointed as a public service, as a public
representative to the board of a company that uses some public money.
So our state funds this company that I am on the board. It's a pollution
prevention center, they work with companies to prevent them, to help
them clean up or not pollute or that kind of thing, and so a lot of state
money goes into that company every year, and they need a public
representative, that's my only involvement.

This response clearly indicates that Covens did not perceive herself as
political or her appointment as political. Yet a further discussion of her
background revealed she was more political than she believed. When
asked how she got appointed to her position, she mentioned that someone she knew through doing community activities asked her. Covens's
volunteer activity was particularly interesting: she was the chair of a taskforce "to assess problems that a proposed road is going to cause for our
community. So our community is up in arms, the neighboring community wants it, so it's a fight between two towns." She was quite concerned
about the new road just as she was concerned about the development of
an interchange more than two decades previously. When discussing who
made up the taskforce, Covens had a hard time not considering it political. She said: "Yeah, different representatives, we have a lot of political
groups in this area, not political I guess public interest groups, we live
in a gorgeous part of the country, and it's also the part of the state where
people want to settle, so there's an endless battle between development
and preservation. And that's the main fight I stay involved in." Although
Covens clearly did not want to be a part of politics, she had a considerable history of advocacy on behalf of herself and her community. She
went on to say that she was too busy with her family, work, and volunteer activities to consider running for elected office or seeking another
appointment.

   Other appointees had a distinct definition of politics as well. Meredith Kincaid, who served on a council serving people with developmental disabilities, felt politics was partisan:

It hurts me to see when the definition that I use for politics, which is
basically when a party comes into power, they will exercise their right to

get rid of whoever they feel does not promote their ideology. And in that process sometimes—or oftentimes—they throw [the] baby out with the bathwater, on some of these boards and commissions, a very good open dialogue that is really honing in and educating all on diverse points of view, making the product actually much better. So that's what I mean—or when others may differentiate what that term politics are, because we have seen the damage that that can do to really good quality outcomes.[3]

Kimberly Schaffley, who served on an engineers and professional land surveyors board, said it was not political "because it is comprised of engineers and land surveyors, and we tend to view the world and be influenced less by politics than by personal and societal ethics and competence, and so I wouldn't consider an engineering board to be political. Although the appointments have come from the governor, so . . . " This comment is particularly telling because this appointee made a distinction between "politics" and "societal ethics and competence." Here she seemed to suggest—similar to the previous appointee, who stated that politics was partisan—that politics was not a positive force in state government. In fact, politics was separate from societal ethics and competence.

This echoes the reasons some high-level appointed women were not interested in elected office because they felt things could not be accomplished there. A high-level female appointee quoted earlier expressed how she felt about being in an appointed position versus an elected position rather pointedly: "For me I think I can get, move issues forward that I care about, and want to work on, more effectively in other ways." Having heard appointees' opinions of politics, we have a sense as to how they arrived at their positions. Let's examine the quantitative evidence in Table 4.2 to see any gender gaps in the motivations to hold public office like those in the qualitative evidence I discussed above.

Table 4.2 breaks up the appointee data by sex, and we see two clear differences in the motivations for holding public office among appointed men and women. Appointed women were about 13 percent more likely to cite career advancement as a reason for accepting or seeking their appointment ($p < 0.01$), and they were 7 percent and 12 percent more likely

3. Another low-level female appointee, when asked about her definition of "political" and whether her board was political, also related politics only to party, notoriety, and elected office.

Table 4.2 Gender Differences in the Motivations for Accepting Political Appointment

Motivation	Men	Women
Career advancement or other reason related to career	25.33%**	38.02%
Interest in policy area or issues	69.78%**	76.92%
Interest in state government	30.22%	27.91%
Opportunity for broadening experience	47.41%**	59.34%**
Opportunity for future elected office	3.85%	3.96%
Opportunity for public service	70.22%	67.25%
Opportunity to work with the governor in his/her administration	21.04%	18.68%
Support for governor's policies	15.85%	16.26%
N	675	455

Note: Chi-2 tests were used to find the difference in means with Fisher's exact test used when observations were less than or equal to five. $^+ p < 0.10$, $* p < 0.05$, $** p < 0.01$.

to cite interest in a policy area/issue and broadening their experience, respectively, than were appointed men ($p < 0.01$). Men and women appointees did not differ as much on the other reasons for accepting their appointments as they did on those first three motivations.

We also know from the qualitative evidence above that not only sex affects motivations for appointed office but also the level of appointment. Figure 4.2 displays the results for motivations for accepting appointment broken down by sex and level of office. A few interesting patterns emerge.

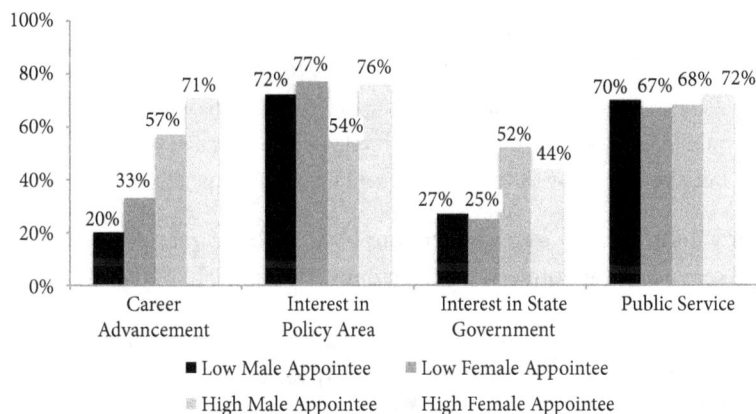

Figure 4.2 Motivations for Appointed Office

First, the gender gap on the career advancement motivation in-creases for high-level appointees. High-level appointed women were 14 percent more likely to say their career was a motivation for accepting their appointments ($p < 0.10$), coinciding with the qualitative evidence above. This updates our understanding of appointee motivations from the CAWP study (1983), which found that female appointees were ac-tually less likely to have accepted their appointments because of their careers. Danielle Whitman, who served on a real estate commission, was an example of an appointee who became involved in state government through her career.

> I was not at all interested in politics until I got involved in the Association of Realtors. And then, as part of being president of the local association of realtors, you are very politically involved, and I started seeing some things going on that I did not like, and so I just got involved and got my say. In the process of doing so I met a lot of politicians, got to be friends with them, and then just one thing led to another.

Whitman became so interested in politics that she decided to run for a city council seat while serving on her state board. She was not recruited for either of these positions. Whitman also held a county-level appoint-ment as a housing authority commissioner. She had a unique perspective because she held both elected and appointed office simultaneously in different levels of government:

> Well, when you are elected, you are answering to your constituents, so you think about your constituents when you vote and you do certain things, when you represent the city and so forth. At the housing commissioner level, which is a county level, we are looking at different things, and then again at the state level we are looking at different things because at the state level I represent all licensed real estate brokers.

For Whitman there were connections between her career as a real estate broker and her appointed and elected positions:

> I can see from a city council level zoning and building places in our town center, in our urban center, for everybody, including people who need help with their housing needs. And then as a realtor I work with people who can afford to buy houses, and then that money that the realtors have

also goes toward homeless people and various things like that, so it's kind of a full circle. If I work with everybody who can't afford a house to live in, all the way up to the millionaires who can afford anything they want. So I work with all those different levels.

Whitman exemplifies how many appointed women become political through their careers.

A second pattern I find when studying the data by sex and level of office is that the gap in policy area motivation is driven by high- and low-level appointed women. High-level appointed women were much more likely than were high-level appointed men to say their interest in a policy area/issue was motivation for accepting their appointments ($p < 0.01$). Although low-level appointed women responded in a similar manner, their responses on this motivational factor were not statistically different from the responses given by low-level men appointees. Third, even though a difference-of-means test between high-level appointed men and women does not reach standard levels of statistical significance on the motivational factor of interest in state government, high-level male appointees were 9 percent more likely than high-level female appointees and 25 percent more likely than all low-level appointees to cite this as a motivation for accepting their appointments. This finding hints at the more political nature of men's interest in state-level appointed office than that of women.

MOTIVATION TO HOLD APPOINTED OFFICE AT THE STATE LEVEL

I argue that understanding internal and external forces on ambition for public office is important if we want to know why some women make it into the political arena and others do not. Chapter 3 reveals the differences in external forces on women who might be poised to run for elected office or seek appointed office. My analysis demonstrates that appointed women continued to be recruited less by key officials in both elected and appointed office, although high-level appointed women were more likely to be recruited.

I have demonstrated that an external force such as recruitment was not enough to explain why some women decided to hold public office and others did not: 219 appointed women, nearly 50 percent of the sample, said they were recruited for either appointed or elected office, but only 42 percent of those women—compared with nearly 50 percent of the appointed men—sought an appointed office or ran for elected office ($p < 0.10$). Why did women turn down the opportunity to be in public office even when they had the opportunity and the support to do so? Furthermore, were the women holding elected and appointed office at the state level really exhibiting what we traditionally define as political ambition, or was it ambition for something else?

My analysis of appointed official motivations to hold public office has demonstrated that women in appointed positions defined politics differently than did appointed men and had more negative views of politics. These findings are important because women might be participating in politics in ways political scholars do not normally take under consideration, such as through political appointments. They also matter because it might mean that women are telling themselves something different than men are about what it means to be a political person. Democratic participation might be defined differently for women because they do not believe they are being political, when in fact they are being quite political.

These findings are both surprising and unsurprising. They are unsurprising because prior studies demonstrate American disavowal of the political. In *The Civic Imagination,* Gianpaolo Baiocchi and his colleagues (2014) found that community activists in the city of Providence, Rhode Island, did not see their actions as political and were vehemently against being in politics. The authors said, "When Americans claim they are not political, they are not simply defining themselves by what they are not. They are *disavowing politics*—rejecting knowledge of, connection to, or responsibility for the processes and consequences of the political—and simultaneously self-identifying with a more positive ideal of public engagement and social change" (40). The authors cited scholars that have found skepticism about politics in the United States (Bellah et al. 2008; Calhoun 1998; Craig 1993; Herbert 2005; Keane 2009; Macedo 2005; Norris 2011; Offe 2006; Pharr and Putnam 2000; Putnam 1995), but argued that "rather than posing a threat to democracy, disavowal of the political allows people to creatively constitute what they imagine to be appropriate and desirable forms of citizenship and civic participation" (Baiocchi et al. 2014, 38).

My quantitative analysis reveals that men and women in appointed positions had different motivations for holding public office and that many of the women, in both high- and low-level appointed office, disavowed politics in the same way local community activists did in Baiocchi and his colleagues' work. This is important for two reasons: (1) it is the first evidence to show that the disavowal of politics is *gendered,* and (2) it shows that the disavowal of politics goes far beyond that of local community activists, all the way to the governor's cabinet. Finding the extent to which the disavowal of politics is gendered and just how far up the political career ladder it affects officeholders helps us to understand why women do not see themselves as political and do not want to be in politics. It also demonstrates that recruitment is not enough. It is not enough to make a woman believe she is capable of running for or holding public office. Instead, it must be recruitment for the *right* office, and it must be pitched in a way that will make the woman believe she will be effective at accomplishing something important to her, not just participating in the unsavory mess of politics. It is clear that specific policy areas motivate women in appointed and elected office. Political recruiters and scholars of women's political ambition need to take that into consideration if we want to see more women publicly serve.

Scholars in the political field must do more to understand why women seek or do not seek public office and how their individual definitions of politics and the real-world nature of politics factor into their interest or disinterest in public office. Without understanding the motivation to hold public office, or to hold only low-level public office, or not even to see a political appointment as a public office at all, we misunderstand and perhaps overinflate the barriers present for women who could be in the political arena. Chapter 5 continues the story of women's interactions with politics through the study of their political ambition for higher office.

5. Where Do I Go from Here?
The Political Ambitions of
Appointed Officeholders

I have had some offers on the federal level, and I have turned them down because I don't want to leave my home and so for personal reasons I have decided that—and I have a lot of colleagues that have relocated to DC and/or travel there, work during the week, and travel home on the weekends, but I am just not willing to have that kind of lifestyle.
—Lillian Fox, commissioner of a mental health department

Lillian Fox has both an interest in politics and a dedication to the field of mental health. Her interest in mental health came both from having family members affected by mental health conditions and a bachelor's degree in developmental psychology as well as a master's degree in counseling psychology. Early in her career, she was hired "to [work on] a federal model demonstration grant that demonstrated either the effectiveness or [in]effectiveness of a model, basically to influence government spending, and that got me very interested in how public policy is actually formulated." Her exposure to public policy in this position pushed her to attain a law degree, which then qualified her to become the deputy director of internal affairs in the department of mental health in her state. This position put her on the radar of the outgoing commissioner, who recommended her to the governor for his post. As commissioner, Fox oversees

an operation budget of 738 million dollars, 3,200 employees, [and runs] an entire continuum of mental health services from seven in-patient psychiatric hospitals to about 260 million dollars of contracted community-based services, really from soup to nuts, from your lightest touch—maybe a weekly phone check—to group living, group homes, to in-patient hospitalization. I'm responsible for informing and speaking on behalf of the governor on issues as they relate to mental health, responsible for licensing all the private psychiatric facilities in the [state]—there's about 2,600 beds, private in-patient acute psychiatric beds—we're responsible [for] licensing, we're responsible for advising the [state] health office on their formularies for psychiatric medication, and we fund 62 court clinics across the commonwealth that do forensic evaluations, such as competency to stand trial, and things like that.

Despite being a Canadian citizen, Fox wants to pursue her US citizenship and potentially pursue her interest in running for elected office one day despite the frustrating experiences she had as a high-level appointee. She had this to say about what it was like being an appointee in her state:

> I think you need to have an incredibly high frustration tolerance, and you need to not take things personally, and you need to pick your battles, and sometimes you need to realize what your endgame is to continue to work towards those, and you need to be able to make compromises, and politics can be very frustrating, can be a very, very dirty business. It's not always fair, let me put it that way. And the media is a wildcard that they like to report the bad story and they're—more often than not, the stories are more inaccurate than they are accurate. So that's a challenge also.

On the one hand, Fox exemplifies yet another appointed woman who sees politics in a negative light. Unlike many of the other women appointees from my analysis, however, she still wants to publicly serve via elected office so that she can "influence public policy and build and strengthen communities."

Although women such as Fox are interested in seeking public office, the advancement of women to public office in the United States has stagnated over the past fifteen to twenty years. Some scholars thought that after women made gains into areas believed to be springboards for public office, such as law and business, gender parity in elected office would soon follow (Darcy, Welch, and Clark 1994). This has proven not to be the case. Even though more women are climbing the career ladder in the private sphere into areas traditionally dominated by men, women continue to have lower ambitions to hold public office at all (Lawless and Fox 2005).[1] Research has even shown how these lower ambitions are present among the youngest generations in the United States (Lawless and

1. It is still important to note that despite the inroads women have made in the private sphere, significant gender differences remain in the fields women tend to go into compared with those men choose (Coontz 2012; Hegewisch et al. 2010).

Fox 2015). Why is this the case? Lawless and Fox (2005) suggest it was a result of differences in how women assess their abilities to seek or hold public office, with women believing they are less qualified to seek and hold political office (Lawless and Fox 2005). Carroll and Sanbonmatsu (2013) argue that it is a combination of lack of recruitment and beliefs about how office holding will affect their personal lives and relationships that affects women's ambition for public office. Carroll and Sanbonmatsu (2013) see gender as both a political and a social construct that has created a masculinized political sphere that makes women feel less qualified to hold public office (see also Lawless and Fox 2005).

Studying ambition for elected versus appointed office can help us better understand how women perceive office holding. The process of being elected versus appointed to public office might require different connections, qualifications, and beliefs about what is political and whether individuals want to take part in the political process (as seen in Chapter 4). This process requires a different calculus to decide if seeking public office is the right step for a woman to take. Chapter 3 shows that external forces such as recruitment are lacking for women in low-level appointed office, and Chapter 4 reveals that appointed women feel differently about the political world (and even the definition of *political*) than do appointed men. These women might serve in an appointed position that happens to be political but cannot or will not hold an expressly political position (such as an elected one) in what they define as a partisan and hostile environment.

It is also important to study political ambition to understand the role of state-level positions as an avenue to national positions. For high-level appointees and state senators, this is particularly relevant because many of them have advanced as far as they can in state-level politics. Unsurprisingly, more is known about how state-level elected positions are a pathway to national elected office. Joseph Schlesinger (1966) described the state legislature as the "breeding ground for political ambition" to national office (72). This appears to be true: 266 US House and Senate members are former state legislators (Congressional Research Service 2018). Furthermore, Fulton and colleagues (2006) found that although female state legislators are less ambitious than male state legislators for national office, they still run for the US House as often as their male counterparts. Female state legislators' lower ambitions are ameliorated by the expected benefit they perceive from becoming a member of the US Congress.

Not as much is known about how state-level appointed positions are a pathway to federal appointed positions. Susan Carroll (1986) studied high-level appointees in the Carter administration and found that 28 percent of the appointed women and 23 percent of the appointed men had held an appointive or administrative position in state government at some point in their careers. In Borelli's (2002) study of US cabinets from Roosevelt to Clinton, she found that on average 14 percent of secretaries-designate came from state or local government. Of the twenty-one women she studied who held cabinet or cabinet-level presidential appointments from 1933 to 2001, only four had come from a state-level appointment. It would appear that, on average, fewer than a quarter of high-level federal appointees came directly from state government appointments. Keep in mind these studies overlook lower-level federal appointments that might be viewed as a career advancement by many state appointees. In short, understanding the next step in state appointees' careers—namely, deciding whether to seek higher office—provides important insights not only into political ambition but also into the future of national-level appointments.

If it is true that candidate emergence is relationally embedded and that this has formed an environment in which women have less confidence in their qualifications for higher office (Carroll and Sanbonmatsu 2013; Lawless and Fox 2005), then we need to understand if the relational calculus that affects initial interest in public office holding continues to affect women's decisions to consider higher public office. Seeking higher office should continue to test a woman's opinion of herself and how pursuing or holding a higher office might affect her relationship with others. Considering a different kind of office altogether (covered in Chapter 6), such as an appointed official considering elected office, also helps us understand which variables tend to affect women's interest in office holding and what about specific positions dissuades women from pursuing public office. Studying the progressive ambition patterns of elected and appointed officials can reveal if ambition changes after an individual holds office and what factors, both politically and socially, affect women's interest in holding higher public office.

Several questions spring from this analysis: First, how do the differences in recruitment patterns Chapter 3 reveals affect ambition for higher office (also known as progressive ambition)? In fact, how does

ambition function within appointed office in the first place? Thus far, all
ambition studies have focused on interest in seeking elected office, or the
progressive ambitions of elected officials. I argue that self-assessed qualifications continue to have a strong positive effect on interest in higher
office, just as they have a strong positive effect on the initial interest to
run for elected office, as discovered by Lawless and Fox (2005). I also
argue that gendered perceptions, or women's lower self-assessment of
their qualifications to hold public office, decrease their progressive ambitions, but that this relationship is conditioned by the individuals' levels
of office. Based upon the evidence in previous chapters, I do not expect
appointed women to be overly ambitious to hold higher public office because they might consider it more political. Despite this earlier finding,
we also saw the ability of some women, even serving in higher appointments, to consider their positions nonpolitical simply because they were
nonelected and nonpartisan. It is therefore possible that we might see
female appointees' unique expressions of political ambition that seem
political in nature but are really related to their careers or interest in
specific policies.

The first half of this chapter is devoted to finding the differences in
appointee ambition for higher office among men and women as well as
self-perceived qualifications that can affect this interest. Using logistic regression analysis, I predict progressive political ambition for appointees
focusing on the effects of sex, self-perceived qualifications, recruitment,
and the interaction of sex and self-perceived qualifications (referred to
as gendered perceptions). The chapter concludes with a discussion of
why appointed women who view themselves as qualified to hold higher
public office exhibit less progressive ambition than do women who have
lower self-qualification scores.[2]

APPOINTED OFFICIALS ON QUALIFICATIONS AND INTEREST IN HIGHER OFFICE

Much like voting, calculating whether to seek political office is a balanc-
ing act of weighing the costs and benefits. What can one accomplish by

2. See Chapter 7 for the analysis predicting elected official progressive ambition.

seeking this position? Will seeking this position adversely affect one's family? Is one even capable of running for political office or seeking a higher appointment? Many of the barriers women have faced in climbing the political career ladder include electoral gatekeepers, institutional barriers (such as the kind of election being held), and most importantly themselves (Arceneaux 2001; Lawless and Fox 2005; Sanbonmatsu 2006; Carroll and Sanbonmatsu 2013). More often than not, when women look in the mirror, they do not see themselves as qualified for political office. Lawless and Fox (2005, 2010) have shown that more than three thousand of the most qualified women in the United States, including lawyers, political activists, educators, and business leaders, systematically rate themselves lower on qualification scales when it comes to pursuing elected office (see also Lawless 2012). Furthermore, their self-perception of lower qualifications for elected office contributes to disinterest in running for political office at all. This means women are saying no to themselves when it comes to elected office before anyone else can tell them yes.

Thankfully an electoral gatekeeper's positive reinforcement can counteract this negative self-evaluation. Despite the positive effect electoral gatekeepers can have on women's political ambitions, they are still not encouraging women to run for elected office at anywhere near the same rates as they do men, as the analysis in Chapter 3 shows (Lawless and Fox 2005; Oxley and Fox 2004; Sanbonmatsu 2006; Welch 2008).[3] The low number of women in political office suggests that even beyond institutional barriers, women face significant hurdles, such as ambition and recruitment, depleting the number of them willing to enter the arena.

Recruitment or the lack thereof has serious effects on the political viability of women in elected politics (Fox and Lawless 2010; Sanbonmatsu 2006). Less political recruitment can feed into lower ambitions for political office. Although the individuals I surveyed already expressed some form of what we traditionally perceive as political ambition because they already held elected or appointed office, we must remember that political ambition does not end at the first office held. Politics, like any career, has

3. See Carroll's (1984) article on how recruitment functions for state cabinet secretaries and Bullard and Wright's (1993) piece, which argues that instead of trying to break through the glass ceiling by climbing the career ladder in one department, female appointees circumvent the glass ceiling by seeking appointments to new departments and agencies.

a ladder, on which those more often marginalized—such as minorities and women—are less likely to be found at the top. If recruitment occurs at lower rates for women even after they have achieved public office, are those women going to be interested in seeking higher office?

Interest in Higher Office

How might the appointees at the state level rate their interest in seeking higher political office? According to Table 5.1, it would seem appointees have different levels of interest for higher political office. Only 4 percent of appointed officials were "very interested" in higher office. About a third were "somewhat interested," and most appointees, regardless of level of office, were not at all interested in pursuing higher office.

Table 5.2 shows that much of the difference in interest for higher office might not be because of sex. Only one category, "Not interested at all," showed a statistically significant difference between appointed men and women in their interest in higher office ($p < 0.10$), although the category of "Somewhat interested" barely missed statistical significance for a difference between appointed men and women ($p = 0.101$).

Table 5.1 Interest in Higher Office

	All Appointees	High-Level Appointed	Low-Level Appointed
Not interested at all	63.83%	60.00%	64.41%
Somewhat interested	32.05%	33.55%	31.84%
Very interested	4.12%	6.45%	3.75%
N	1,117	155	961

Note: Comparisons are between high- and low-level appointed officials. $^+ p < 0.10$, $^* p < 0.05$, $^{**} p < 0.01$.

Table 5.2 Interest in Higher Office by Sex for Appointed Officials

	Appointed Men	Appointed Women
Not interested at all	61.56%+	67.18%
Somewhat interested	33.95%	29.27%
Very interested	4.50%	3.55%
N	666	451

Note: Statistical comparisons are between males and females. $^+ p < 0.10$, $^* p < 0.05$, $^{**} p < 0.01$.

Part of the reason appointees seem disinterested in seeking higher appointed office or elected office might be the nature of their current appointments. Many appointees at the board and commission level expressed their love of politics or public service without the ambition for public office for themselves. A man from a commerce board stated:

> I am currently employed and very busy in my position as a manager in the energy industry. My appointment by the Governor as Chairman of the Workforce Development Council is based upon my interest in Workforce Development and in my past experience in creating partnerships with private industry, education, unions, and state agencies in improving the skill, quality, and quantity of workers in the energy industry. My role as chairman is not monetarily compensated and part time. It is more a labor of love. I have no political ambitions but am seeking to provide better work opportunities in [my state] for our young people.

A woman on a Louisiana health works commission said something similar:

> I first began in politics when I was seven and [my] father ran for office; [I] have one MS in campaign management and another in public administration. I love politics and loved running campaigns—but never wanted to run for office. At present [I] work for an organization, and [my] work encompasses policy and lobbying. My appointments are in areas where I have the greatest interest—workforce, education, and health care. [I] have worked at all levels—city, state, and as a congressional staffer—and loved every position.

These two appointees pointed to specific personal passions: one for workforce development and the other for career politics. These appointees demonstrated the ability to separate being political from taking part in the political process. Other appointees accepted their positions purely because of their specific qualifications related to their job or education.

Still other appointees expressed an active interest in pursuing higher office and even elected office, but age, self-doubt, and lack of support from family members got in the way. This active interest was much less common. A woman on a special commission on postpartum depression expressed her difficulties in feeling confident as an appointee on her commission:

I am a perfect example of someone who never considered running for office even though I am passionate, articulate, and have leadership skills. I advocated to be appointed to [my] commission for over a year. When I finally was appointed I was terrified to participate at that level of our government, having no former experience. I have thrived there and have been one of the leaders despite the fact that I am out-experienced by almost everyone there. I also am from Western MA, which is a huge obstacle to real political engagement. Despite that, I have been a key leader on the committee, and my leadership has grown. I am not clear what my own next steps might be at the state level, and I'm interested in pursuing more opportunities.

Chapter 4 demonstrates how many of the feelings associated with holding public office are gendered. Many of the appointed women had specific definitions of what was "political," with even high-level appointed women saying they did not pursue their position because it was political but because it was related to their professional field or interests. Although both men and women expressed negative feelings toward the political process, only the women in the open-ended section of the survey made the connection between the competitive, hostile nature of politics and their disinterest in being in politics. Seven appointed men and five appointed women expressed negative views of politics in the open-ended section of the survey. All five of the female appointees made the connection between the negativity in politics and their disinterest in being in politics, with one woman from a naturopathic medicine board saying the following: "I am generally disgusted by politics and want to have nothing to do with it. I serve on my profession's board because we are a small profession and my children are older and so I have more time to do it than many of my colleagues." Men stated their dislike of politics but did not say this made them disinterested in being in politics, like this man from a real estate appraiser board: "Most appointees now are basically political hacks who appear to not know what they are doing—as is the case of the board upon which I sit. I have lost my faith in government and its ability to effect change for the better." These feelings about politics might be part of the reason men and women in appointed positions have slightly different ambitions for higher office. But do self-assessed qualifications continue to be different for men and women in appointed positions, as they are for individuals positioned to run for elected office?

Self-Assessed Qualifications

As we know, many highly qualified individuals never get over the "terror" of participating, and more importantly, might never recognize that their own skills and abilities uniquely qualify them for public office. Lawless and Fox (2005, 2010) have shown this was particularly true among women when it came to qualifications for elected office. How did appointed officials at the state level see themselves when I asked them about qualifications for higher office? Table 5.3 represents the breakdown of appointed officials' responses, by level of office, to the question "Overall, how qualified do you feel you are to attain a higher level of political office?" To specify exactly what I meant by "higher office," I gave two to three examples of high-level offices within their own pathway (such as, for appointed officials, deputy agency leader and full-time political appointee).

For every single response, high-level appointed officials were statistically different than low-level appointed officials. This statistical significance comes from the low-level appointees' lower self-assessed qualifications compared with the higher self-assessed qualifications of high-level appointees. When grouped together we can see that appointees overall saw themselves as "qualified" or "very qualified" for higher office. High-level appointed officials were much more likely to rate themselves "very qualified" compared with low-level appointees. Low-level

Table 5.3 Appointed Officials' Qualifications for Higher Office

	All Appointees	High-Level Appointed	Low-Level Appointed
Not at all qualified	9.29%	1.94%**	10.51%
Somewhat qualified	25.96%	13.55%**	27.92%
Qualified	31.88%	22.58%**	33.44%
Very qualified	32.88%*	61.94%**	28.13%
N	1,097	155	942

Note: Statistical comparisons are between all high- and low-level appointed officials.
$^+ p < 0.10$, $^* p < 0.05$, $^{**} p < 0.01$.

Table 5.4 Appointed Officials' Qualifications for Higher Office by Sex

	Appointed Men	Appointed Women
Not at all qualified	6.44%**	13.45%
Somewhat qualified	19.63%**	35.20%
Qualified	35.74%**	26.23%
Very qualified	38.19%**	25.11%
N	652	446

Note: Statistical comparisons are between males and females. $+ p < 0.10$, $* p < 0.05$, $** p < 0.01$.

appointees were much more ambivalent about their qualifications. This is particularly interesting because, according to Table 5.1, high-level appointees did not deviate much from low-level appointees when it came to interest in higher office. Although self-assessed qualifications might have been a key factor in limiting nascent ambitions for public office (Lawless and Fox 2005), self-assessed qualifications might not have been a factor in progressive ambition for high-level appointees to state positions.

Table 5.4 goes a bit deeper into the self-perception of qualifications among appointed officials. Unsurprisingly, appointed women were significantly more likely to feel unqualified for higher office, whereas appointed men were more likely to feel qualified for higher office ($p < 0.01$). Apparently, even when they had been elected or appointed to a high position, women still rated themselves lower on qualifications for higher office than did similarly situated men. Table 5.5 shows this was particularly true at the lower levels of office.

Approximately 77 percent of high-level appointed women—compared with 89 percent of high-level appointed men—rated themselves in the top two categories (qualified and very qualified) when assessing themselves for higher public office. We still see a gender gap when it comes to qualifications for higher office in high-level political appointees, but it is particularly stark among low-level political appointees. Nearly half of low-level appointed women said they were "not at all" or "somewhat qualified" for higher office, but less than a third of low-level appointed men rated themselves the same way. These results are particularly important in light of the incredibly high levels of education and professional experience both men and women had.

Qualifications continue to be an area in which gender gaps are common, particularly at low-level appointments in state government. The

Table 5.5 Appointed Officials' Qualifications by Sex and Level of Office

	High Appointed Men	High Appointed Women	Low Appointed Men	Low Appointed Women
Not at all qualified	3.23%	0%	6.98%**	15.67%
Somewhat qualified	7.53%**	22.58%	21.65%**	37.08%
Qualified	29.03%*	12.90%	36.85%**	28.46%
Very qualified	60.22%	64.52%	34.53%**	18.80%
N	93	62	559	383

Note: Statistical comparisons are between males and females within high-level appointed office, then between males and females in low-level appointed office. $^+ p < 0.10$, $^* p < 0.05$, $^{**} p < 0.01$.

following analysis of progressive ambition for higher office takes into consideration how self-assessed qualifications and sex interact as well as how they interact with level of office. Additionally, my analysis will look at the effects of recruitment on political ambition because both prior studies and Chapter 3 found significant differences in the recruitment patterns of men and women in appointed positions.

PREDICTING PROGRESSIVE POLITICAL AMBITION FOR HIGHER OFFICE AT THE STATE LEVEL

The main area of ambition Lawless and Fox (2005, 2010) discuss is nascent ambition, the initial interest in pursuing public office before the decision of whether to run for public office takes place. Because the public officials in my study already pursued—and at the very least accepted—their positions, I am specifically looking at the ambitions of officeholders, which can be progressive (attempting to seek higher office), static (trying to maintain their current office), or discrete (wanting to leave public office). If qualifications are such an important predictor of the initial calculations for considering public office, do self-assessed qualifications continue to be a hurdle after an individual has attained public office and is considering higher office? Put simply, if women assess themselves lower on a qualification scale without having held public office, which in turn highly influences their ambitions for public office, do women who already hold public office continue to self-assess their qualifications as lower, and does that continue to affect their ambitions for higher office? I expect self-assessed qualifications will have a strong positive effect on interest in higher office (progressive ambition) for appointed officials. I also expect gendered perceptions, in the form of women officeholders having lower perceptions of their qualifications for higher office, will affect the progressive ambitions of appointed women, with women with higher self-assessed qualifications displaying increased progressive ambitions.

We already know that women in appointed office, particularly in low-level appointments, have lower self-assessments of their qualifications for higher office (Table 5.5). Because self-assessed qualifications differ based upon whether an individual holds a high- or low-level appointed office and based upon his or her sex, I also expect the effects of gendered perceptions on progressive ambition to be conditioned by the level of office the individual holds. How much do these qualification self-assessments matter in light of other personal, structural, and political variables?

Dependent and Independent Variables

The dependent variable for the regressions in Tables 5.6 and 5.7 is *interest in higher office,* where 1 denotes interest in higher office and 0 indicates no interest in higher office. Table 5.6 predicts the ambitions for *interest in higher office* for appointed officials, and Table 5.7 predicts ambition for higher office for appointed officials with the interactions of *sex and self-qualifications* and *sex, self-qualifications, and level of office.*

The independent variables are broken down into five major categories: the demographic measures (or controls), such as sex, education, and race; family dynamics, including marital status and responsibility for household tasks; political dynamics, such as party identification and issue passion; personal political characteristics, including number of elected offices sought and position value; and finally, state-specific variables, such as political opportunity structure and culture. All variable descriptive statistics and explanations for coding are located in Appendix C.

Predicting interest in higher office was completed using logistic regression with robust standard errors. Next to the coefficient column is the "impact" column, which predicts the change in probability for the variables that were statistically significant using Clarify. All dichotomous variables were set to their most frequent response, and continuous vari-

Table 5.6 Baseline Logistic Regression Model for Interest in Higher Office

	Full Model		Impact
Demographics			
Sex 1 = Female	−0.568*	(0.227)	−8.88%
Education	0.009	(0.075)	
Family income	−0.262**	(0.088)	−10.46%
White 1 = White	0.502	(0.333)	
Age	−0.087**	(0.011)	−31.63%
Family Dynamics			
Married/long-term relationship	−0.641*	(0.293)	−13.81%
Majority household responsibilities	0.276$^+$	(0.151)	+10.81%
Children over eighteen	0.496*	(0.215)	+7.96%
Parental suggestion	0.205$^+$	(0.113)	+12.81%
Personal encouragement	0.806**	(0.190)	+17.67%
Political Dynamics			
Recruited since position	0.366$^+$	(0.196)	+7.31%
Republican	0.171	(0.234)	
Democrat	−0.371	(0.256)	
Percent Obama vote 2012	−0.679	(0.843)	
Sexism	0.165	(0.115)	
Issue passion	0.020	(0.188)	
Political participation	1.324**	(0.381)	+21.75%
Political interest	−0.009	(0.109)	
Political efficacy	−0.073	(0.077)	
Personal Political Characteristics			
Number of years in position	−0.008	(0.011)	
Prior position sought	0.504*	(0.207)	+10.42%
Position value	0.009	(0.014)	
Difficulty of attaining position	0.812**	(0.271)	+17.66%
Qualifications	0.400**	(0.109)	+19.60%
Lower-level position	0.374	(0.252)	
Had sponsor or mentor	0.074	(0.219)	
State-Specific Variables			
Traditionalist	−0.210	(0.211)	
Governor congruence	−0.232	(0.297)	
State legislature congruence	−0.004	(0.307)	
State opportunity structure	0.005$^+$	(0.003)	+7.53%
Local opportunity structure	−0.0003	(0.0002)	
Constant	2.211$^+$	(1.243)	
N	865		
Pseudo-R^2	0.2181		

$+ p < 0.10$, $* p < 0.05$, $** p < 0.01$.

Table 5.7 Logistic Regression on Interest in Higher Office for Political Appointees

	Full Model		Impact
Demographics			
Sex 1 = Female	2.905	(1.999)	—
White 1 = White	0.437	(0.331)	—
Education	0.021	(0.075)	—
Family income	-0.284**	(0.089)	-8.89%
Age	-0.088**	(0.011)	-26.86%
Family Dynamics			
Married/long-term relationship	-0.622*	(0.295)	-11.36%
Majority household responsibilities	0.251+	(0.151)	+7.93%
Children over eighteen	0.218	(0.261)	—
Parental suggestion	0.193+	(0.113)	+10.10%
Personal encouragement	0.833**	(0.191)	+15.44%
Political Dynamics			
Recruited since position	0.364+	(0.196)	+5.97%
Republican	0.193	(0.238)	—
Democrat	-0.395	(0.260)	—
Percent Obama vote 2012	-0.792	(0.853)	—
Sexism	0.166	(0.116)	—
Issue passion	0.048	(0.190)	—
Political participation	1.309**	(0.385)	+17.47%
Political interest	-0.006	(0.111)	—
Political efficacy	0.077	(0.078)	—
Personal Political Characteristics			
Number of years in position	-0.010	(0.011)	—
Sought appointment prior to position	0.522*	(0.209)	+9.18%
Position value	0.009	(0.015)	—
Difficulty of attaining position	0.828**	(0.280)	+15.47%
Qualifications	0.635	(0.452)	—
Low appointee	1.133	(1.687)	—
Had sponsor or mentor	0.033	(0.220)	—
State-Specific Variables			
Traditionalist	-0.240	(0.213)	—
Governor congruence	-0.265	(0.296)	—
State legislature congruence	-0.032	(0.311)	—
State political opportunity structure	0.004	(0.003)	—
Local political opportunity structure	-0.0003	(0.0002)	—
Interactions			
Sex × children over eighteen	0.725*	(0.362)	+13.58%
Qualifications × sex	-0.939+	(0.558)	-15.55%

continued

Table 5.7 *continued*

	Full Model		Impact
Interactions (continued)			
Low level × sex	-3.473[+]	(2.091)	-15.53%
Low level × qualifications	-0.135	(0.462)	—
Sex × qualifications × low level	0.755	(0.594)	—
Constant	1.598	(1.953)	
N	865		
Pseudo-R²	0.2261		

Note: The predicted probability of *Sex × qualifications* represents going from a woman who rates herself with low qualifications for higher office to a woman who rates herself with high qualifications for higher office. [+] $p < 0.10$, * $p < 0.05$, ** $p < 0.01$.

ables were set to their means. When predicting the change in probability for categorical variables, I went from their lowest level (for example, setting self-assessed qualifications to not at all qualified) to their highest level (very qualified). For continuous variables, I went from one standard deviation below the mean to one standard deviation above the mean.

The variables of main interest here are *sex, recruitment,* and *qualifications for higher office.* However, I do have some expectations for how other variables might behave in the regressions. The normal controls of education, family income, race, and age are included, and we should expect that those who are older and those who are wealthier might be less interested in pursuing higher office. Some appointees specifically commented on how their age has affected their ambitions for elected office, so age might be a particularly important variable for appointees.

Family dynamics include *marital status, majority of household responsibilities, having children over eighteen, parental suggestion,* and *personal encouragement.* Although scholars in the women and politics field have speculated about the effects of marital status on ambition—specifically that those who are married or in a long-term relationship might not have the support to seek office or might have more responsibilities associated with running a household—marital status itself has not been a significant predictor of political ambition (Fulton et al. 2006; Lawless 2012; Lawless and Fox 2005). Even when Lawless and Fox (2005) added the dimension of household responsibilities to better examine the effects of being responsible for more household duties, neither marital status nor household responsibilities were significant. Furthermore, having young children or increased child-care responsibilities was also not significant when predicting nascent ambitions for elected office (Lawless 2012; Lawless and Fox 2005). Having children in the household was not significant when state legislators considered running for congressional office (Fulton et al. 2006), although women having children at home was significant and negatively associated with congressional ambition (Fulton et al. 2006).[4]

I expect marital status and increased household responsibilities to have the same effects as in previous studies, but I think it best to look beyond having young children at home, to being a parent to children already out of the house. First, much of the literature that focuses on women in elected office already demonstrates that they tend to be older than elected men, making it more likely that women are simply waiting until their children have grown up before dedicating time to a political career (Carroll 1985a; Diamond 1977; Dolan and Ford 1997). Second, having children might expose individuals to situations and issues they had never encountered or thought about before. This might be especially true at the local and state levels concerning the areas of education and welfare programs; for example, the woman who requested appointment to a board in the health department that dealt specifically with a disability her daughter had or the other woman who had a severely disabled adult daughter who spurred her to represent the special needs population on a council in North Dakota. I would expect having *children over eighteen* to have less of an effect on appointed women because they are on average four and a half years younger than elected officials and appointed men, even though I still expect having *children over eighteen* to have a positive effect on interest in higher office by all state-level officials.

The *parental suggestion* for elected office is meant to cover the area of political socialization, in which those respondents told by their parents that one day they could or should run for elected office were taught to think about politics not only positively but in relation to their accom-

4. Sapiro (1982) also found that women with young children at home were much less likely than men with young children at home to be politically ambitious. Furthermore, both Lawless and Fox (2005) and Carroll and Sanbonmatsu (2013) found qualitative evidence from women discussing the effect holding public office or running for public office might have on their families, demonstrating that being a mother is still a hurdle for women who want to hold public office.

plishments. Suggestion to run for political office by a parent and political socialization in general are found to have a positive influence on ambitions for elected office. Soule's (1969) study on the political ambitions of state legislators finds that earlier political socialization was associated with higher political ambitions, and we know that growing up in a political household has a positive effect on the nascent ambitions of individuals in business, law, education, and political activism (Lawless 2012; Lawless and Fox 2005). Finally, Moore (2005) found that both activity in student government and experiencing gender bias had a positive effect on the political ambitions of political activist women. As a result of the large effects of socialization, I expect *parental suggestion* to have a strong and positive effect on both elected and appointed officials' interest in higher office.

Like the effects of *parental suggestion,* encouragement to seek public office is also found to have strong positive effects on the ambitions of those considering elected office (Lawless 2013). Previous *personal encouragement* variables, however, have not taken into account encouragement concerning political appointment. *Personal encouragement* in this model includes encouragement from a spouse or family member for either elected office, appointed office, or both, and I expect this to have a positive effect on ambitions for higher office.

Political dynamics involve the political identification of respondents and their levels of participation, interest, and efficacy and for appointed officials whether they feel *sexism* is present in the boards, commissions, and/or departments with which they are involved. The variable of highest interest within political dynamics is the *recruitment* variable; it specifically measures political recruitment for appointed or elected office since respondents attained their positions. Lawless and Fox (2010) show the importance of political recruitment to interest in elected office, and Sanbonmatsu (2006) demonstrates how electoral gatekeepers are less likely to recruit women. I expect political recruitment to continue to positively affect appointed officials, but particularly appointed officials who might require the political support or attention of others to be considered for appointment at all, especially if the appointment is competitive. *Political participation, efficacy, interest,* and *issue passion* are included as controls because more involvement, interest in, or passion for particular areas of politics might spur ambitions for higher office.

It is not clear what effect party identification might have on interest in higher office. We know that women have been more likely to be appointed at the state level when their parties match those of the governors (Riccucci and Saidel 2001), and we also know that women—in the electorate and as elected officials—are much more likely to be Democrat than Republican (Fiorina and Abrams 2008; Levendusky 2009; Norrander and Wilcox 2008). In general, I do not anticipate party identification to affect interest in higher office, but gendered effects may be present with closer analysis.

Experiencing or feeling as if one's organization exhibits, or has previously exhibited, sexist behavior might be a real barrier for women considering higher office. Moore (2005) considers experiencing sexism part of political socialization and finds that experiencing sexism increases ambition for elected office among women. For the purposes of this model, *sexism* is treated as a political dynamic of the position of each respondent. Feelings of having experienced sexism might inhibit ambitions for higher office, or they might spur women to push harder, as they did in Moore's 2005 study.

Beyond general political dynamics, personal political characteristics such as the *number of years in their current position, position value,* and most importantly, *self-assessed qualifications for higher office* might have large effects on ambitions for higher office. Two variables in this area are particularly important: having *sought appointed office* and *self-assessed qualifications.* I expect that a history of holding appointed office has a significant impact on ambitions for higher office. Furthermore, I expect *qualifications for higher office* to have a particularly strong effect on political ambition because I do not think doubts over one's qualifications simply disappear after the initial calculation of running for elected office or seeking political appointment. In fact, Lawless and Fox (2005) demonstrate how higher self-assessed qualifications for elected office still have a positive effect on those who have already run for elected office (those who exhibited expressive ambition). The following model will show if this is true for the ambitions of appointed officials in addition to applying the effects of self-assessed qualifications to progressive ambition.

Finally, I test several state-specific variables, including *political culture* and the opportunities available at the local and state level to hold public office.[5] *State legislature congruence, state political opportunity struc-ture,* and *local political opportunity structure* are based on variables Law-less and Fox (2010) use to see if higher availability of public offices in-crease the ambitions of those considering public office. Lawless and Fox (2010) do not find any support for these variables among those most likely to run for office, but the effects of these variables might be differ-ent for those already holding office because they are more knowledgeable about the kinds of public offices available to them. In addition to *state legislature congruence,* I add *governor congruence* because I expect those appointees who belong to the same party as their governor to feel more ambitious because it would seem more likely they could be appointed.

Tables 5.6 and 5.7 present the results of predicting political ambition for higher office among appointees and then a deeper analysis of ap-pointees, respectively. Using logistic regression with robust standard er-rors and Clarify to predict the change in probability of each significant variable, we can see what affects progressive ambition among state-level appointed officials.

Progressive Ambition for Higher Office at the State Level

In general there are four major patterns. First, what predicts interest in higher office for elected officials in prior studies is not the same as what predicts interest in higher office for appointed officials. Second, all of the family dynamics variables are significant when predicting interest in higher office for appointed officials. Third, *sex* is a statistically significant predictor of progressive ambition for political appointees. Finally, *self-assessed qualifications* are a significant predictor of progressive ambition for appointed officials.

Appointed women are almost 9 percent less likely than appointed men to exhibit interest in higher office. Unlike in previous analyses of elected officials, being married is a significant predictor of progressive ambition for appointees. Being married or in a long-term relationship

5. I ran the regressions with different combinations of dummies for the four po-litical cultures (moralist, individualist, pluralist, and traditionalist), and none was statistically significant. I left in traditionalist as a control for political culture because traditionalist cultures have lower rates of female representation.

depresses ambition by 14 percent. Two family dynamics variables are significant: *parental suggestion* and *having children over eighteen*.[6] The first hint of the effects of having children over eighteen is present in Table 5.6: appointees with children over eighteen were 8 percent more likely to be progressively ambitious. These findings confirm my theory on the effects having grown-up children might have on an individual's political ambitions. Also note that the political socialization variable of parental suggestion increases progressive ambition by 13 percent.

Recruitment was significant for appointees. Appointees recruited since attaining their positions were 7 percent more likely to be progressively ambitious than appointees not recruited at all. The variable of greatest interest, *self-assessed qualifications,* is highly significant for appointed officeholders ($p < 0.01$), confirming my earlier expectation. Appointees who assesses themselves as very qualified are more than 19 percent more likely to be interested in higher office than appointees who assess themselves as not at all qualified for higher office.

Finally, the majority of state-specific variables is insignificant, with one notable exception. Progressive ambition appears to be affected by the opportunity structure within the state for appointees (*state political opportunity structure* significant at the $p < 0.10$ level). Why would appointees be more ambitious if there was a high number of offices at the state level? The more positions open, the higher the opportunity to participate, especially if these positions are low level and less political.

To test my earlier expectations, which predicted that gendered perceptions would affect women's ambition for higher office and that those ambitions would be conditioned by their levels of office, I extend the baseline model in Table 5.6 to include four interaction variables: *qualifications × sex, low level × sex, low level × qualifications,* and *sex × qualifications × low level.* Additionally I include a final interaction for *sex × children over eighteen* to pinpoint my earlier theory that women with adult children exhibit more ambition. I conduct this analysis for appointees above.

Table 5.7 provides the results for the full model for appointees with the addition of the five interaction variables. See Appendix D for mod-

6. *Family income* and *age* were negatively related to interest in higher office among appointees; respondents with higher incomes and higher ages were less interested in higher office.

els that show the addition of each interaction to see how each interaction changes what predicts interest in higher office for political appointees. The results in Table 5.7 show the continued effects of self-assessed qualifications, except that this time they are affected by the sex of the appointees.

Low-level female appointees are more than 15 percent less likely to have progressive ambition (Table 5.7). Most interesting is the divide between *sex and qualifications* and *sex and level of office.* Both the interaction of *sex and level of office* and *sex and qualifications* are significant at the $p < 0.10$ level, which partially confirms my earlier theory that gendered perceptions exist for the progressive ambitions of appointed state officials.

Table 5.7 also shows the lack of support for my theory that gendered perceptions are conditioned by the level of office women hold. The triple interaction of *sex, self-assessed qualifications,* and *level of office* fails to attain standard levels of statistical significance. This suggests that gendered perceptions do exist among the lower-level appointees because the interaction between *sex and self-qualifications* is significant, but these gendered perceptions are not related to the individuals holding low-level appointed office because neither the interaction between *qualifications and level of office* nor the triple interaction of *level of office, sex, and self-qualifications* is significant. It is important to note that the interaction for *sex and low appointee* is significant: low-level appointed women are 15 percent less likely to be interested in higher office. Again, because the triple interaction of *level of office, sex, and self-qualifications* is insignificant, this lower ambition among women on boards and commissions does not seem to be a result of the level of their office.

Significantly, the gendered perceptions go in the opposite direction I would expect. Gendered perceptions studies tend to find that women tend to have lower perceptions of their own abilities, which negatively affects their ambitions (Fox and Lawless 2011; Lawless and Fox 2005). Therefore, when women express more confidence in their abilities and qualifications to hold higher office, then they will express higher levels of political ambition. If this were true, then I would expect the coefficient for the interaction *sex × qualifications* to be positive because qualifications are measured from "Not at all qualified" to "Very qualified." However, the coefficient of the interaction *sex and self-assessed qualifications* is negative, which means that as women rate their own qualifications higher, they become less progressively ambitious. In fact, a female appointee who assesses herself as very qualified for higher office is more than 13 percent less likely to be progressively ambitious than a female appointee who assesses herself as not qualified at all for higher office. In this sense, having a higher perception of one's qualifications is not an asset to progressive ambition but a deterrent—at least in the appointment realm. Why this is the case clearly requires further study because these results are so unexpected. It should also be noted that the coefficient for *sex × children over eighteen* is significant and positive, meaning that women who have children over eighteen are more progressively ambitious.

WHY WOMEN WITH HIGH SELF-QUALIFICATION SCORES ARE DISINTERESTED IN HIGH OFFICE

My analysis of the State Political Pathways Survey pertaining to ambition demonstrates that what explains the progressive ambition of elected officials does not explain the progressive ambitions of appointees. In other studies of nascent ambition, gendered perceptions are a major factor for men and women considering elected office (Lawless and Fox 2005). I argue that gendered perceptions persist in calculations of progressive ambition for appointed men and women at the state level. (I further argue that higher self-qualifications increase a woman's interest in higher office, although her level of office would condition this.) The results demonstrate the strong positive effect self-perceived qualifications have on appointed officials' progressive ambitions, but they also demonstrate the negative effect sex has on appointed officials' progressive ambitions.

My deeper analysis of progressive ambition for appointees tests the theory that gendered perceptions exist, with higher perceptions increasing interest in higher office, and that they are influenced by the individual's level of office. This analysis shows not only that gendered perceptions exist independently of the individual's level of office in the appointment arena but also that gendered perceptions work in the opposite way one would expect. Instead of appointed women with high self-assessed qualifications having increased interest in higher office, they exhibited lower levels of interest in higher office.

Why might an appointed woman who sees herself as qualified for higher office be less interested in higher office than a woman who assesses her qualifications as lower? The answer might be that with more confidence and a better perception of their abilities comes a deeper sense of what they are interested in dedicating their life's work to. The words from the appointees themselves in Chapter 4 point to a deep sense of public service with no interest in holding a public office with more responsibility—specifically an elected office, which has the weight of elections and partisan politics behind it. In fact, many appointees, both high and low level, argued that their positions were not political at all, even though a political body appoints them and state governments fund their boards, commissions, or departments.

The women in my sample were a highly motivated and successful group of women, holding positions where they could make a real difference. These women had both a proven track record of success in their own lives and a glimpse into the world of state politics through their appointments, which again, many of them did not think were political. This put them in a unique position of having personal experience in state-level politics, dedicating their time and energy to an issue they cared about without having to take part in the competitiveness or "dirtiness" of politics. In this sense, these women were the most informed about what it takes to hold a higher elected or appointed office and acknowledged they might be qualified for it but still opted out.

This could also suggest that many of these women had a different definition of what is political and, most importantly, at which level or type of office "politics" begins. For example, even though there were many women in high-level appointed positions within state government, most did not see their positions as political, echoing what the low-level appointees said. Some of the disinterest in higher office among these women might not have been because they did not feel they were qualified for higher office (although the earlier analysis showed low-level female appointees did feel this way) but because higher office was considered more political and therefore not of interest to them. In this sense, low-level female appointees were not interested in higher public office because they saw it as explicitly political. High-level female appointees might also have felt this way, but because many of them did not see their positions as political, this might have led them to believe that higher public office, specifically higher appointed public office, was not political either. This belief allowed them to exhibit higher ambitions for public office than did low-level female appointees, but only ambitions that were *not political but something else entirely.* These results suggest that we cannot assume that women with high self-assessed qualifications will automatically be interested in higher public office, nor should we take political ambition as a given.

Many of the women in high-level appointments took these positions because they were related to their career in the private sector, meaning the women had ambitions to be directors or deputy directors of state agencies not because they were political but because they were moving up *their* career ladder—not the political one. In this sense, high-level appointed women in state government concurrently supported and confounded Carroll and Sanbonmatsu's (2013) argument that "ambition and candidacy may arise simultaneously" because many of these women had expressed interest in public office after someone had recruited them but had taken the job not for political ambition but an ambition related to their own careers or personal interests (44). A few of the women, for example, went on to express ambition for higher appointed office or another high-level appointed office not because they wanted to be in politics but because they wanted to continue the work they were doing at the state level. Madison Williams, a commissioner in a commerce department, said the following when asked about her interest in another appointment:

> I think for me it would be who was leading. I have been really lucky in
> my career to work with and for people that I admire greatly, and I have
> learned a lot, and I have grown in each of those positions, and I feel
> people that have integrity, they want to get things done, they have the
> same values, and that's really important to me. . . . I would definitely
> prefer to stay at the state level; I think you can get stuff done here. And
> this is the whole level of bureaucracy, it's all interesting kind of watching
> FEMA, and we've had a lot of interactions with several other agencies
> after Irene, and so I think I prefer to work at state level. It's a small state,
> and you really can get things done, and you know people and you know

how you treat people and people might not agree with you this time, but they'll still want to work with you again if you dealt with them fairly.

Elizabeth Goldman, a deputy director in a natural resources department said something similar when asked about accepting a federal appointment: "Right now I'm number two or three in the department of Natural Resources at the state level. Would I consider doing that at the federal level? Yes, if I believed in the philosophies of the administration. If I felt that person was consistent with my beliefs and I wasn't selling out, then I would do that." According to these women, there is something unique about being in the appointment realm; it is a place where they can contribute to a field about which they are passionate without having to deal with the politics many elected officials must battle on a daily basis. If it is true that appointed women have a disinterest in offices they consider political, then we would expect appointed women to be less interested in an office considered very political, such as elected office. Chapter 6 will further explore appointees' interest in elected office. If it is true, as the qualitative evidence has shown, that women are less interested in public office because they do not like politics, then we should expect being a woman to be a negative predictor of ambition for elected office, just as it was a negative predictor for ambition for higher office.

6. Considering the Other Pathway
Appointed Officials' Interest in Elected Office

> I've worked with the entire legislature in my current position, state
> legislature, and I've worked with our congressional delegation offices,
> both in my past work with the city as well as with the past work with
> the state, and this work, and frankly I've never found it very appealing
> as a career.
> —*Riley Cunningham, high-level appointee, natural resources department*

Riley Cunningham has had a long career working with and in government. She worked for the Portland City Council as well as setting up a
program for the Endangered Species Act. She worked at the federal level
for the Peace Corps as a country director, which was not a political appointment. She found out from friends and colleagues about the direc-
torship position open in her state. They felt she should apply: "There was
a standard application process and interview process that included four
other, or three other, very big finalists; I have no idea what the pool was
to begin with, so it was more of a competitive application process for the
job I currently hold." When asked about her motivations to seek out this
position, she said:

> I thought it would be a really interesting job. It's a fascinating agency, and
> so I thought the work would be really interesting, and I definitely thought
> it would be interesting to work at really the higher levels of policymaking
> in the state; obviously when you are working for the three highest elected
> officials, you get to be involved with some of those broad big-scope
> policy decisions, which was of interest to me.

Despite this clear interest to influence policy, Cunningham was not interested in affecting policy through elected office. She went on to say
about seeking elected office:

I was going to say . . . if people approached me, I probably wouldn't. If somebody approached me from the president's office, whoever that might be, and said would you like to be the Peace Corps director of the world? I definitely, I would take that on. But that's not an elected position, that's an appointed position. Or if somebody said would you like to be ambassador to France? I would take that on, but in terms of actually running for office, no, I have no interest in that.

As her quote from the opening of this chapter suggests, she has had a front-row seat to what it means to be in an elected position and is not interested in serving in that capacity, even though colleagues have suggested she seek an elected position. Cunningham discusses her position and how she must be both responsible to statute and to her elected bosses:

As appointed officials, [we] are not political in the sense that we haven't gone out and won an election, but we are . . . still very aware of the political nature of pretty much everything we do, and so while we work to maintain the integrity of the standards that we are hired to implement, we also are aware of and work as much as possible, as best as possible I guess, that's a poor way to say it but, in terms of making sure that we are moving within the agenda of the political officials who have hired us. And in my case, that's particularly complicated because I have a part of my job that is directly responsible for implementing the desires, the programs, the goals of the state land board, who are these three elected officials, and then I have an entire other part of my job that is my responsibility under statute that does not have anything to do with them . . . and there are times when politically they want one thing, and from my, under my hat of implementing the statutes, which is my legislative bosses, I have a responsibility to do something that doesn't necessarily fit with their political agenda, and I feel like I have to have the integrity to be able to explain that but still meet that responsibility. So that's a tricky part of being an appointed official, particularly one that has both responsibilities under the appointee authority and then on another level in another direction, to other elected officials, in reality.

Cunningham exemplifies the position of many appointed women in state government. They have constant interaction with elected officials and must work with and for them daily. For many of these women, working with elected officials only affirms their disinterest in electoral politics.

I establish in Chapter 5 that women are less progressively ambitious than men, specifically women who see themselves as qualified to hold higher office. The analysis in this chapter tests this gender gap further, moving beyond predicting progressive ambition to predicting appointed officials' interest in the traditional political pathway, elected office. I expect appointed women to be less ambitious for elected office because of my qualitative evidence revealing women are less interested in politics, revealed in Chapters 4 and 5.

Previously, it was assumed that women are generally not found in US public office because they are not interested in running for elected office (Lawless and Fox 2005), or if they are interested, they come across too many barriers to nomination and election. I have made the case in this book that the usual method of answering why women are not publicly serving at the same rates as men is flawed because it almost always focuses upon the ambition for elected office. Rarely have scholars considered appointed office a viable entrance into politics for women, and they have not considered appointed office part of the political career ladder. This mentality and methodology overlook thousands of women who do publicly serve and who wield an impressive amount of power in state politics.

Chapter 5 seeks to rectify this oversight by trying to understand how progressive ambition functions within the appointment realm, but in Chapter 4 I uncover a distinct disdain for politics among female appointees to the point that they insist that their service as appointees is different from elected, or "normal," politics. This disavowal of politics leads me to believe that appointed women would be even less ambitious for elected office, which many of them said was the kind of politics they tried to avoid, than they would be for higher office in general. If this is the case, then it would explain why there is such a large number of women in political appointments who have gone unnoticed by the scholars of women in politics: they are unlikely to be studied in the first place, and not enough are crossing over into elected positions to signal to scholars that appointments are a common jumping-off point to elected office. This is important because it means we might have been simplifying the story of women's ambition for politics. It is not simply that women feel they are less qualified for elected office, or they are recruited less, and these issues lead to a lower ambition for elected office. It might be that women are disinterested because of their personal definitions of *political,* which almost always encompass elected office and generally do not include appointed office, particularly their own office. They can either be actively ambitious for an appointed office, or, when the opportunity presents itself, they convince themselves that what they are doing is *not actually political.* At the very least it would suggest that the story of women's ambition for political office is considerably more complicated than originally theorized.

POLITICAL AMBITION FOR ELECTED OFFICE AMONG APPOINTEES

There are many examples of prominent elected officials later seeking political appointment (e.g., Hillary Clinton, Christine Todd Whitman) and appointees later running for elected office (e.g., Janet Reno, Robert Reich, Donna Shalala, Elizabeth Warren). Unfortunately, not much is known about those who cross over from elected to appointed office (or vice versa), nor is there any understanding of the ambitions of such a political move. More than 18 percent of the political appointees in my sample had run for elected office, with slightly more low-level appointees (19.5 percent) than high-level appointees (13.4 percent) who held elected office ($p < 0.10$). Yet, appointed men were 10 percent more likely than were appointed women (23 percent versus 13 percent, respectively) to have run for office ($p < 0.01$), suggesting a gendered component to appointees running for elected office. The appointees ran for local elections such as school board or town council, and some even ran for and achieved positions in the state legislature (forty appointees ran for state representative, and fifteen of them won). Figure 6.1 shows that most appointees do not run for any elected positions and that men are more likely to run, and if they do run they are more likely than women are to run for multiple elected positions. We know that some appointed officials not only consider the opposite pathway to public office but also have already held or at least sought positions on the other political path. There is little difference between the appointed men and women in having sought prior appointed office. Overall 21 percent of appointees said they had sought

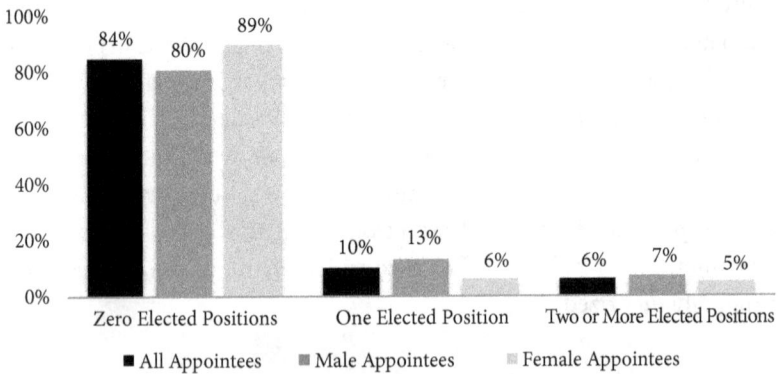

Figure 6.1 **Number of Elected Positions Appointees Sought**

an appointment prior to their position. Slightly fewer than 23 percent of male appointees versus 19 percent of female appointees had sought an appointment—not a statistically significant difference. The percentages are the same even when I break down the data by high- and low-level appointees. These data suggest that ambition for appointed office is different from ambition for elected office.

Although a considerable number of the appointed women from the interviews were firm in their disinterest in elected office, a few appointees had already held elected office or expressed an interest in it for the future. Two women—Lillian Fox, a high-level appointee discussed in Chapter 5, and Donna Abramson, a low-level appointee discussed in Chapter 2—had never run for elected office but expressed ambitions to run in the future. Danielle Whitman, discussed in Chapter 4, was an elected and appointed official and expressed interest in higher elected or appointed office. For her it depended on her health and what she would be willing to give up in order to run. Wendy Jenkins, a low-level appointee from Connecticut, had previously run and served as a town council member. She was ambivalent about serving in elected office again:

> I don't know if I would seek elected office, but I would probably look at serving on some various committees or whatever; I mean I already am, but I could see that right now I'm doing it because I'm appointed somewhat as a staff person, where I would look at it more being appointed as a member of the community, which is a little bit different—I

have the expertise from my work as a staff person, but I think could see my role stepping up more.

Even for Jenkins, who has held elected office, the appointment route was of more interest to her for the future. The final appointee from the interviews, Carol Swanson, had a long history in politics. Carol had an interest from a young age—serving in student government and becoming the first female student body president of her high school. This interest in government as well as the environment and natural resources led her to her first position, an appointment to her town's parks and recreation commission. She served on that commission (which required reelection) for twelve years, until someone encouraged her to run for the township board. She was the first woman to be elected to the board. Swanson also served six years as a state representative, followed by another eight years as a state senator, the maximum number of years for both chambers in a term-limited legislature. During her entire time as legislator and during the time of the interview, she was an appointee on the Great Lakes Protection Fund Board. Before she semiretired after her legislative service, she worked in a natural resources office as a high appointee for two years. When asked if she harbored any interest in running for a seat in Congress, her answer was:

> No, I was asked a couple of times. . . . I thought, well number one, it is more difficult for women to raise money than it is for men, especially when I started in government. And even when I left the Senate it's always been more difficult for women to raise money than it is men. And it is so dominated by money now that I just felt I could not be as effective as I would have liked to have been. So I decided I did not want to do that.

Swanson's career was much more similar to those of the other state legislators from my study than to those of other appointees. And it is important to note that she had a long history of appointed and elected office; her interest in government and the environment pushed her to seek opportunities to serve in whatever capacity she could. This lack of limitation on public service is what made Abramson, Fox, Swanson, and Whitman unique in this study of appointee political ambition.

Because the women in appointed office had lower progressive ambitions compared with those of men and exhibited a potent dislike for politics, I anticipate that *female appointees are less ambitious for elected office than are male appointees.* I also expect that *individuals' self-assessed qualifications will continue to exert a strong positive influence on appointed officials' interest in elected office.* Put simply, the more confident they are in their abilities, the more ambitious they are for the other political pathway compared with those who perceive themselves as having lower qualifications. As I do in Chapter 5, here I examine public officials' interest in seeking elected office as a first test of my theory that appointed women are less ambitious for elected office.

Interest in the Other Political Pathway

I asked the appointed officials who had never held an office different from their own (appointees never holding elected office) if they had ever considered holding elected office. The results are presented in Table 6.1. Fewer than half of the appointees in this sample had thought about elected office. However, more than half had never even thought about it or had no interest. There is little difference when I break down the data by high- and low-level appointees; they are equally disinterested in elected office.

Moving to the gender differences within each office (Table 6.2), appointed men who had never held elected office were more likely than appointed women who had never held elected office to have seriously considered running for elected office; additionally, appointed women were significantly more likely to have no interest in elected office at all than were appointed men ($p < 0.05$).

Table 6.1 Prior Thoughts on Running for Elected Office by Political Appointees

	All Appointed	High Appointed	Low Appointed
Yes, I seriously considered it.	6.77%	7.91%	6.56%
Yes, it has crossed my mind.	40.17%	41.73%	39.90%
No, I had not thought about it.	10.70%	10.79%	10.68%
No, I have no interest.	42.36%	39.57%	42.86%
N	916	516	400

Note: Statistical comparisons are between high- and low-level appointees. This question was asked only of those who had never run for elected office. $^{+} p < 0.10$, $^{*} p < 0.05$, $^{**} p < 0.01$.

Table 6.2 Prior Thoughts on Running for Elected Office by Sex

	Appointed Men	Appointed Women
Yes, I seriously considered it.	8.33%*	4.75%
Yes, it has crossed my mind.	42.05%	37.75%
No, I had not thought about it.	10.68%	10.79%
No, I have no interest.	38.95%*	46.75%
N	516	400

Note: Statistical comparisons are between men and women in appointed office. This question was asked only of those who had never run for elected office. $^+ p < 0.10$, $* p < 0.05$, $** p < 0.01$.

Table 6.3 Prior Thoughts on Running for Elected Office by Level of Appointment

	High-Level Appointed Men	High-Level Appointed Women	Low-Level Appointed Men	Low-Level Appointed Women
Yes, I seriously considered it.	9.76%	5.26%	8.06%$^+$	4.66%
Yes, it has crossed my mind.	41.46%	42.11%	42.17%	37.03%
No, I had not thought about it.	13.41%	7.02%	10.14%	11.37%
No, I have no interest.	35.37%	45.61%	39.63%*	46.94%
N	82	57	434	343

Note: Statistical comparisons are between males and females in each level of appointed office. This question was asked only of those who had never run for elected office. $^+ p < 0.10$, $* p < 0.05$, $** p < 0.01$.

The pattern stays the same in Table 6.3 when we look at the data by sex and level of office. High- and low-level female appointees were less likely than male appointees to have an interest in elected office. Although the difference was not statistically significant, it was particularly pronounced between high-level appointees. High-level female appointees were 10 percent more likely to have no interest in running for elected office than were high-level male appointees.

Just as there were appointed women who expressed interest in elected office despite most women having no interest in it at all, there were also men who had no interest in elected office. Notice that almost half of all men appointees had no interest in elected office or had never thought about running for elected office. Although the evidence thus far shows that men had more political ambitions than did appointed women, there was also a considerable number of men who had no ambitions for elected office. In the open-ended question of the survey, twenty-two men and seventeen women listed similar reasons for how they received their appointments, and some of the men were clear that the offices in which they served were not political. A male deputy director of the health department said, "I'm not really political. My career advancement led me to the level of this agency where appointments are political. I would have little interest in a political appointment otherwise." A male appointee on a land conservation and development commission said something similar: "By statute the commission is required to include a historian, and there are not a lot of us in this state. So I felt obliged to say yes when asked." A man from an oil recovery commission was firm in his disinterest in public service beyond his appointment: "I'm on a very specific commission, which oversees a very specific state organization. I am a scientist, and my education and work experience are directly related to the work of said state organization. My appointment to the commission was a function of my background and an inherent interest that I have in the work of the state organization. I have no political ambitions and work full time in the private sector." Similarly, a male appointee from a state board of architectural examiners said, "I have zero political ambition. I have enjoyed giving back to my profession and take great pride in my work on committees helping shape what the architects test should be to license new young professional[s]. This board is certainly monocentric on architecture and is certainly not a stepping-stone to a political career." Male appointees, too, can have less ambition for elected office and land their appointments for professional or personal reasons. The qualitative evidence for these male appointees does not reveal a dislike of government as a reason for this lack of ambition. Both the interviews of the female appointees and some of their statements in the open-ended portion of the survey hint at a deeper dislike and distrust of politics as a reason for their lower political ambitions.

The difference between appointed men and women's interest in seeking elected office might have been a result of the differences in their motivation to hold public office, as discussed in Chapter 4. If women appointees had a different definition of politics, and if their motivations for seeking their appointments were not politically driven, then we should not be surprised that appointed women were less interested in elected office because it is very political. In fact, high- and low-level women appointees were similarly disinterested in elected office, with low-level appointed women perhaps slightly more disinterested than high-level appointed women.

As I mentioned above, two female appointees I interviewed who had never run for elected office before did express an interest in elected office. Fox, who served in a health department, said she was interested in elected office because it would allow her to influence public policy and "build and strengthen communities." Abramson, a low-level appointee, always had an interest in running for elected office:

> I've always wanted to run for office, ever since I can remember, but there
> are things in my life that led me to believe I wasn't ready; if that's true or
> not I'm not sure, but I wanted to get my kids raised first, and I wanted
> to be financially stable, and have some community experience before I
> ran, and I know that those aren't requirements per se, but I just felt like it
> would make me a better official, so that's what I decided to do.

The responses of these two women, high- and low-level political appointees, respectively, suggest that some women feel they can do more in elected office. Abramson in particular pointed to a lifelong ambition for elected office that was markedly more similar to that of the elected officials in my sample who had a positive view of politics and did not mind being political (see Chapter 7). Bear in mind that these two women were the outliers of my interviews; most of the women were quite clear about not being interested in elected office, usually because they did not like politics, felt they could do more in their appointments, or did not want their personal lives invaded by the election process.

Suzanne Richards, discussed in Chapter 4, cited her experience observing and working with her state legislature and how it "turned her off to it." Darlene Vesko, who served on a commission for the blind, spoke of the personal costs of entering the electoral arena:

> I think for me an elected position scares me a little bit more, and I'll tell
> you why: because you have to be much more openly out there in the
> public. You already lose. I mean at each layer of politics you lose your
> personal life, and that is just a facet and a factor that exists. And when
> you have children who really like to have privacy, and you have loved

ones that really need privacy, and really their quiet, solitude times, and quiet family times, that makes it very challenging. . . . So you have to weigh, is that a wise move as a parent? The downside of that would be detrimental to my family, and I would not do that.

Once again, these appointees referred negatively to costs associated with elected office that make them disinterested in running. This negativity does not seem to extend to appointed office, or at least not their own office.

I also asked all appointees about their interest in pursuing elected office in the future. I asked political appointees the following question: "Which best characterizes your attitudes toward running for elected office in the future?" Table 6.4 provides the breakdown of appointee responses by sex. The general pattern remains the same: female appointed officials were less ambitious for elected office than were male appointed officials, just as female appointees who had never run for elected office were less likely to have considered elected office than were their male counterparts. The results in Tables 6.1 and 6.4 offer support for my first expectation, that female appointees are less ambitious for elected office than male appointees are.

I asked a series of questions to the appointees who said running for office was something they would not do or that they currently had no interest in but would not rule it out. These questions asked if they were more likely to consider running if a certain condition were met, such as if someone from work suggested they run, if there were issues they were more passionate about, or if there were a lot of support for their candidacy. Their answers could have been "Yes," "Possibly," or "No." The appointees who had no interest in running for elected office were firm in this belief. For almost every one of these conditions, except for support for candidacy, more than half and oftentimes more than two-thirds of the appointees said they were not more likely to run for office despite more spousal support, campaign experience, or free time. More than half of the appointees said they were more likely to consider running for elected office if they "knew there was a lot of support" for their candidacy. The only other two factors that seemingly had an effect on appointees' calculations of running for elected office were having more free

Table 6.4 Ambition for Future Elected Office among Appointees

	All Appointed	Appointed Men	Appointed Women
It is something I definitely would like to undertake in the future.	4.03%	4.50%	3.34%
It is something I might undertake if the opportunity presents itself.	16.40%	18.29%*	13.59%
I would not rule it out, but I currently have no interest.	41.58%	41.38%	41.87%
It is something I would not do.	37.99%	35.83%+	41.20%
N	1,116	667	449

Note: Statistical comparisons are between men and women in appointed office.
$^+ p < 0.10$, $^* p < 0.05$, $^{**} p < 0.01$.

time and being more passionate about certain issues. Male and female appointees answered the majority of these questions similarly. The only areas in which female appointees deviated from male appointees were in not being as influenced by a spouse/partner suggesting they run and in being slightly more influenced by having more experience working on campaigns. In short, the data derived from these questions provide an understanding of what might persuade those not interested in running for office to take the plunge. The overall message was pretty clear: most appointees would never consider running for elected office regardless of their gender and the circumstances.

PREDICTING POLITICAL AMBITION FOR THE OTHER PATHWAY

Table 6.5 predicts the ambitions of appointees for elected office. The dependent variable for Table 6.5 is *interest in elected office*, where 1 signifies interest in elected office and 0 represents no interest in elected office. The variables contained in these regressions are similar to the earlier regressions predicting interest in higher office, with only a few notable differences. I change the *recruitment* and *personal encouragement* variables to specifically reflect recruitment and encouragement for elected office. I

Table 6.5 Logistic Regression of Ambitions for Elected Office by Appointees

	Ambition for Elected Office		Impact
Demographics			
Sex	−0.772**	(0.265)	−14.46%
Education	0.047	(0.088)	—
Family income	−0.106	(0.109)	—
Race (white)	1.088**	(0.423)	+19.16%
Age	−0.104**	(0.014)	−40.63%
Family Dynamics			
Married/long-term relationship	−0.475	(0.344)	—
Majority household responsibilities	0.285+	(0.172)	+11.68%
Children over eighteen	0.183	(0.246)	—
Parental suggestion	0.363**	(0.137)	+6.86%
Personal encouragement for elected office	0.516+	(0.267)	+10.61%
Political Dynamics			
Recruited for elected office	0.562*	(0.262)	+11.49%
Republican	−0.370	(0.276)	—
Democrat	−0.902**	(0.328)	−18.01%
Percent Obama vote 2012	−1.764	(1.633)	—
Sexism	0.247+	(0.133)	+7.98%
Issue passion	0.466*	(0.216)	-
Political interest	0.023	(0.140)	—
Political efficacy	−0.134	(0.472)	—
Political participation	1.336**	(0.472)	+25.17%
Personal Political Characteristics			
Number of years in position	−0.001	(0.013)	—
Ran for elected office before	0.071	(0.311)	—
Current position value	0.021	(0.016)	—
Difficulty of being appointed	−0.048	(0.086)	—
Qualifications	0.481**	(0.133)	+26.93%
High-level position	−0.400	(0.316)	—
Had sponsor or mentor	0.168	(0.262)	—
Term limits for appointment	0.024	(0.219)	—
Likely to win if ran	0.106	(0.063)	—
Financial concerns regarding elected office	3.875**	(0.478)	+52.53%
Family concerns regarding elected office	−1.670**	(2.018)	−27.26%
State-Specific Variables			
Traditionalist culture	−0.285	(0.272)	—
State legislature congruence	0.156	(0.367)	—
Governor congruence	−0.712*	(0.356)	−14.45%
State political opportunity structure	0.0001	(0.005)	—

continued

Table 6.5 *continued*

	Ambition for Elected Office		Impact
State-Specific Variables (continued)			
Local political opportunity structure	0.003	(0.0003)	—
Legislature professionalism	-0.206	(0.370)	—
Legislature term limits	-0.173	(0.305)	—
Midwest	-0.388	(0.420)	—
Constant	1.549	(2.018)	—
N	811		
Pseudo-R^2	0.3633		
Percent Correctly Predicted	81.13%		

Note: Standard errors in parentheses. Difficulty of becoming appointed is the subjective answer the respondent gave to how difficult, in general, he or she felt it was to attain their position, from very difficult (1) to very easy (7). $^+ p < 0.10$, $^* p < 0.05$, $^{**} p < 0.01$.

include three new variables. The first measures the respondents' opinions on the *likelihood of winning an election* if they did run for elected office. This is meant to capture any doubts respondents might have about the viability of their candidacies, with the expectation that those who did not believe they would win would be less likely to have had an interest in elected office. The answer to this question was gendered. More than 40 percent of male appointees, compared with 28 percent of female appointees, said they were likely to win office if they decided to run. This continues the pattern earlier in this chapter in which female appointees were less likely than males were to be confident in their abilities to hold higher office ($p < 0.01$).

Regarding two other specific costs individuals might incur when running for elected office, I asked those appointees who had no interest in elected office if they were more likely to run for office if they had fewer *family responsibilities* or they were more *financially secure*. Those who answered that they would be more interested in elected office or could possibly be more interested in elected office if they had fewer family responsibilities or were more financially secure are coded as 1. Those who said they still would not be interested and those who expressed an interest for elected office already are coded as 0.

Both of these variables assume that those who expressed an interest in elected office from the start might not have had the worry of family obligations or finances, or that family obligations or finances did not affect their interest in elected office. It is also a way to test the relationally embedded model of candidacy Carroll and Sanbonmatsu (2013) favor. The effects of running for office on women's families and finances are two major reasons that might affect their interest in elected office. Considerations of family and finances can be different for each woman, depending on whether she has young children and whether she has spousal support.

Introducing variables controlling for these considerations can help us understand how such personal considerations might affect a person's interest in elected office in general and a woman's interest in elected office specifically. A simple difference-of-means test on these two new variables of *family responsibilities* and *financial concerns* did not reveal any gender differences. Appointed women were only slightly more likely (3 percent) than appointed men were to say that they would consider running for office if they had fewer family responsibilities, but this difference did not reach standard levels of statistical significance. The difference between men and women on *financial concerns* was even smaller; women were less than 1 percent less likely than men were to be interested in running for elected office if they did not have financial concerns. I ran the regressions with the interactions of *sex and family responsibilities* and *sex and financial concerns.* Neither of the interactions was significant, which means I cannot provide statistical support that appointed women are more concerned with family responsibilities and finances than are appointed men.

The costs-of-running variables (*family responsibilities and financial concerns*) are part of appointed officials' calculus of interest in elected office. Those who would be more interested in running if they were more financially secure (Table 6.5) were 52 percent more likely to express an interest in elected office than were those who did not have such concerns to begin with or were still not interested in elected office.

Interestingly enough, those more interested in running for elected office if they had fewer family responsibilities were still less likely to have an interest in elected office, which might be an indication that other variables affecting family life might have been negatively associated with interest in elected office. It also might suggest that modeling political ambition for elected office when candidate emergence is relationally embedded is difficult because trying to capture all of the ways in which issues such as family concerns or financial support affect political ambition is nearly impossible. This might be a reason so many quantitative studies have found that a woman having young children does not affect political ambition, even when the follow-up interviews of women put family concerns in the forefront of considerations in running for elected office (Fox and Lawless 2014; Lawless and Fox 2005; Norrander and Wilcox 2008).

As I said earlier, running the models with an interaction between family and financial concerns and sex does not make either of these variables or their interactions significant. Appointed women were not more likely to be interested in running for elected office than appointed men were, even if they had fewer family responsibilities or felt more financially secure.

Personal encouragement for elected office and *recruitment for elected office* were significant predictors of interest in elected office, and as before, higher assessment of one's *qualifications* was associated with more interest in elected office.[1] Appointed officials who had the highest self-assessment of their qualifications were nearly 27 percent more likely to have ambitions for elected office than appointed officials who had the lowest self-assessment of their qualifications.[2] Many of the variables that measure the value of staying in the appointment arena are not signifi-

---

1. I use the same *self-assessed qualification* variable that predicted interest in higher office for interest in elected office and appointed office. Although the survey question did not specifically ask about qualification for either office but more broadly asked about qualification for higher office, I believe it is still a good representation of the self-assessment the respondents did of their own qualification in general.

2. I also run this model with interactions for *sex and qualification, sex and low-level office, low-level office and qualification,* and the triple interaction of *sex, low-level office,* and *qualification,* mirroring the analysis in Chapter 5, which predicted interest in higher office. When the interaction of *sex and qualification* is introduced, *sex* drops out of significance and the interaction never reaches standard levels of statistical significance. After adding the other interactions leading up to the triple interaction of *sex, level of office,* and *qualifications,* the variance inflation factor (VIF) goes over 15, suggesting high levels of multicollinearity, particularly after the triple interaction is included in the regression. This problem never occurs in the regression analysis of progressive recruitment. Because the multicollinearity is so high with the triple interaction, further model specification or data collection might be necessary to tease out the effects of gendered perceptions and levels of office on appointees' interest in seeking elected office.

cant, specifically the *number of years* in their position and their *position value.* Having *run for elected office* before was not a significant predictor of interest in elected office in the future. The results from the analysis of predicting political appointees' interest in elected office confirm both of my expectations: being an appointed woman decreases the ambition for elected office, but having higher self-qualification evaluations increases ambition for elected office. Overall these results point to the continued effects of self-perceived qualifications, recruitment, and sex on appointee ambition.

I think it is important to take a moment to compare the results of predicting progressive ambition from Chapter 5 with the results of predicting interest in elected office among appointees. One important difference is in the effects of sex. Not only does sex become statistically significant when predicting interest in elected office compared with progressive ambition but also it has an even larger negative impact on interest in elected office. Appointed women were about 9 percent less likely to be progressively ambitious than were appointed men, but women were more than 14 percent less likely to be ambitious for elected office, which earlier analysis indicates is because of disinterest in political office.

Beyond sex, several variables stand out when we compare the progressive ambitions versus ambitions for elected office of appointees. First, being white was not statistically related to progressive ambition, but it was statistically related to ambition for elected office. What is it about elected office that made white appointees more interested than were appointees from underrepresented groups? Second, two of the family dynamic variables are no longer significant when predicting ambition for elected office: *being married* and having *children over eighteen.* Third, many of the political dynamic variables become significant when predicting ambition for elected office, perhaps providing more proof that being politically oriented is more important in the elected arena than in the appointment realm. Finally, *self-assessed qualifications* has a larger impact on ambition for elected office than on progressive ambition. Considering oneself highly qualified increased ambition for elected office among appointees by nearly 27 percent but increased ambition for higher office by only 15 percent. This is not surprising because *self-assessed qualifications* had a much higher effect on the progressive ambitions of elected officials than on appointed officials, as Chapter 7 shows.

Table 6.6 Appointee Interest in Specific Public Offices

	All Appointees	Appointed Men	Appointed Women
Mayor	6.19%	7.70%*	3.96%
State senator	13.54%	16.15%**	9.67%
Statewide elected office	5.00%	4.89%	5.05%
Governor	2.65%	3.56%*	1.32%
US representative	8.14%	9.19%	6.59%
US senator	4.16%	5.04%+	2.86%
Appointment to state board	19.38%	20.59%	17.58%
Appointment to state department	18.85%	19.85%	17.36%
Appointment to a federal agency or department	16.11%	15.70%	16.70%
	1,130	675	455

$+ p < 0.10$, $* p < 0.05$, $** p < 0.01$.

Specific Political Office Interest

As a final analysis of women appointees' reticence to seek elected office, I include the data from the questions that asked appointees about their interest in specific public offices. It is important to note that these percentages are all low. Even for state-level appointed positions, most appointees did not note an interest. However, there is still interesting variation even among the smaller number of appointees interested in future office holding. Note, for example, that for all of the elected positions, male appointees were more interested then female appointees were (see Table 6.6). Although men were slightly more likely to be interested in appointment at the state level than were women, female appointees' interest in future appointed offices was double that of their interest in elected offices. One has to wonder if female appointees' interest would have increased had they been asked about specific boards, commissions, or departments that directly affect their professions or personal lives.

UNDERSTANDING THE POLITICAL AMBITIONS OF PUBLIC OFFICIALS AT THE STATE LEVEL

I was the most qualified person I knew in the state to perform the function designated in the commission. So I could not turn it down.

Giving back to the public was the only reason. No expectations or aspirations.

—Male member of a mining commission

Some men I wouldn't listen to, some women I would . . . and vice versa. Two equally qualified people, a man and a woman . . . have equal chances. The problems come with how we prepare our girls [and] women to speak up, prepare logic, etc. Our pool of who chooses to run is smaller because of how we prepare them. So they are equally likely to get appointed/be elected if they are similarly trained. But that probably isn't what you were really asking.

—Female member of an accounting board

The State Political Pathways Survey provides a better understanding of who is appointed at the state level, how progressive ambition functions for appointees versus elected officeholders, and how men and women think about the other types of offices. This chapter contributes to the literature on political ambition in a number of ways. We now have a clearer understanding of the ambitions of appointed officials from the lowest boards and commissions to the secretary of a governor's cabinet. Although many of these boards and commissions require little time commitment and offer no compensation, they fulfill the public service desire for many of their members.

The man from a North Carolina board mentioned above was one of many appointees who expressed their interest in politics and wanted to give back to their community in some way, whether professionally or politically. Although most appointees were not at all interested in higher office, more than one-third of both high- and low-level appointees did express interest in going beyond their positions, and a similar number of respondents articulated their interest in elected office.

Beyond contributing to the general understanding of how ambitious appointed officials were for elected office, we have a sense of what affected those ambitions and how they compared with the progressive ambitions of elected officials. For appointed officials, their sex was negatively associated with progressive ambition (see Table 5.7). Women were less likely to feel they were qualified for higher office (see Table 5.6) and reported lower levels of political recruitment prior to their position as well as since attaining their position (as seen in Chapter 3). Both recruitment and self-assessed qualifications were statistically significant when predicting appointees' progressive ambitions, so it is no surprise that on average appointed women were 8 percent less likely than appointed men were to have progressive ambition.

Lawless and Fox (2005) revealed the profound effect self-assessed qualifications have on nascent political ambitions, especially among women. My analysis extends the study of self-assessed qualifications even further to include progressive ambition. Perhaps most fascinating is how important self-assessed qualifications are for both elected and appointed officials and how these perceived qualifications are also important for ambition when they are considering a different pathway to public office.

I discuss at length throughout this chapter how women might be less ambitious for elected office specifically because they do not like politics and do not want to hold a political position. We hear the words of the women themselves that they harbor ambition unrelated to politics. As scholars keep trying to improve our understanding of political ambition, we need to end the assumption that ambition means political ambition. In fact, many women might appear to be climbing the political career ladder when in fact they are pursuing offices or jobs related to their primary career or area of interest, with no thought of politics. We scholars need to broaden our definition of ambition and begin to question how men and women define politics. With state-level appointments, there is no clear consensus of what constitutes politics and what does not. We need to understand why this is the case, how sex factors into these different definitions, and how these definitions affect political ambition.

If there is one takeaway from the findings in this chapter, it is that when we focus solely on elected office, half of the picture is missing; both the opportunities available to women politically and how women operate in various political positions are not understood. A small body of literature has focused on men and women in civil service and appointed roles (Bowling et al. 2006; Bullard and Wright 1993; J. Dolan 2000a, 2000b; 2004; Gilmour and Lewis 2006; M. A. Newman 1994; Riccucci and Saidel 2001). This area not only should be expanded but also should be examined in conjunction with studies of elected office. Doing so acknowledges the power and influence women can have in nonelected positions and can provide a more comprehensive understanding of how variables such as ambition operate within different institutional structures and throughout different levels of public office.

7. A Different Perspective
Recruitment, Motivations, and Ambitions of State Elected Officials

> I was always raised to be a participant—don't sit on the sidelines—so I
> was very, very involved in community activities, and when the city clerk
> retired, many people—but specifically my husband—assumed or felt that
> I would be a good representative because this position was the only full-
> time elected position that dealt directly with the public.
>
> —*Serena Dickinson, state senator*

Serena Dickinson has always been interested in politics. This attentive-
ness to politics comes from her mother and manifested itself in her
schooling as well as her engagement in local politics. When the city clerk
of her community retired, her husband was the first to suggest that she
apply for the position, followed shortly by many of her colleagues on
the Chamber of Commerce Board. Because the clerk retired, it was an
appointment, which involved an interview process. The encouragement
from both her husband and colleagues was important to seeking the position: "I do not believe that on my own I would have ever pursued anything
like this or a career in politics; I was very happy being a businesswoman
and involved in that community and involved with my family." Serving as city clerk was just the beginning of twenty years of public service:

> Once bitten, I was completely infected by the governmental process, so
> I went from being city clerk to also running for a position on our local
> waterway board. . . . But I decided I really wanted to be in a leadership
> position, and so I ran for mayor and I won, and as mayor I learned many
> new lessons, one of them being if you couldn't agree with your neighbors
> on specific transportation projects or regional projects, the state typically
> ignored your requests for monetary assistance. So I put together a
> collaboration of mayors, and we prioritized all of our transportation
> projects, and then that kind of led into prioritizing all regional projects,
> whether it was for open space or conservation, or whatever, and then

again, when my state senator was diagnosed with a life-threatening illness and stepped down, a lot of my mayors—whether they were Democrats or Republicans—went to the Republican Party, which is the appointment process, and strongly recommended—as did my senator himself—that I be appointed in his stead.

Dickinson's political trajectory was different from that of State Senator Betty Johnson:

> I had no interest in getting involved in politics, and in May of 2004, I got a phone call one evening from a man who's on the community council—who was on local assembly. And I knew him because I was involved with community councils . . . and he asked me to run, and I said, "Hell no, why would I do that?" But I was kind of persuaded, but when I did run, and said I would run, I kept telling people, "Yeah I'll do it, but don't stop looking for somebody better, and you find somebody better I'll step down because it's not something I really wanted to do." And I never thought I would win, I just was willing to spend the summer knocking on doors and talking to neighbors about the things I cared about, and anyways, to an odd circumstance I did win, and I was terrified. . . . Anyway, so I just found out I loved it, and that was ten years ago.

Although Johnson also started at the local level through membership on community councils, to her, as opposed to Dickinson, this was a low-key endeavor. Dickinson and Johnson represent the importance of recruitment and the fact that interest in politics is not a prerequisite for landing in elective office. In many ways, their paths mimic how many of the women in political appointments obtain their positions. Yet simultaneously those paths are different because appointed women are often firm in their disinterest in elected politics. In this chapter I provide the results and analysis of elected officials' recruitment, motivations, and ambitions for higher office. The analysis mirrors the pathways of appointees in Chapters 3–6 and confirms much of what has already been found in previous studies of elected officials. However, including the elected official analysis in this book highlights the unique position women in appointments hold in state government and further emphasizes the choices women make about their careers and politics.

ELECTED OFFICIALS AND RECRUITMENT

In Chapter 3, the data show that more than half of the appointees in my study had been recruited for elected or appointed office. This number was even higher for elected officials: more than 75 percent of the elected officials said they were recruited for elected or appointed office at some point in their lives. Furthermore, levels of recruitment were not noticeably different based upon the sex of the elected official: elected women were only 3 percent more likely to be recruited compared with men. Whether the elected official was a senator or representative did not seem to significantly affect levels of recruitment either (see Figure 7.1).

I argue in Chapter 3 that scholars not only have neglected to study appointees in general but also they have not considered how women are recruited to appointments or how appointees can act as recruiters. A considerable number of the appointed women in my sample who were recruited for elected office had also been recruited for appointed office. Most importantly, I found that more than a third of the women who were not recruited for elected office *were* recruited for appointed office. This means that a substantial number of women has been overlooked by prior recruitment studies. The story is no different for elected women, although my sample is smaller. Nearly a quarter of the women state legislators who were never recruited for elected office *were* recruited for appointed office. More importantly, half of those women had held political appointments at some point in their careers, demonstrating not only the

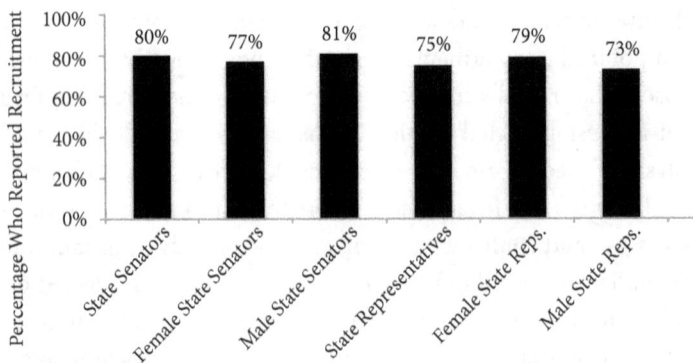

Figure 7.1 Political Recruitment among State Legislators

presence but the effectiveness of political recruitment to and from appointed positions.[1]

The elected officials in my sample also revealed the need to include the appointment arena in studies of women holding elected office. Nearly 38 percent of elected women were recruited for appointed office at some point in their careers. This is 10 percent higher than for elected men at only 28 percent ($p < 0.10$). Furthermore, studies of the political recruitment of elected officials have excluded political appointees as potential recruiters and have instead focused on party leaders, other elected officials, and women's organizations as the primary recruiters of candidates for elected office. This is extremely problematic because more than a quarter of my elected official sample was recruited for appointed or elected office by an appointed official.

The differences in recruitment for elected and appointed officials might be a result of differences in their levels of political activity. In Chapter 2, the data show that elected officials were more likely to have been politically active, especially in their attendance of party events. More than 88 percent of elected officials had attended a party event compared with only 55 percent of appointees. This could be because many appointees in the sample held their positions because they were the most qualified people in the state and thus attained their appointments through professional notoriety. Many low-level appointees expressed their disinterest in politics along with professional or personal reasons for accepting their appointments. However, even when the data are divided by level of office, assuming that higher-level political appointees were more "political," political participation did not vary enough. High-level appointees were only slightly more likely than low-level appointees to have attended a party event, so that disinterest in politics—and therefore decreased political activity—cannot be the only reason for party officials recruiting fewer appointees than they did elected officials.

Do recruiters pursue elected men and women differently? Table 7.1 contains the breakdown of recruitment of elected men and women. A few patterns emerge from these data. First, elected women reported higher levels of recruitment from elected officials and women's organiza-

1. Of the thirty-four women state legislators who were never recruited for elected office, eight were recruited for appointed office and four had held appointed office previously.

Table 7.1 Political Recruitment by Recruiter: State Legislators

Recruiter	Elected Official	Elected Men	Elected Women
Elected official	67.81%	66.90%	70.00%
Appointed official	27.52%	27.87%	26.67%
Party official	52.33%	55.75%	44.17%*
Governor's staff	18.56%	18.60%	18.49%
Women's organization	22.22%	16.49%	35.83%**
N	407	287	120

Note: Chi-2 tests were used to find the difference in means. $^{+} p < 0.10$, $* p < 0.05$, $** p < 0.01$.

tions. Women's organizations recruited female elected officials considerably more than they did male elected officials, although this is to be expected. More interestingly, elected women were more than 10 percent less likely to report recruitment from a party official, which echoes what other studies find regarding the "good old boy" network of political parties (Sanbonmatsu 2006).

Table 7.2 looks more generally at recruitment to appointed office versus elected office. More than 30 percent of all elected officials were recruited for appointed office versus the 71 percent recruited for elected office. These percentages do not preclude recruitment for the other type of office, but as can be seen in the second to last row of the table, it was not common for an elected official to have been recruited to both offices. The results from the appointees in Chapter 3 show that elected officials were less likely to be recruited to appointed office than appointees were, but they were substantially more likely to be recruited to elected office. Fewer than a quarter of appointees were recruited to elected office, but nearly three-quarters of elected officials were recruited to elected office. Furthermore, women state legislators were more likely than men state legislators were to be recruited to appointed office, suggesting a gendered dimension to recruitment—depending upon the office for which the individual was being recruited.

Elected women might have been recruited for appointed office at higher rates than were elected men because of many state governments' need for appointing members of underrepresented groups to their cabinets and departments. We know from the data in Chapter 1 that only 35.1 percent of high-level appointees are women (Center for Women in Government and Civil Society 2008). Although this percentage is higher

Table 7.2 Recruitment for Elected versus Appointed Office: State Legislators

	All Elected Officials	Elected Men	Elected Women
Recruited for appointed office	30.86%	27.97%	37.82%+
Recruited for elected office	71.25%	71.08%	71.67%
Recruited for both	26.17%	24.13%	31.09%
N	405	286	119

Note: Chi-2 tests were used to find the difference in means. $^+ p < 0.10$, $^* p < 0.05$, $^{**} p < 0.01$.

than for any other office, it is still far from gender parity. Moreover, it is not uncommon to see governors prioritize attracting more women and other underrepresented groups to their administrations.[2] Elected women are uniquely positioned because they have experience in state-level government and might be considered experts on issues directly related to the states' departments or agencies. This might make elected women attractive candidates for appointed office.

Predicting State Legislator Recruitment

The data from my study show us the differences in who gets recruited, which offices they get recruited for, and who is recruiting them. The analysis reveals the following:

- There are major differences in the recruitment patterns between elected and appointed officials. Elected officials report higher levels of recruitment than do appointed officials.
- There are differences in who recruits elected and appointed officials. Elected officials are more likely to be recruited by other elected officials and party officials.
- There are gendered dynamics in this recruitment story. Both appointed and elected women are more likely to be recruited compared with men by women's organizations and are less likely to be recruited by party officials than men are.

2. Also, if the appointed positions need senate confirmation, a woman coming from the state legislature might be more easily confirmed.

- Finally, there are differences in the positions for which elected and appointed officials are being recruited. Elected officials are much more likely to be recruited for elected office, whereas appointed officials are more likely to be recruited for appointed office.

To compare the factors that predict recruitment for elected versus appointed officials, I run the same regression analysis for elected officials as for appointed officials in Chapter 3. Each model uses a different dependent variable that represents recruitment by a specific political actor when the elected official attained his or her position (0 equals no recruitment; 1 equals recruitment). More than 53 percent of the state legislators reported being recruited while in their position (55 percent of male state legislators were recruited versus 51 percent of female state legislators). Each model uses logistic regression with robust standard errors and has associated predicted probabilities using Clarify. In most cases I use the identical independent variables from the appointee analysis, with a few exceptions. Instead of using a composite political participation variable as for the appointees, I use each individual component (volunteered for a candidate, attended a city council/school board meeting, etc.) for the elected official analysis because the Alpha test is not high enough. I also include a legislative professionalism variable in case legislators in more professionalized chambers were more likely to be recruited. Table 7.3 contains the regression analysis, and Table 7.4 provides the predicted probabilities.

Some interesting patterns emerge from my elected official analysis. First, being a woman state legislator depressed recruitment from elected and party officials and increased recruitment from women's organizations. Yet being a woman did not reach standard levels of statistical significance when predicting recruitment by all of these gatekeepers. Second, none of the political participation variables mattered for increasing recruitment of state legislators. Having held prior elected or appointed office as well as length of service in a position did matter for elected official recruitment. The longer state legislators held their positions, the more likely they were to be recruited. Surprisingly, having held appointed office consistently increased an elected official's chances of recruitment. This might have been because a person who has served in appointed office has a larger network of recruiters who might see them as a good candidate for another office. This finding further underscores

Table 7.3 Recruitment of Elected Officials

	Recruited by Elected Official	Recruited by Appointed Official	Recruited by Party Official	Recruited by Women's Organization	Recruited by Any Official
Demographics					
Female	-0.437+ (0.260)	-0.0560 (0.319)	-0.731** (0.275)	0.831** (0.296)	-0.206 (0.261)
Age	-0.037** (0.011)	-0.032* (0.0146)	-0.045** (0.012)	-0.0140 (0.016)	-0.0314** (0.011)
Nonwhite	-0.394 (0.399)	-0.173 (0.462)	-0.549 (0.404)	0.195 (0.444)	0.0325 (0.409)
Family income	0.149 (0.102)	0.144 (0.124)	-0.070 (0.105)	0.0991 (0.130)	0.124 (0.099)
Education	0.093 (0.083)	-0.010 (0.104)	0.041 (0.090)	-0.088 (0.106)	0.0583 (0.085)
Political Environment					
Republican	-0.281 (0.412)	-0.407 (0.479)	0.171 (0.445)	-1.515** (0.508)	0.0150 (0.384)
Democrat	0.220 (0.402)	-0.171 (0.455)	0.374 (0.431)	-0.485 (0.491)	0.393 (0.373)
Volunteered for a candidate	0.198 (0.363)	-0.133 (0.453)	0.0443 (0.389)	0.102 (0.498)	-0.130 (0.360)
Attended a city/school meeting	0.046 (0.508)	0.193 (0.662)	-0.312 (0.519)	-0.504 (0.666)	0.0676 (0.476)
Attended party event	-0.305 (0.411)	0.425 (0.546)	0.868+ (0.491)	0.097 (0.564)	-0.099 (0.387)
Attended state legislative session	0.420 (0.300)	0.0502 (0.384)	0.254 (0.329)	0.239 (0.427)	0.231 (0.303)
Served nonprofit board	-0.059 (0.295)	-0.059 (0.369)	0.663+ (0.342)	-0.056 (0.434)	0.222 (0.284)
Moralistic	-0.445 (0.281)	0.011 (0.340)	-0.529+ (0.297)	-0.324 (0.380)	-0.094 (0.284)
Local political opportunity structure	-0.0001 (0.0003)	-0.0007* (0.0003)	-0.00005 (0.0003)	0.00004 (0.0004)	0.00001 (0.0003)
State political opportunity structure	-0.003 (0.004)	0.004 (0.005)	-0.005 (0.004)	-0.007 (0.006)	-0.007+ (0.004)
Percent female state legislature 2012	-1.787 (2.380)	-3.166 (3.104)	-0.120 (2.477)	-0.776 (3.145)	-0.389 (2.392)
Percent female appointees 2007	-1.528 (1.707)	-1.428 (2.260)	0.324 (1.778)	-0.524 (2.228)	-1.342 (1.686)
Current Office Characteristics					
Had mentor/sponsor	0.105 (0.239)	-0.0176 (0.291)	0.356 (0.250)	0.659* (0.328)	0.257 (0.233)
Number of years in position	0.043* (0.021)	0.075** (0.025)	0.044+ (0.023)	0.059* (0.028)	0.0273 (0.021)
Senate	-0.162 (0.285)	0.444 (0.348)	0.325 (0.295)	0.135 (0.376)	-0.0201 (0.288)
Number of elected offices held	0.248+ (0.143)	-0.0103 (0.173)	0.222 (0.155)	0.103 (0.182)	0.266+ (0.142)
Held appointment	0.532* (0.253)	0.824** (0.311)	0.457+ (0.269)	0.181 (0.325)	0.663* (0.261)
Professionalism	0.114 (0.284)	0.0304 (0.327)	0.430 (0.292)	0.502 (0.369)	0.380 (0.293)
Constant	1.027 (1.329)	0.0783 (1.597)	-0.987 (1.328)	-1.380 (1.762)	-0.0115 (1.292)
N	369	369	369	369	369
R^2	0.0943	0.0817	0.1092	0.1191	0.0815

Note: Standard errors in parentheses. + $p < 0.10$, * $p < 0.05$, ** $p < 0.01$.

Table 7.4 Predicted Probabilities of Elected Official Recruitment

	Recruited by Elected Official	Recruited by Appointed Official	Recruited by Party Official	Recruited by Women's Organization	Recruited by Any Official
Female	−10.59%	—	−16.05%	+12.68%	—
Age	−20.71%	−9.39%	−25.42%	—	−18.05%
Republican	—	—	—	−9.44%	—
Attended party event	—	—	+17.54%	—	—
Served on nonprofit board	—	—	+14.56%	—	—
Moralistic	—	—	−12.00%	—	—
Local political opportunity structure	—	−11.95%	—	—	—
State political opportunity structure	—	—	—	—	−20.29%
Had mentor	—	—	—	+9.02%	—
Number of elected offices held	+5.80%	—	—	—	+6.69%
Held appointed office	+11.70%	+13.72%	+11.26%	—	+14.96%
Number of years in position	+12.08%	+11.53%	+12.56%	+7.82%	—

Note: For predicted probabilities, Democrat and political participation variables were set to one. Sex, nonwhite, having a sponsor/mentor, Republican, senate, moralistic, and held appointment were set to zero. All other variables were set at their means. Most predicted probabilities went from one standard deviation below the mean to one standard deviation above the mean. Number of elected offices was predicted based upon going from having held one to two prior elected offices, and number of years in position was predicted based upon going from one to thirteen years.

how important it is to consider appointed office a potential position for which to be recruited as well as a position that might help individuals become targets of recruitment.[3]

MOTIVATIONS TO SERVE IN ELECTED OFFICE

Recruitment is an important external motivation to serve in elected office. What other kinds of motivations do state legislators have to serve in elected office? Table 7.5 contains a list of motivations for state legislators

3. When I mirror the analysis of the appointed officials by predicting recruitment by all recruiters except for women's organizations, the results do not change significantly. Sex is still not significant, and having held prior elected or appointed office is still significant (length of service drops from significance). When I include an interaction to account for women senators, it does not become significant, and neither does sex.

to serve in elected office. The top three motivators for state legislators were interest in a policy area, opportunity for public service, and interest in state government. Chapter 4 reveals that the top three motivators for appointees accepting appointment included the opportunity for public service and interest in policy areas, but instead of interest in state government, appointees saw their positions as broadening their experiences. Furthermore, there is some interesting variation between appointed and elected officials on the other motivators. For example, more appointees saw their positions as career advancement, whereas few elected officials saw their elected offices in this way. Although still a small portion of the sample, more elected officials sought their positions as stepping-stones to future elected office, whereas fewer than 5 percent of appointees accepted their positions for this reason. There is also little to no variation in motivations for elected office between senators and representatives. There is much more variation in motivations to serve in appointed office, depending upon whether the appointee was in a low- or high-level position.

Nearly a quarter of the elected officials who expanded upon their motivations to run for public office said they wanted to "change the direction of government" or "reform state government."[4] In comparison, only

Table 7.5 Motivations for Seeking Elected Office

Motivation	All Legislators	Senators	Representatives
Interest in policy area or issues	78.38%	78.89%	78.23%
Opportunity for public service	78.87%	75.56%	79.81%
Interest in state government	62.41%	65.56%	61.51%
Support for my party's policies	39.07%	37.78%	39.43%
Opportunity for broadening experience	37.59%	36.67%	37.85%
Opportunity to work with others in government	35.63%	35.56%	35.65%
Career advancement/reason related to career	5.65%	5.56%	5.68%
Opportunity for future elected office	13.27%	13.33%	13.25%
N	407	90	317

Note: Chi-2 tests were used to find the difference in means. $^+p < 0.10$, $^*p < 0.05$, $^{**}p < 0.01$.

4. Fifty-four elected officials wrote in an answer for the reasons they decided to run for office; twenty-one of these elected officials were women, and thirty-three were men.

3 of the 155 appointees who expanded upon their motivations to accept their appointment said they wanted to change or reform government.[5] In fact, the most common words used by appointees when describing their motivations for accepting their appointment were "advocate," "interest in," and "support." Many appointees' comments were regarding specific issues or professions, whereas many of the elected officials' comments were broader, for example, about running for office to "make a difference," and "solve problems with sound policy." Interestingly, a few public officials mentioned political recruitment as a reason they ran for or accepted public office. Three men and four women state legislators said they ran because they were recruited, with one woman pointedly saying, "I had never thought of doing it before someone asked me to challenge the incumbent." These statements echo the findings of prior studies about the effects of recruitment on individuals' interest in public office and connect to what the women said in the follow-up interviews. A senator from the Midwest said she did not think she would have "run if I hadn't had that encouragement." In contrast, only three female appointees said recruitment was a reason for accepting their appointment compared with the six male appointees who said recruitment was a major reason for accepting their appointment.

Are there gender gaps in motivation for elected office among state legislators? Yes and no. Men and women state legislators had similar motivations when running for their elected offices on five of the eight motivational factors questioned (see Table 7.6). Two motivations were career advancement and interest in a policy area/issue, which provided two of the major deviations in motivations for appointed office among male and female appointed officials. Male and female state legislators deviated on the motivations of "Interest in state government," "Opportunity for future elected office," and "Support for my party's policies."

It seems that women state legislators were following the same pattern as women appointees were and not expressing political motivations for running for office. Women state legislators were about 15 percent less likely than were men state legislators to say interest in state government was a reason they ran for office and were also 7 percent less likely to say

5. Of the 155 appointees who wrote in an answer, 58 were women, and 97 were men.

Table 7.6 Gender Differences in Motivations When Running for Elected Office

Motivation	Men	Women
Career advancement or other reason related to career	5.92%	5.00%
Interest in policy area or issues	77.70%	80.00%
Interest in state government	66.90%	51.67%**
Opportunity for broadening experience	35.89%	41.67%
Opportunity for future elected office	15.33%	8.33%+
Opportunity for public service	78.75%	79.17%
Opportunity to work with others in government	35.19%	36.67%
Support for my party's policies	35.54%	47.50%*
N	287	120

Note: Chi-2 tests were used to find the difference in means with Fisher's exact test used when observations were less than or equal to five. $^+ p < 0.10$, $* p < 0.05$, $** p < 0.01$.

that they ran for office as an opportunity for future elected office. However, this pattern breaks down for the last motivational factor chosen, "Support for my party's policies." Women were about 12 percent more likely than men to say that they ran for elected office because they wanted to support their party's policies, a politically motivated response ($p < 0.05$).

This finding is surprising because none of the qualitative evidence shows that either men or women state legislators considered their party's policies significant motivators for public office. Only one woman from a general assembly said, "Support for the minority opinion of my party" was a reason for her seeking elected office. Only two men mentioned their party as motivation for seeking their offices, and not in ways we would expect. One man said the following:

> My wife and I have been active in the Republican Party for a long time. I did a lot of driving for Coy Privette when he ran for Congress in 1992. Our family worked very hard for Robin Hayes when he ran for Congress and every time he ran for reelection. My wife has served on the county and state GOP Executive Committees. She and our youngest child talked me into running for the state House. She is now my legislative assistant. I would not be in office if not for the local Tea Party group, who worked very hard to get me first appointed and then elected to my current position. I had asked them a few years before to stop attacking the Republican Party and get involved and take it over, instead. In 2013,

they did take over leadership of our county GOP. The first time I ran for any office was in 2001 for city council, only because our county GOP chairman at that time asked me to do it. Until I got angry enough to run against my predecessor, I never really thought about running for office myself.

This legislator was not recruited by a political party, as is more common, but by another organization that tapped into his dissatisfaction with his party and pushed him to run.[6] The other man, a senator from North Dakota, made it clear that his party did not push him into the legislature by saying the following:

> I was asked many times to consider running for this seat and turned them down. Then I was asked to have a meeting and visit about it; I agreed. I had thought that my ace in the hole was to let them know that I had never voted party lines in my life and was not going to start now, so, if that is what was going to be asked of me, we could stop the discussion about me running for office early and go home. They still wanted me to do it, and I am very glad that it worked out as it has.

The four women senators who took part in my follow-up interviews also gave reasons not related to their party for their motivations to seek office; three of them were interested in government or liked the work they were doing in lower political office. As Serena Dickinson explained at the beginning of this chapter, she sought and accepted the appointment to the state senate because she wanted to apply what she had learned at the local level to state government. She said she wanted to use the

> opportunity to take everything that I had learned at the local level and translate that into activity at the state level, a desire to change, just that general evolution, of both job/career as well as my life circumstances. And I had been also a special education teacher for seven years—that's my background, my degree and my masters are in special education— and so again, with all of that I felt that maybe it was time for me to take what I knew what was happening in a local perspective and take that to

6. See Theda Skocpol and Vanessa Williamson's 2016 book *The Tea Party and the Remaking of Republican Conservatism* about the rise of the Tea Party more generally. Melissa Deckman's *Tea Party Women* (2016) provides a good example of how women feel more comfortable coming to power outside of the establishment.

the state level and be able to be that kind of communicator in between the two units of government.

Another woman senator from the Midwest said something similar:

> I had found local government really, really interesting, you know, after my local issue was resolved, but it's just a smaller set of issues. And so when there was the opportunity I just thought it would be very interesting and it would be another way to make a difference because I thought I made a difference locally. And that was very rewarding, and I think my community is better for it, so it was just a great opportunity to be able replicate that on a bigger scale.

The other female state senator cited her desire to be able to do more as an elected official. She said because the seat was contested in a special election, she did not have to give up her House seat and that she "would be able to do more as a senator, which is absolutely true. I have a lot more influence as a senator than I did as a House member." All three of these women demonstrated how their work in a lower elected office spurred them to seek higher elected office. In fact, although Carroll and Sanbonmatsu (2013) argue that elected women tend to not follow the political career ladder model that men often use to ascend to higher office, these women legislators followed the more traditional ambition model.

Interestingly, like most of the female appointees, Betty Johnson could see how elected office was a turnoff to many people outside the arena. When asked about her involvement in politics, she said the following:

> I guess my takeaway is that it's far more fun than it looks like, and though the publicity and comments and stuff give a sense of major hostility—which certainly there is hostility and there's arguments—but that's not the whole story, that's just the news part, but it is fun. It's really interesting and because of that, because so many people don't understand that, I'm very involved in recruitment, because I knew nothing, I mean I really knew nothing, and I certainly didn't know I could do it when I ran, so I like to call people and tell them that, that years ago when my kids were in school and I was asked to go to Juneau and talk to the legislature about education issues, I could not imagine myself doing that and always declined immediately, but you know what? I could have done it, and I tell people you could, too, and when people come to my office, women come

and talk about PTAs and their school funding whatever, I always, if they are smart and articulate and passionate, I always try to plant the seed that they could run for office; it's amazing how often they say, "Oh, not me."

If we learn one thing from my analysis of appointee motivations, it should be that both sex and level of office can have an effect on the motivation to hold public office. Therefore, I include an additional figure showing the breakdown in motivation to run for the state legislature by sex and legislative chamber (Figure 7.2). As with appointees, elected officials varied in their motivations to run for the state legislature based upon their level of office and their gender. For example, I discuss above the finding that female state legislators were more likely to cite support for their party's policies as a motivation to run for the state legislature than were their male counterparts. Figure 7.2 reveals that this was a particularly strong motivation for female House members, 49 percent of whom said support for their party's policies was a motivation for them running for the state legislature ($p < 0.05$). This might not be surprising because most state general assemblies tend to have a larger number of representatives than do the upper chambers and are more likely to be dominated by party rules. State senates—the more elite chambers—are smaller and more personable and therefore might not be as party dominated as the lower chambers.

Although the numbers for party motivation were much smaller among women state senators, we can see that they, like appointed women,

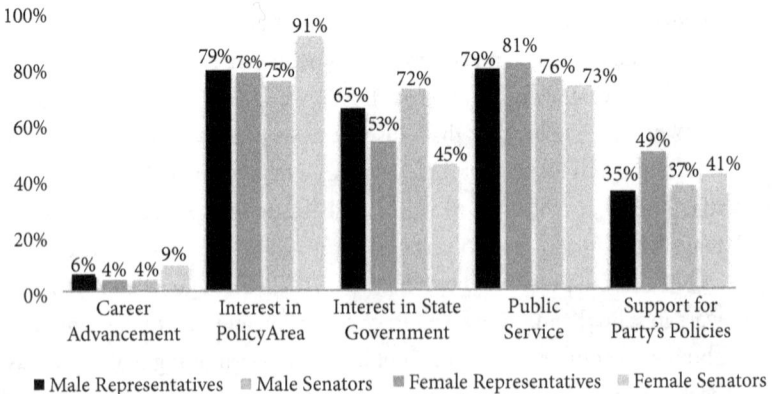

Figure 7.2 Motivations to Serve in the State Legislature

were much more likely to say they ran because of their interest in a specific policy area or issue. However, the female state senators were much less likely to say they ran because they had an interest in state government. These women were also slightly less likely to cite public service as a motivator to serve in the state legislature.

The analysis of motivations to serve in appointed and elected offices reveals important differences. Most of these differences are based on holding elected versus appointed office, but many of these differences are gendered as well. The analysis reveals the following:

- Both elected and appointed officials cited interest in policy areas and public service as their top two motivations to pursue their positions.
- Elected and appointed officials diverged in interest in state government and career advancement as reasons they wanted their positions. In particular, high-level appointed women cited career advancement as a major motivation.
- Many of the appointed and elected women were not actively seeking their positions but benefitted from recruitment (elected women) or an opportunity to advance their career in a new area (appointed women).
- The appointee analysis reveals a distinct separation between what they considered political and what their positions entailed. There was no attempt to move away from politics among state legislators.

Understanding the internal impetus to seek elected office is important if we want to grasp why some women land in elected or appointed office. Oftentimes the scholarship on women and public service suggests that women lack agency in seeking public office. If they are not overly affected by political socialization (Lawless and Fox 2005, 2010), then they disproportionately need to be asked by a political recruiter (Sanbonmatsu and Carroll 2013). Although both socialization and recruitment are variables that influence a woman's path to public service, we cannot forget that many of these women are also making decisions based upon their careers, ambitions, and interests. My analysis of the elected data emphasizes some key differences between men and women elected officials as well as between elected and appointed officials more generally. The final portion of this chapter delves into the ambitions of elected officials both for higher office and for appointed office to further underscore the importance of studying elected and appointed officials so we can better understand the pathways to power in the United States.

AMBITIONS FOR HIGHER OFFICE

Numerous studies of elected officials' political ambitions have been conducted. From Lawless and Fox's (2005, 2010) results showing the effects of gendered perceptions to the null findings of the effects of children on ambition (Fulton et al. 2006; Lawless 2013; Lawless and Fox 2005), we now have a much deeper understanding of the factors that influence ambition for elected office as well as the more specific ambitions of elected officials. I revisit this analysis below to provide the complementary findings to the appointee analysis of progressive ambition in Chapter 5. I also provide new analysis on the subject of elected officials' ambition for appointed office, more specifically similar to how in Chapter 6 I predict appointee ambition for elected office. I find that appointed women are less ambitious for higher appointed office and are especially less ambitious for elected office. Furthermore, appointed women with a high estimation of their own qualifications are less ambitious than appointees with lower self-qualification scores. This further suggests that women are not simply ruled by gendered perceptions—that in fact many women fully recognize their skills and abilities and are simply not interested in certain positions. When we look at interest in higher office for the elected official sample in Table 7.7, we see quite a bit of difference depending upon the chamber in which the legislators serve.

State senators were particularly uninterested in seeking higher office. This might be a result of the fact that the next step for state senators is most likely Congress, an expensive and difficult office to win. Addition-

Table 7.7 State Legislator Interest in Higher Office

	All Legislators	State Senators	State House
Not interested at all	39.40%	50.56%*	36.22%
Somewhat interested	47.63%	37.08%*	50.64%
Very interested	12.97%	12.36%	13.14%
N	401	89	312

Note: Comparisons are between state senators and state representatives. $^+ p < 0.10$, $^* p < 0.05$, $^{**} p < 0.01$.

ally, state legislators in general were more ambitious for higher office than state appointed officials were. Whereas 39 percent of state legislators were not at all interested in higher office, 64 percent of appointees were not interested in higher office ($p < 0.01$; see Table 5.1). Although female state appointees were slightly less ambitious for higher office, there is almost no difference in ambition among elected officials based upon sex (Table 7.8).

The second component of this story is the role of self-perceived qualifications. Past studies look to the effect of self-qualification scores on the ambitions of those most likely to run for elected office (Lawless and Fox 2005, 2010). But how do self-qualification scores function for those already holding elected office? Table 7.9 provides the data on self-perceived qualification scores for state legislators by chamber. First, it is important to note that there is a small amount of variation in state legislators' evaluation of their qualifications for higher office. This would suggest that even those who have decided to run for elected office still have some doubts about their qualifications. However, it is important to note that few state legislators do not feel they are unqualified for higher office (note that not a single senator felt he or she was unqualified). Second, beyond

Table 7.8 Interest in Higher Office by Sex for Elected Officials

	Elected Men	Elected Women
Not interested at all	38.30%	42.02%
Somewhat interested	48.23%	46.22%
Very interested	13.48%	11.76%
N	282	119

Note: Statistical comparisons are between males and females. There were no statistical differences between male and female elected officials at the state level. $^+ p < 0.10$, $^* p < 0.05$, $^{**} p < 0.01$.

Table 7.9 Elected Officials' Self-Qualifications for Higher Office

	All Elected	State Senate	State Representatives
Not at all qualified	2.23%	0%	2.87%
Somewhat qualified	16.63%	13.48%	17.52%
Qualified	37.22%	34.83%	37.90%
Very qualified	43.92%	51.69%$^+$	41.72%
N	403	89	314

Note: Statistical comparisons are between state senators and state representatives. $^+ p < 0.10$, $^* p < 0.05$, $^{**} p < 0.01$.

Table 7.10 Elected Officials' Self-Qualifications for Higher Office by Sex

	Elected Men	Elected Women
Not at all qualified	1.41%[+]	4.20%
Somewhat qualified	14.79%	21.01%
Qualified	34.86%	42.86%
Very qualified	48.94%**	31.93%
N	284	119

Note: Statistical comparisons are between males and females. [+] $p < 0.10$, * $p < 0.05$, ** $p < 0.01$.

a slight difference in the category of "Very qualified," state senators and representatives are not much different when self-evaluating.

Table 7.10 reveals that although there is little variation in self-qualification scores by level of office, there is more variation by sex. Elected men were much more likely to say they were very qualified for higher office. These findings are important because they demonstrate that gendered perceptions existed for those who took the plunge to run for and win elected office. However, it is important to recognize that, overall, elected women had higher self-qualification scores than did appointed women. Only a quarter of appointed women said they were very qualified for higher office, as seen in Chapter 5.

Thus far, we know that state legislators are more ambitious for higher office compared with state appointed officials. We also know that state representatives are more ambitious than state senators, but there is no difference in the level of ambition between men and women. When we look at self-perceived qualifications for higher office, a major explanatory variable for political ambition, we see that few legislators see themselves as unqualified for higher office. In particular, senators and male state legislators see themselves as very qualified for higher office. Here I use the self-qualifications for higher office variable to predict progressive ambition for elected officials in the same way that in Chapter 5 I predict progressive ambition for appointees. I use similar variables measuring demographics, family dynamics, political dynamics, personal political characteristics, and state-specific characteristics, reported in Table 7.11. I run logistic regression with robust standard errors and predicted probabilities using Clarify, reported in the "Impact" column (0 represents no interest in higher office and 1 represents somewhat or very interested in higher office).

Table 7.11 State Legislator Logistic Regression Model for Progressive Ambition

			Impact
Demographics			
Sex 1 = Female	0.430	(0.396)	
Education	−0.006	(0.097)	
Family income	−0.040	(0.146)	
White 1 = White	−1.504*	(0.659)	−20.85%
Age	−0.096**	(0.020)	−46.21%
Family Dynamics			
Married/long-term relationship	0.116	(0.501)	
Majority household responsibilities	0.351	(0.259)	
Children over eighteen	0.741$^+$	(0.443)	+16.91%
Parental suggestion	0.542**	(0.206)	+25.59%
Personal encouragement	−0.165	(0.291)	
Political Dynamics			
Recruited since position	0.381	(0.295)	
Republican	−0.153	(0.366)	
Independent	0.142	(0.509)	
Percent Obama vote 2012	0.390	(2.471)	
Issue passion	1.067$^+$	(0.636)	−21.17%
Political participation	−0.440	(0.394)	
Political interest	0.450*	(0.192)	+30.40%
Political efficacy	0.016	(0.139)	
Personal Political Characteristics			
Number of years in position	−0.052$^+$	(0.027)	−13.57%
Prior position sought	−0.032	(0.167)	
Position value	−0.137	(0.116)	
Difficulty of attaining position	0.313*	(0.132)	−39.90%
Qualifications	0.787**	(0.198)	+49.58%
Lower-level position	−0.393	(0.387)	
Had sponsor or mentor	0.243	(0.282)	
State-Specific Variables			
Traditionalist	0.334	(0.430)	
State legislature congruence	0.817*	(0.413)	+18.55%
State political opportunity structure	−0.007	(0.006)	
Local political opportunity structure	0.0004	(0.0003)	
Professionalism	0.318	(0.505)	
Term limits	0.370	(0.453)	
Constant	2.648	(2.739)	
N	339		
Pseudo-R^2	0.3128		

$+\, p < 0.10,\ *\, p < 0.05,\ **\, p < 0.01.$

Several patterns emerge from my analysis. First, sex is not a statistically significant variable for predicting progressive ambition among state legislators. Second, the variable that has the largest effect on progressive ambition is self-perceived qualifications. Moving from "Not at all qualified" to "Very qualified" increases a state legislator's progressive ambitions by 50 percent. The next closest variable to have such a substantial effect is age, where a higher age depresses progressive ambitions. Lastly, just as for political appointees, having children over eighteen increases progressive ambitions. This is yet another hint that although having young children does not depress ambition, having older children might increase it.

As in the appointee sample, I also include a series of interaction variables to measure female self-qualification scores as well as interactions with the level of office of the legislator. Because my sample size of elected officials is much smaller, a few variables have to be removed to keep the integrity of the model. However, even when the number of variables is decreased to accommodate the interaction variables, multicollinearity tests for the elected official model still do not pass standard levels of acceptability. Therefore, I narrow the model to include only two interactions, *sex and qualifications* and *lower level and sex.*[7] Neither interaction becomes significant; sex remains insignificant from the baseline model, and the effect of self-qualifications decreases to 44.3 percent.[8] Except for these minor changes, there is little variation between the baseline model and the model with the interaction variables.

The analysis of elected officials' progressive ambition and appointee's progressive ambition reveals important findings:

- Although appointed women had a slightly lower interest in higher office than men did, there were no sex-based differences for interest in higher office among elected officials.
- Overall, elected and appointed men had higher self-qualifications for higher office than did elected and appointed women.
- Self-perceived qualifications had a positive effect on progressive political ambition for both elected and appointed officials.

7. Again, because of modeling limitations, it also does not include the interaction for *sex × children over eighteen.*

8. Issue passion also drops out of significance.

- Sex never affected progressive political ambition of state legislators. Being a woman appointee led to lower ambition in general.
- Gendered perceptions never became significant among elected officials. However, appointed women with high self-qualification scores had lower ambition than appointees with lower self-qualification scores did.

After men and women were elected to the state legislature, self-assessed qualifications continued to matter but no longer differed based upon the sex of the elected official. This raises the question of how much gendered perceptions decrease the numbers of women in elected office. Lawless and Fox (2011) argue that gendered perceptions prevent women from even considering elected office, which suggests that those women who attain elected office do not suffer from gendered perceptions. Following this logic, we would not expect gendered perceptions to have persisted in progressive ambition for elected officials because those women who achieved elected office never suffered from self-doubts in the first place. However, in reality, we still do not know if electoral success decreased gendered perceptions or if those women with higher self-assessed qualifications were self-selecting into elected office. It could also be, as Carroll and Sanbonmatsu (2013) argue, that the women who went into elected office did so because they received the support they needed from those in their personal lives and believed that their being in an elected position would not adversely affect their family and friends. Additionally, gendered perceptions were not present in the progressive ambitions of elected officials at all.

AMBITIONS FOR APPOINTED OFFICE

To provide further understanding of the political ambitions of elected officials, I completed an analysis of state legislator ambition for appointed office. The evidence from the sample is clear: the majority of appointed women was disinterested in electoral office. I want to understand if there are gendered perceptions regarding appointed office among elected officials. A good portion of the elected official sample had been involved with appointed office in some form. More than 27 percent of elected officials had actively sought an appointment, and even more had held appointed office at some point in their careers—close to 35 percent. Unlike those of appointed officials, there were no gender differences between elected men and women having sought office: approximately 27 percent of elected men sought appointment compared with 28 percent of elected women. More female state legislators than male state legislators reported holding appointed office: 33 percent of male state legislators held appointed office, and just more than 39 percent of female state legislators held appointed office (a chi-2 test does not reach standard levels of statistical significance). These appointments were at all levels, although most appointments were either for local and city appointments or state boards and commissions. Table 7.12 reports elected officials' prior thoughts on being politically appointed.

Fewer than half of the elected officials in my sample had considered appointed office. Nearly 10 percent had seriously considered it, and it had crossed the minds of 35 percent of state legislators. Furthermore, there is little variation by sex. I also asked the state legislators a similar question: "Which best characterizes your attitudes toward holding appointed office in the future?" Table 7.13 contains the breakdown of responses from the elected officials. Again, the pattern remains the same as in Table 7.12: elected women were no different from elected men in their ambition for appointed office. During the phone interviews, when I asked the state legislators if they had ever considered seeking appointed office instead of elected office, I received three different answers. We see one example in this response from Betty Johnson:

> No, I didn't think about elected office either. And even the community council, the only reason I was involved in the leadership there and PTA was because I felt like I had to take a turn, if I believed in what they did, and somebody had to do it, ok well then I'll take a turn. Once I was elected to a board or something, I thought my first job is to find the person who's going to do it next year, or the year after if it was a two-year term. That was always my first thing, you find somebody who's coming next, it's part of your job.

Johnson made it clear that she was not interested in public office in general. She provided the only evidence of an official considering both elected and appointed office positions, but she also demonstrates how a

Table 7.12 Elected Officials' Prior Thoughts on Being Politically Appointed

	All Elected	Elected Men	Elected Women
Yes, I seriously considered it.	9.67%	9.60%	9.86%
Yes, it has crossed my mind.	34.57%	35.86%	30.99%
No, I had not thought about it.	42.01%	40.40%	46.48%
No, I have no interest.	13.75%	14.14%	12.68%
N	269	198	71

Note: Statistical comparisons are between males and females within elected office; there were no statistical differences. This question was only asked of those who had never sought or held appointed office. $^+ p < 0.10$, $^* p < 0.05$, $^{**} p < 0.01$.

Table 7.13 Ambition for Future Appointed Office among State Legislators

	All Elected	Elected Men	Elected Women
It is something I definitely would like to undertake in the future.	8.50%	9.54%	5.98%
It is something I might undertake if the opportunity presents itself.	43.00%	43.11%	42.74%
I would not rule it out, but I currently have no interest.	41.75%	39.58%	47.01%
It is something I would not do.	6.75%	7.77%	4.27%
N	269	198	71

Note: Statistical comparisons are between men and women within elected office; there were no statistical differences. $^+ p < 0.10$, $^* p < 0.05$, $^{**} p < 0.01$.

woman can seem as if she is behaving in a politically ambitious manner when circumstances and recruitment are the only reasons she moved up in politics.

The two remaining women said something different when asked about their interest in appointed office. A state senator who said she had been approached for an appointment in the Bush administration was not interested because it would have been a short-term appointment and because she had "invested a lot of time and energy in state issues. So that was kind of where my heart was and my interest level as well." The other state legislator said she was never attracted to appointed office; she liked being in the legislature. Unfortunately, the size of my interview sample for state legislators was small, but these three women hint at the calculus behind elected officials' consideration of appointed office versus elected office. It appears the first elected official could have landed in appointed office if the circumstances were right, whereas the other two seem to have had an interest only in elected office or state issues, which prompted their disinterest in appointed office.

When we use ambition for appointed office as a dependent variable for predicting state legislators' political ambitions, we get a much clearer picture of the political ambition of elected officials. Unlike in the appointee sample, where *sex* was a negative predictor of interest in elected office (women were 14 percent less likely than men were to be interested in elected office), *sex* was not a significant predictor of interest in appointed office for the elected officials (Table 7.14). There were distinct differences in the predictors of interest in appointed versus elected office. *Value of current position* was not important for appointees, but it was important for legislators. Elected officials who were very satisfied with their policy influence were 32 percent less likely to be interested in appointed office compared with those who were very dissatisfied with their policy influence. Furthermore, many of the state-specific variables that were insignificant for appointees were significant for elected officials in their interest for appointed office. Those with less *professional legislatures* and those with *term limits* were much more likely to express an interest in appointed office than those in professional legislatures without term limits.

Self-assessed qualifications was even more important for legislators than it was for the appointees considering elected office. Legislators who assessed themselves as very qualified were 44 percent more likely to be interested in appointment than were legislators who assessed themselves as not qualified at all. For both appointed and elected officials, qualification self-assessment was a key factor in the interest for both a higher office and the opposite type of office.[9]

We should also take note of another interesting comparison between

9. An interaction between *sex and qualifications* does not reach standard levels of statistical significance, nor does the interaction for *level of office and sex*. The smaller number of observations for the elected sample limits the number of variables that can be included in the regression. After I drop a few variables to be able to add in the interactions for *sex, qualifications,* and *level of office,* the coefficient and standard error for the interaction *sex and level of office* becomes high. I also find that the variance inflation factor (VIF) is slightly high at 7.26, suggesting the same multicollinearity problem present in the prediction of interest in elected office for appointed officials.

Table 7.14 Logistic Regression of Elected Official Ambitions for Appointed Office

	Elected Official Ambition for Appointed Office		Impact
Demographics			
Sex	0.116	(0.353)	—
Education	0.048	(0.095)	—
Family income	0.028	(0.129)	—
Race (White)	−0.613	(0.497)	—
Age	−0.074**	(0.017)	−33.36%
Family Dynamics			
Married or long-term relationship	0.194	(0.450)	—
Majority household responsibility	−0.134	(0.247)	—
Children over eighteen	0.885*	(0.367)	+20.16%
Personal encouragement for appointment	1.056+	(0.635)	+14.35%
Parental suggestion	0.142	(0.165)	—
Political Dynamics			
Recruited for appointment	−0.181	(0.338)	—
Republican	−0.064	(0.457)	—
Democrat	0.074	(0.455)	—
Percent Obama vote 2012	5.644*	(2.259)	< +1%
Issue passion	−0.381	(0.560)	—
Political interest	0.065	(0.196)	—
Political efficacy	0.047	(0.135)	—
Volunteered for a candidate	−0.132	(0.389)	—
Personal Political Characteristics			
Number of years in position	0.010	(0.024)	—
Held appointment prior to position	0.216	(0.319)	—
Current position value	−0.330**	(0.104)	−32.05%
Difficulty of being elected	0.024	(0.122)	—
Qualifications	0.697**	(0.186)	+44.10%
Senate	−0.370	(0.332)	—
Had sponsor or mentor	0.691*	(0.271)	+15.25%
State-Specific Variables			
Traditionalist	−0.092	(0.377)	—
State legislature congruence	−0.010	(0.421)	—
Governor congruence	0.669+	(0.394)	+15.06%
State political opportunity structure	−0.016*	(0.006)	−35.65%
Local political opportunity structure	0.0006	(0.0005)	—
Professionalism	1.065*	(0.476)	+43.08%
Term limits	0.676+	(0.381)	+10.90%
Midwest	−1.165+	(0.619)	−26.62%
Constant	−1.706	(2.347)	—
N	336		
Pseudo-R^2	0.1887		
Percent Correctly Predicted	69.35%		

Note: Standard errors in parentheses. $^+ p < 0.10$, $^* p < 0.05$, $^{**} p < 0.01$.

elected and appointed officials' political ambition: having *children under eighteen* ceased being significant in predicting ambition for elected office among appointees, and just as it had been in predicting appointees' progressive ambitions, it actually became more significant when predicting elected officials' ambition for appointment. Why this is the case is not yet clear, but it could be a result of the increased amount of time elected officials might have to dedicate to full-time appointments, especially if they are coming from a citizen legislature. What is clear is that the debate about the effects of having children on public office holding and ambition cannot be put to rest until we further test parenthood's effects on all kinds of political ambition.

UNDERSTANDING THE RECRUITMENT, MOTIVATIONS, AND AMBITION OF STATE LEGISLATORS

The analysis in this chapter reveals important differences in the recruitment, motivations, and ambitions between appointed and elected officials. The main contribution of this book is to help understand appointees. By completing the complementary analysis of the elected officials, I further underscore how critical it is to look beyond the ballot. Political appointees are uniquely positioned in US government, particularly if they are in less visible and therefore less studied positions. They have consistent—and at times significant—interactions with government through their appointments, which in turn color their feelings toward government. For many individuals, appointments are where they get their start. For some elected officials, they are where they end their political careers. Yet despite the more often studied pathway of elected office, women in appointments and the legislature have similarities. Both report lower recruitment, specifically from other elected officials and party officials. Both cite public service and interest in a policy area as the main motivation for accepting their office. And both have lower perceptions of their own qualifications for higher office than do their male colleagues.

There are also important differences between appointed and elected officials in general and women public servants more specifically. Elected officials overall are much more politically involved than their appointee counterparts are, as well as being older and less educated. Gendered perceptions are not a significant predictor of progressive ambition for legislators as they are for appointees. And most importantly, there is a considerably different outlook on government and public service between the two types of officials that is especially prominent in appointed women. These are significant disparities that have been missed until now and must be explored further.

8. How to Be the Nonpolitical Public Servant

Right at the top was something buried in my heart of hearts—I really didn't *want* to run. I'd had enough of Washington. I'd never yearned for a life in politics.

—*Elizabeth Warren*

Following her service on the National Bankruptcy Review Commission (NBRC) in 1997, Elizabeth Warren went back to what she loved: teaching and research. She did this until Washington, DC, came knocking on her door again, via a phone call from Majority Leader Harry Reid (D-NV) asking her to join a congressional oversight panel (COP) that would monitor the money distributed from the Troubled Asset Relief Program (TARP), which had been passed in October of 2008. Warren (2015) found herself making frequent trips to Washington, writing reports, and becoming involved in the political world that oftentimes let her down. This position put her on the radar to help establish the Consumer Financial Protection Bureau (CFPB), an agency she long wished to come into fruition. Although she was integral to the bureau's creation, she was not well liked by Republicans, who would refuse to confirm her if she was nominated to direct the bureau. So in 2011, less than a year after she helped to create the CFPB, Warren resigned from her position.

Back home in Massachusetts, Warren had the opportunity to jump back into the political arena through a pathway she had never considered before: elected office. Scott Brown had been elected to the US Senate via special election in 2010 after Senator Ted Kennedy passed away. Many felt Warren should challenge him in 2012. But Warren was not so sure: "Although I appreciated the support, no one could pretend that I didn't have a stack of liabilities. I had never run for *any* office, let alone a highly contested national office like this one. Even before Martha Coakley's defeat, women had not done well in statewide races in Massachusetts, and conventional wisdom held that this was a man's game" (2015, 209). As the epigraph above shows, Warren was not interested in politics. Yet what is so interesting about her story is that time and again—despite a deep dislike of politics cultivated from firsthand experience—she got involved. And each time, from the very first appointment to the NBRC to the COP to the CFPB to the US Senate, Warren did so because the position was tied to her profession as a scholar of bankruptcy law and her personal conviction to see the system do better for the citizens it serves. Although elected office seems to be the line many of the appointees in this study will not cross, their motivations to serve in their appointed positions are remarkably similar to Warren's.

At the start of this book I ask how we can better understand women's pathways to public office and how we can better understand how women think of the political world. The short answer is as I suspected: by including appointed offices. The long answer, however, is somewhat unexpected. When we think of public officeholders—especially those most visible to us—such as members of Congress, high-level political appointees, and governors, we assume that each public officeholder reached his or her position intentionally. We might also assume that they deliberately sought out any prior positions they held as they aspired to the top of the political career ladder. That we refer to public service ambition in terms of a political career ladder suggests an ambition inextricably tied to the political world.

These assumptions occur in the literature of women and politics as well. Every time we ask why there are not more women in government, we are making the assumption that government and politics is something to aspire to. Every time we narrow the scope of ambition to only political ambition and constrict our view of the individuals we study to only those in elected office, we assume that those holding public office did so only for political reasons and that elected office is the only way in which one can be ambitious. We do not yet understand the nonpolitical motivations to publicly serve, and at the same time we ignore a considerable number of public offices that women (and men) might fulfill both for political and for nonpolitical reasons.

I have tried to rectify this by broadening the research on types of offices we normally study regarding ambition for public office. In this book, I include an analysis of high-level appointed offices in boards, commissions, and departments at the state level. I have also tried to represent, as much as possible, the appointees' reasoning for their interest in public office. Oftentimes, especially among appointed women, what might look like political ambition is really ambition that is not politically motivated. The women in my study had ambitions related to specific issues; perhaps wanting to give a greater voice to those largely ignored by the political world or wanting to do something different with their expertise in the areas of health, the environment, or commerce. Many of the appointees had highly specialized careers, which means these individuals were ambitious for success in their area of expertise. Political appointments could be an unintended result of their career advancement. This is also a way women convince themselves to get involved in politics, *by redefining what they do as nonpolitical.*

I argue throughout this book that moving beyond elected office is essential to getting an accurate picture of the status of women in US politics. I also argue that studying women in nonelected positions should not be done separately but in tandem with research on elected officials. My comparison illuminates why women are motivated for appointed versus elected office, why more women are appointed than elected, and what affects women's ambitions for public office. The analyses in Chapters 3–7 support this argument. Women in nonelected positions think differently about politics, have different political aspirations, and are recruited for public office in different ways than are elected women. The following summary of the findings further highlights why studying nonelected positions is just as important as studying elected positions, especially when it comes to public service motivations and ambition for public office.

SUMMARY OF FINDINGS

Who Holds State-Level Appointed Office?

Chapter 2 begins this study with a simple question: Who are the men and women appointed and elected to state government? Through comparison in three major areas—demographics, family life, and political involvement—I present a snapshot of elected and appointed officials from the statehouse to the governor's office, all the way down to the boards and commissions that advise on the needs of specific populations within states.

Women held 40 percent of all the state appointments I surveyed. This was 10 percent higher than the percentage of women from my state legislature sample, and more than 10 percent higher than the proportion of women serving in all state legislatures across the United States as of 2019 (Center for American Women in Politics 2018b). Furthermore, these appointees were highly educated, even more so than the state legislators. This is not surprising because many of the members included in my survey were on boards and commissions that regulated professions such as medicine or accounting. Beyond professional licensing boards, many of the boards and commissions dealt with specific issues or populations (e.g., the Traumatic Brain Injury Council) that usually require medical personnel to serve.

My analysis in Chapter 2 also finds that appointees were younger than elected officials, specifically high-level appointed women. The qualitative and quantitative data show that appointed women had lower progressive ambitions and were less likely to be interested in their positions because of their political aspect, and in fact many of the higher-level appointees had to be convinced to take their positions because the positions *were* political. The lower age of appointed officials, particularly the high-level female appointees, fit with the quantitative and qualitative data suggesting that these appointments were just another part of their *nonpolitical* careers. We know, for example, that many women in elected office tended to be older because they wanted to wait until they raised their children before they pursued politics. This suggests that having a family and pursuing or holding elected office are not easily done. However, if high-level appointments are not seen as political but as just another job, then being appointed and having children might not be as large of an obstacle as being elected and having children. Multiple women in high-level appointed positions said their office *happened* to be political, but that was unrelated to the reason they took the position. If women in appointments do not have political ambition and think of their positions as nonpolitical, then they will be less likely to feel as if they have to wait to have children or wait until their children are old enough before accepting appointment. Elected women might feel the need to juggle such personal and political concerns and therefore wait to enter public office later or simply forgo having children altogether.

Appointed and elected officials also exhibited gaps in their party identification and political activities. Once again, these differences support the belief many appointees expressed: politics is not a part of the appointed realm. Barely any state legislators identified as Independents, but a considerable number of appointees did. Additionally, elected officials were much more likely to have taken part in political activities outside their elected positions, with appointed officials trailing far behind. Identifying political affiliation as being outside of the two major parties and expressing decreased levels of political participation might be two ways appointees demonstrate how nonpolitical (nonpartisan) they are in their personal lives in addition to being nonpolitical in their appointments.

Public Service Motivations for Appointed Officials

In Chapters 3 and 4 the gender gaps continue as we move into the study of political recruitment and motivation for public office. Like prior studies, my analysis continues to demonstrate the decreased recruitment of women for public office. However, my analysis expands on previous studies in three significant ways. First, it expands recruitment studies to political appointments, an important inclusion because more than 50 percent of political appointees said they had been recruited for elected or appointed office. Second, I introduce a new political actor, political appointees, as a source of political recruitment, again showing the shortcomings of the narrow definition of political recruitment to elected positions only. Third, I unravel political recruitment to understand who is recruiting elected versus appointed officials and for which offices they are being recruited.

Appointed women revealed lower levels of recruitment than did men. Female appointees were recruited less often by elected officials compared with male appointees. My regression analysis further confirms the disparities in recruitment between men and women. Being a woman depresses appointee recruitment by elected officials and party officials. Further analysis finds that women were recruited more after they made it to the high appointment level. Chapter 3 exposes the recruitment that occurs beyond elected office. The findings reveal the political opportunities available to women. They also show how women, even with high levels of representation in the appointment arena, are still recruited less often than men are, at least until they reach a certain level of state government.

Like the external motivation of recruitment, the internal motivations to hold public office in Chapter 4 complement the findings for recruitment. Female appointees revealed a different definition of politics, usually involving partisanship, and demonstrated a near total disavowal of politics. For many women, their appointments were not political but simply a part of their careers or a way to advocate for an issue or people they felt needed representation. This shows up in the follow-up interviews, where female appointees expressed higher motivations to hold appointed office because of their careers or issues in which they were interested. It also surfaces during the qualitative analysis, in which appointed women had a definition of politics that did not include their own appointments. This allowed them to feel like they were giving back and doing something important for their careers without having to be a part of the partisan and negative world of politics. My analysis suggests that disavowal of politics is not only gendered but also is present in the highest offices of state government. It also suggests a new avenue for attracting more women into public service: find a position that matters to them and downplay its political nature; simultaneously, highlight how it connects to their careers, expertise, or personal interests.

(Non)political Ambitions of Appointed Officials

Following the findings in Chapters 3 and 4, I find decreased levels of progressive ambition among female appointees in general in Chapter 5 and a strong disinterest in elected office in particular in Chapter 6. Women appointees had a lower interest in higher office and were less likely to believe they were qualified to hold higher office. However, my statistical analysis reveals that the women who believed they *were* qualified for higher office were less interested in seeking higher office. Although perplexing at first because it is a reversal of previous findings, it fits with the findings from Chapters 3 and 4 upon second examination, as well as with the statements of female appointees throughout my entire survey about their disinterest in politics.

Some women reached for higher appointments because they convinced themselves the positions were not political. This does not mean we should assume that they want higher office or that if they do it will be a result of sudden political ambitions. There might be a threshold after which appointments are undeniably political or are outside women's ambitions, which might be the point at which these women lose interest in the positions. Remember, the low-level appointees met irregularly and had careers outside of their appointments. They already exhibited ambition within their careers. Holding higher political appointments might not factor into these ambitions. Also keep in mind that high-level female appointees most often said their political appointments were natural progressions of their careers—careers *not* devoted to politics. This made their appointments just another job, which is also likely how they viewed appointments above their current positions. We should not assume that wanting to be in a higher office is the ambition of every woman. The results from Chapter 6 provide further support for female appointees' disinterest in explicitly political offices. Being a woman appointee depresses ambition for elected office. Viewed altogether, the findings throughout Chapter 6 paint a unique picture of what public service looks like to the women who go into appointed versus elected office.

Finally, Chapter 7 addresses the motivations, recruitment, and ambitions of elected officials. This chapter reveals important gender differences in addition to the differences as a result of being in elected versus appointed office. Elected women were less likely to report being recruited by party officials compared with elected men. My regression analysis also reveals that elected women were 10–17 percent less likely to be recruited than elected men. In contrast with appointees for whom achieving a high appointment led to more recruitment, female state senators did not increase recruitment to higher public office by already having held office. Elected officials also exhibited similar reasons in motivations to publicly serve. Like those of appointees, their top two motivations were interest in a policy area as well as the opportunity for public service. Unlike appointees, they were not as motivated by advancing their career or broadening their experience. Elected men in particular cited interest in state government as a motivation for elected office. Although elected men were slightly more likely than were elected women to say they were motivated to serve in order to achieve higher elected office, sex does not become significant when predicting progressive ambition or ambition for appointed office. Self-perceived qualifications, however, continues to affect both kinds of ambition.

WHY EXPANDING THE POLITICAL PIPELINE IS IMPORTANT

Our research clearly suggests that those interested in electing more women to office should operate with an expanded notion of the pool of women who could be tapped to run. . . . We conclude that the pool of eligible women to run is both wider than commonly perceived and more than sufficient for women to achieve parity in state legislatures. Widespread social change in women's occupational status, their family roles, or their socialization is not a necessary prerequisite for increasing the numbers of women in office. Those interested in increasing women's representation need not wait for a social revolution. (Carroll and Sanbonmatsu 2013, 124)

We began this book by asking why highly accomplished and politically minded women like Cheryl Perry and Tricia Moniz demonstrated no ambition to run for office, whereas their similarly situated male counterparts, Randall White and Kevin Kendall, confidently spoke about their prospects of entering the political sphere as candidates. We end this book with an answer to that question: deeply embedded patterns of traditional gender socialization pervade U.S. society and continue to make politics a much less likely path for women than men. (Lawless and Fox 2005, 156)

The road to political power is closely studied by scholars of political science and yet is only partially understood. Although Carroll and Sanbonmatsu (2013) make the case for a broader understanding of who is eligible to run for elected office, they are still operating under an assumption that political power is mainly sought and achieved in elected office. Lawless and Fox (2005) similarly underestimate positions of political power through their study of elected ambition alone, which leads them to conclude that women are socialized to believe they are unqualified to run and hold political office. I consistently argue that focusing a study of women's political careers, recruitment, and ambition solely on elected office distorts the true story of women in US politics. It ignores the offices they are most likely to hold, which in turn overlooks the considerable amount of power they can wield in nonelected positions. Additionally, it leads us to believe that women are more often victims of forces they cannot control—socialization, discrimination, and family dynamics.

My book proves that not only do women take part in the political process in a unique and influential way but also that they make conscious decisions to do so as part of their careers, personal interests, or areas of expertise. They are telling themselves that what they do is not political, in the sense of it being partisan or electoral, but that they hold positions that feed their unique kind of ambition while giving back to the public in ways they might not have been able to do outside of their appointed positions. My findings reveal that women are engaging in politics in a way we have barely considered before. This would suggest that the way to get more women to seek public office is to personalize it for them—how does it factor into their expertise, career, or interests?

My findings are also troubling, though, in that women do not see what they do as political and struggle to consider certain appointed or elected offices for themselves because they seem more explicitly political. In one way, this might not matter because women are still pursuing positions that make a difference in citizen's daily lives, even if scholars of women in politics understudy those positions. In another way, it concerns me that women in our democracy are more likely to renounce politics and that this disavowal can be found in the highest levels of public service in states. We should be concerned that women's view of politics is so negative that they feel certain routes to political power—electoral routes—are simply not the way to accomplish anything in state government. If they feel this way about state government, then we can only imagine how those feelings increase when they face a decision to serve at the federal level. In fact, in the beginning of Chapter 1, this is exactly the fear Elizabeth Warren (2015) expressed: "I didn't know anything about Washington, but the bits I picked up from the press made it sound pretty awful" (49). It was only after former US representative Mike Synar recruited Warren by persuading her how much of a difference she could make that she truly considered, and then accepted, the appointment on a federal commission.

Perhaps worse is that the political climate has become even more hostile and negative since I began my study. The Pew Research Center (2018) finds that nearly 75 percent of Americans feel debate among political leaders is disrespectful. In 2015, the center reported that only 19 percent of Americans trusted the federal government to do the right thing, a steadily downward trend since the 1970s. Most importantly, women are disproportionately turned off by the negativity of politics. Kaid and Holtz-Bacha (2000) find that women are disproportionately affected by negative television broadcasts, Fridkin and Kenney (1999, 2011) find that men are more tolerant of uncivil and irrelevant messages than women are, and King and McConnell (2003) find that when women are over-exposed to negative campaign advertisements, they have more negative reactions to the sponsoring candidate instead of the target of the advertisement. Deborah Jordan Brooks (2010) reports the presence of a "negativity gap" in which men are more mobilized by negative campaign messages compared with women.[1] Shauna Shames (2017) finds that some of the most likely people to run for elected office—law students from prestigious institutions—are uninterested, in part because of dislike of politics and the belief that they can get more accomplished outside of the electoral arena. These findings—in conjunction with the psychology literature indicating that women tend to be less aggressive, less confident, risk averse, and avoid conflict (Byrnes, Miller, and Schafer 1999; Gneezy, Niederle, and Rustichini 2003; Kling et al. 1999; Niederle and Vesterlund 2007, 2010, 2011; Ors, Palomino, and Peyrache 2013)—show an environment ripe for gender differences in political ambition and views on politics. It is important to take these findings into consideration when studying female officeholders because it helps to explain why there are so many women in political appointments despite their aversion to politics.

CONTINUING TO UNRAVEL WHY WOMEN CHOOSE PUBLIC SERVICE

Much is left unknown about how and why women hold public office. Even with what we learned through my survey about appointed officials and their perspectives on politics, I never outright asked them for their definition of politics. I also never asked my respondents their feelings toward government—whether they believed government could be a positive force or if their overriding view of government was negative. I believe that receiving such a clear picture of their views on politics without explicitly asking about it is further proof that my findings are accurate. It is still incumbent upon scholars, however, to ask these more

1. See also Deborah Jordan Brooks and John G. Geer, "Beyond Negativity: The Effects of Incivility on the Electorate," *American Journal of Political Science* 51, no. 1 (2007): 1–16.

direct questions so that we can further tease out the gender differences in political negativity and public service. Moreover, my book focuses only on the state level. Although I expect even more disinterest from women to serve in the federal government (even in appointments) because of its more political nature, we need to test this and discover whether local office is considered more or less political. It might be easier for women to see local public service as less political and more personal, and we have to consider how their view of appointments versus elected office factors into this.

My study inadvertently reveals another area of future research. Although much is known about federal appointments and high-level state appointments, little is known about lower-level state appointments as well as nearly all appointments at the local level. The scope of these boards and commissions, who serves on them, and exactly what they can do is uncharted territory. Any differences in how men and women serve on these boards are also unknown. Clearly this is problematic because state and local boards and commissions can have a real and direct impact upon citizens. They decide the requirements for who becomes an acupuncturist, barber, chiropractor, or dentist. They inspect and approve the use of specific lands and state funds and can also decide who becomes the head of certain agencies and departments. They also have the power to educate the governor and legislature on important issues that affect vulnerable populations, influencing policy for all. Viewed together, boards and commissions across state and local government matter in the day-to-day lives of people and are an important area of focus for future research on political and nonpolitical ambition, political participation, and substantive representation.

Finally, it is incumbent upon scholars to expand this study to other departments in addition to the other thirty states. Although my sample of appointees was representative, I did not capture any appointees from education or police or corrections departments. It is important to study these departments because they are two areas of strong state control. Moreover, large portions of state budgets go to both education and law enforcement, so studying these departments means capturing an even better view of how state governments work. Additionally, police and corrections are known to be highly male-dominated departments, whereas education is female dominated. It would be quite enlightening to study these departments side-by-side to see if motivations and recruitment for women in these appointments differ in significant ways. Although I feel my study does capture significant differences in male and female appointees' recruitment patterns and motivations by including commerce, health, environmental, and natural resources departments, I suspect that the differences might be even more significant in more male-dominated departments such as corrections, fire protection, police, or possibly even transportation.

As students of government, we need to better understand all the political offices by which citizens are affected and in which they have the opportunity to publicly serve. Elected positions at all levels of government are incredibly important, and we should continue to study them and advance our understanding of how women view elected office in terms of their own ambitions. However, we should not study elected offices to the exclusion of other kinds of public service. Doing so ignores the impact thousands of women have at the local, state, and federal levels of government. It distorts our understanding of the offices truly available to women to hold and most importantly alters how we understand political and nonpolitical ambition as it pertains to public office. Studying women's ambitions and motivations to accept particular appointments is incredibly important to fully grasp why women are more likely to be in appointed instead of elected positions and why they accept these appointments. How appointments factor into the overall conceptualization of political participation among women is crucial as well. There are many paths to political power in the United States, and it is our duty to study and recognize all of these paths equally.

Appendix A: State Political Pathways Surveys

Part I. I would like to begin by asking a few questions regarding your work history.

Q1. *Have you ever worked in the private sector?*
o Yes. Please specify the field:
o No, I did not work in the private sector.

Q2. *Have you ever run for elected office?*
o Yes.
o No.

Q2a. *How many offices have you run for?*

Q2b. *Which offices have you run for? Check all that apply.*
o School board
o Town or city council
o County elected office
o Mayor
o State representative
o State senator
o Other local elected office
o Other state elected office

Q3. *Have you ever held elective public office?*
o Yes.
o No.

Q3a. *How many elective offices have you held?*

Q3b. *Which elected offices have you held? Check all that apply.*
o School board
o Town or city council
o County elected council
o Mayor
o State representative
o Other local elected office
o Other state elected office

Q3c. What year did you win your first election?

Q3d. What position was that?
o School board
o Town or city council
o County elected office
o Mayor
o State representative
o Other local elected office
o Other state elected office

Q4. If you have never run for office, have you ever thought about running for office?
o Yes, I seriously considered it.
o Yes, it has crossed my mind.
o No, I have not thought about it.
o No, I have no interest.

Q5. Prior to your current position, did you ever seek a political appointment?
o Yes.
o No.

Q5a. How many political appointments have you sought?

Q5b. Which positions for political appointment did you seek? Check all that apply.
o Political appointee in a city or local government
o Position on a state board or commission
o Political appointee in a department
o Political appointee in an agency
o Commissioner in an agency or department
o Head of an agency
o Deputy department head
o Department head
o Political appointment for the federal government

Q6. Prior to your current position, have you ever held a political appointment? Please do not include political appointments held due to holding elected office.
o Yes.
o No.

Q6a. How many appointive offices have you held prior to your current position?

Q6b. What year did you attain your first appointed office?

Q6c. *What was the position of the first appointment you held?*
o Political appointee in a city or local government
o Position on a state board or commission
o Political appointee in department
o Political appointee in an agency
o Commissioner in an agency or department
o Head of an agency
o Deputy department head
o Department head
o Political appointment for the federal government

Q6d. *What positions have you held throughout your political career? Check all that apply.*
o Position on a board or commission
o Commissioner in an agency or department
o Department head
o Deputy department head
o Political appointee in a department
o Political appointee in an agency
o Political appointment in a city or local government
o Political appointment for the federal government

Q7. *Prior to your current office, were you ever recruited by any of the following people to run for elected office or be politically appointed? Check all that apply.*
o Someone from a women's organization
o A party official
o An elected official
o An appointed official
o Someone from the governor's staff

Part II. This next series of questions concerns your current position as a political appointee.

Q8. *What year did you get appointed to your current position?*

Q9. *If you are an appointee on a board or commission, are you a public member?*
o Yes.
o No, not a member of a board

Q9a. *Please describe how your compensation works for your position on your board/commission. Check all that apply:*

o Per-diem compensation, please specify:
o Travel expenses
o Salary, please specify:
o No compensation

Q10. *Is your current position full time or part time?*

o Full time
o Part time

Q11. *Do you have term limits?*

o Yes.
o No.

Q11a. *How many terms can you serve?*

Q12. *Who were you appointed by?*

o Governor
o Cabinet secretary
o Someone within my department
o Someone within my agency
o State legislature
o An outside organization
o President of the Senate
o Speaker of the House
o Other, please specify

Q12a. *What was the party of the governor who appointed you?*

o Democrat
o Republican

Q13. *Did you have a sponsor or mentor who has helped you at any point in your political career?*

o Yes.
o No.

Q13a. *If so, was this sponsor male or female?*

o Male
o Female

Q13b. *How important was the sponsor/mentor to your political success?*
o Not important at all
o Somewhat unimportant
o Neither important or unimportant
o Somewhat important
o Very important

Q14. *I am interested in how the following characteristics and experiences have affected your political career. Please select: Hurt my career (1), Neither hurt nor helped my career (2), Helped my career (3), Not applicable (4).*
o Working on campaigns
o Being an aide to an elected official
o Employment in several state agencies
o Having held elected office
o Age
o Employment in different levels of government
o Employment in different branches of government
o Moves between public and private sector
o Relationships with those in the public sphere
o Childbearing/child care
o Spouse's career

Q15. *Including your current position, how many departments/agencies have you been in? If you are or have been on a board or commission, include the agency/department your board or commission falls under.*

Q16. *Why did you accept your appointment? Check all the reasons that apply.*
o Career advancement or other reason related to career
o Opportunity to work with the governor in his/her administration
o Support for the governor's policies
o Interest in policy area or issues
o Interest in state government
o Opportunity for public service
o Opportunity for broadening experience
o Opportunity for future elected office
o Other; please specify:

Q17. *On average, how satisfied are you with your current appointed position in your state?*
o Very dissatisfied
o Dissatisfied
o Somewhat dissatisfied

o Neutral
o Somewhat satisfied
o Satisfied
o Very satisfied

Q18. *How satisfied are you with your compensation for the job you do with the state?*
o Very dissatisfied
o Dissatisfied
o Somewhat dissatisfied
o Neutral
o Somewhat satisfied
o Satisfied
o Very satisfied
o I do not receive compensation

Q19. *How satisfied are you with your influence over policies in your department/agency/board?*
o Very dissatisfied
o Dissatisfied
o Somewhat dissatisfied
o Neutral
o Somewhat satisfied
o Satisfied
o Very satisfied

Q20. *Generally speaking, how difficult is it to get appointed to the office you currently hold?*
o Very difficult
o Difficult
o Somewhat difficult
o Neutral
o Somewhat easy
o Easy
o Very easy

Q21. *Lots of people have a negative view of what is entailed in holding political appointment. How did you feel about . . . ? I was comfortable with it (1), It did not bother me (2), It was a serious consideration (3), It almost deterred me from accepting the appointment (4), Not applicable (5).*
o Spending less time with family
o Loss of privacy

o Less time for personal interests
o The appointment process
o Dealing with members of the press

Q22. *Please mark your level of agreement with each of the following statements: Strongly disagree (1), Disagree (2), Neither agree nor disagree (3), Agree (4), Strongly agree (5).*

o My workload is reasonable.
o Those above me communicate the goals and priorities of the organization.
o In my organization, men receive preferential treatment compared with women.
o Minority women face extra obstacles to advancement.
o The viewpoint of a woman is often not heard at a meeting until it is repeated by a man.
o Once a woman assumes a top appointed position, that position often loses much of its power and prestige.
o My organization is reluctant to appoint women to supervisory or management positions.
o I see myself as a representative for women.
o I am given a real opportunity to improve my skills in my position.
o I feel encouraged to come up with new and better ways of doing things.
o Appointees have a feeling of personal empowerment with respect to work processes.

Q23. *Did any of the following individuals ever suggest that you run for office and/or seek political appointment in the past? Check all that apply. Suggested running for elected office, suggested seeking appointment.*

o Political party member
o Coworker/business associate
o Elected official
o Political appointee
o Friend/acquaintance
o Spouse or partner
o Family member
o Nonelected political activist
o Someone from a women's organization
o Other, please specify

Q24. *Which of the following best describes your plans affecting your career in the next three to five years? Check all that apply.*
o No change planned
o Seek higher appointment within this agency/department or board/commission
o Seek higher appointment within the state government but in another agency/department or board/commission
o Leave the state service to work outside the state government
o Retire from state government
o Seek a position in the federal government
o Take a leave of absence
o Resign from my current job
o It depends on future politics

Part III. I would now like to ask you about your opinions on what it means to be a political appointee in your state.

Q25. *In your view, are men and women equally likely to be encouraged by your party to seek political appointment?*
o Strongly disagree
o Disagree
o Neither agree nor disagree
o Agree
o Strongly agree

Q26. *There are many different qualities that are sought after in an elected official; which of the following do you think are important qualities to look for in elected officials? Check all that apply.*
o Having worked in a government department or agency before
o Having held an appointed position before
o Having held an elected position before
o Public speaking skills
o Having campaign experience
o Having a law degree
o Having policy experience

Part IV. Many people may not be interested in seeking higher office, but I'm interested in your impressions and experiences even if you are not interested in these things.

Q27. *Overall, how qualified do you feel you are to attain a higher level of political office, such as deputy agency leader, full-time political appointee, or commissioner in a department?*
o Not at all qualified
o Somewhat qualified
o Qualified
o Very qualified

Q28. *Which best characterizes your attitudes toward running for elected office in the future?*
o It is something I would not do.
o I would not rule it out, but I currently have no interest.
o It is something I might undertake if the opportunity presents itself.
o It is something I definitely would like to undertake in the future.

Q28a. *Would you be more likely to consider running for office if . . . : Yes, Possibly, No.*
o someone from work suggested you run?
o you had more free time?
o you had more impressive professional credentials?
o a spouse/partner suggested you run?
o you were more financially secure?
o you had fewer family responsibilities?
o there were issues you were more passionate about?
o you knew there was a lot of support for your candidacy?
o you had previous experiences working on a campaign?
o you better understood how to run for elected office?
o your district were less competitive?

Q28b. *Would any of the following resources make you more interested in running for office? Check all that apply.*
o Manuals and articles on campaigns and elections
o Interviews with political operatives and elected officials
o Webcasts on organizing, fund-raising, and media skills
o Training programs sponsored by political organizations

Q29. *If you were to run for public office, how likely do you think it is that you would win your campaign?*

o Very likely
o Likely
o Somewhat likely
o Undecided
o Somewhat unlikely
o Unlikely
o Very unlikely

Q30. *Overall, how interested are you in obtaining a higher office?*

o Not interested at all
o Somewhat interested
o Very interested

Q30a. *I would now like to ask you about your interest in specific public offices. What offices might you be interested in seeking? Check all that apply.*

o City council member
o Mayor
o State representative
o State senator
o Member of the US House of Representatives
o US senator
o Governor
o Statewide office (e.g., attorney general)
o Appointment to a state board or commission
o Appointment to a state agency or department
o Appointment to a federal agency or department
o President
o I am not interested in any of these offices

Q31. *Regardless of whether you are interested in seeking elective office or higher political appointment, have any of the following individuals/groups ever recruited you to run or seek higher office since you obtained your current political appointment?*

o Someone from a women's organization
o A party official
o An elected official
o An appointed official
o Someone from the governor's staff

Part V. Finally, I would like to end by asking you a few questions about your background and family life.

Q32. *How would you describe your party affiliation?*
o Strong Democrat
o Democrat
o Independent, leaning Democrat
o Independent
o Independent, leaning Republican
o Republican
o Strong Republican

Q33. *What is your sex?*
o Male
o Female

Q34. *Besides during your political career, have you ever . . . ? Check all that apply.*
o worked or volunteered for a candidate?
o attended a city council or school board meeting?
o attended a political party meeting, convention, or event?
o observed or attended a state legislative committee meeting or floor session?
o had an elected official as a family member or friend?
o served on the board of a nonprofit organization or foundation?

Q35. *How closely do you follow national politics?*
o Very closely
o Closely
o Somewhat closely
o Not closely

Q36. *What is your age?*

Q37. *What is the highest level of education you have completed?*
o Some high school
o High school graduate
o Attended some college (no degree attained)
o Associate's degree
o Completed college (BA or BS degree)
o Attended some graduate school (no degree attained)
o Completed graduate school

Q38. *In what category does your family income fall?*

o Under $50,000
o $50,001–$75,000
o $75,001–$100,000
o $100,001–$200,000
o Over $200,000

Q39. *What is your race/ethnicity?*

o White
o Black
o Asian
o Latino
o Native American
o Other; please specify:

Q40. *Do you consider yourself to be . . .*

o heterosexual or straight?
o gay?
o lesbian?
o bisexual?

Q41. *What is your marital status?*

o Single
o Long-term or committed relationship
o Married
o Widowed
o Divorced

Q41a. *If you are married or live with a partner, which statement best describes the division of labor on household tasks, such as doing laundry and cooking?*

o I am responsible for all household tasks.
o I am responsible for more of the household tasks than my spouse/partner.
o The division of labor in my household is evenly distributed.
o My spouse/partner takes care of more of the household tasks than I do.
o My spouse/partner is responsible for all of the household tasks.
o Other:

Q42. *Do you have any children? Check all that apply.*

o Yes, I have children over eighteen.
o Yes, I have young children still living at home.
o No, I do not have any children.

Q42a. *How many children under the age of eighteen do you have?*

Q42b. *If you have children, which statement best characterizes your child-care arrangements?*
o I am the primary caretaker of the children.
o I have more child-care responsibilities than my spouse/partner.
o My spouse/partner and I share child-care responsibilities.
o My spouse/partner is the primary caretaker of the children.
o Other:

Q43. *If you do not have children, do you plan on having children in the near future?*
o Yes.
o No.
o I don't know.

Q44. *When you were growing up, how frequently, if at all, did your parents suggest that, someday, you should run for elected office?*
o Frequently
o Occasionally
o Seldom
o Never

Q45. *When you think about politics, how important are the following issues to you? Not important at all (1), Not very important (2), Neither important nor unimportant (3), Somewhat important (4), Very important (5).*
o Abortion
o Education
o Environment
o Health care
o Economy
o Guns
o Crime
o Gay rights
o Women's rights

Q46. *Please mark your level of agreement with the following statements. Strongly agree (1), Agree (2), Neither agree nor disagree (3), Disagree (4), Strongly disagree (5).*
o Taxes are too high.
o More gun control laws should be passed.
o Abortion should always be legal in the first trimester.
o The federal government should provide a pathway to citizenship for undocumented immigrants.
o The government pays attention to people when making decisions.

- It is just as easy for a woman to be elected to a high-level public office as a man.
- It is just as easy for a woman to be appointed to a high-level public office as a man.
- Most men are better suited emotionally for politics than are most women.
- Despite the election of an African American president, the United States still has a long way to go on the issue of race.

Q47. Is there anything else you would like to share with me about your political history or experiences as a public official in your state?

Q48. Would you be willing to take part in a phone interview sometime in the near future to discuss your experiences as a public official at the state level?
- Yes.
- No.

ELECTED OFFICIALS SURVEY

Part I. I would like to begin by asking a few questions regarding your work history.

Q1. Have you ever worked in the private sector?
- Yes. Please specify the field:
- No, I did not work in the private sector.

Q2. How many offices have you run for?

Q2b. Which offices have you run for? Check all that apply.
- School board
- Town or city council
- County elected office
- Mayor
- State representative
- State senator
- Other local elected office
- Other state elected office

Q3. How many elective offices have you held?

Q3b. *Which elected offices have you held? Check all that apply.*
o School board
o Town or city council
o County elected council
o Mayor
o State representative
o Other local elected office
o Other state elected office

Q3c. *What year did you win your first election?*

Q3d. *What position was that?*
o School board
o Town or city council
o County elected office
o Mayor
o State representative
o Other local elected office
o Other state elected office

Q4. *Prior to your current position, did you ever seek a political appointment?*
o Yes.
o No.

Q4a. *How many political appointments have you sought?*

Q4b. *Which positions for political appointment did you seek? Check all that apply.*
o Position on a board or commission
o Commissioner in an agency or department
o Head of an agency
o Department head
o Deputy department head
o Political appointee in a department
o Political appointee in an agency
o Political appointee in a city or local government
o Political appointment for the federal government

Q5. *Prior to your current position, have you ever held a political appointment? Please do not include political appointments held due to holding elected office.*
o Yes.
o No.

Q5a. *How many appointive offices have you held prior to your current position?*

Q6b. *What year did you attain your first appointed office?*

Q5c. *What was the position of the first appointment you held?*
o Political appointee in a city or local government
o Position on a state board or commission
o Political appointee in department
o Political appointee in an agency
o Commissioner in an agency or department
o Head of an agency
o Deputy department head
o Department head
o Political appointment for the federal government
o Other; please specify

Q6. *What positions have you held throughout your political career? Check all that apply.*
o Position on a board or commission
o Commissioner in an agency or department
o Department head
o Deputy department head
o Political appointee in a department
o Political appointee in an agency
o Political appointment in a city or local government
o Political appointment for the federal government

Q7: *If you have never sought a political appointment, have you ever thought about seeking a political appointment?*
o Yes, I seriously considered it.
o Yes, it has crossed my mind.
o No, I have not thought about it.
o No, I have no interest.

Q8. *Prior to your current office, were you ever recruited by any of the following people to run for elected office or be politically appointed? Check all that apply.*
o Someone from a women's organization
o A party official
o An elected official
o An appointed official
o Someone from the governor's staff

Part II. This next series of questions concerns your current position as an elected official in your state.

Q9. *What year did you get elected to your current position?*

Q10. *Is your current position full time or part time?*
o   Full time
o   Part time

Q11. *Do term limits apply to your current position?*
o   Yes.
o   No.

Q11a. *How many terms can you serve?*

Q12. *Did you have a sponsor or mentor who has helped you at any point in your political career?*
o   Yes.
o   No.

Q12a. *If so, was this sponsor male or female?*
o   Male
o   Female

Q12b. *How important was the sponsor/mentor to your political success?*
o   Not important at all
o   Somewhat unimportant
o   Neither important or unimportant
o   Somewhat important
o   Very important

Q13. *Select the explanation indicating the extent to which each activity affected your political career: Hurt my career (1), Neither hurt nor helped my career (2), Helped my career (5), Not applicable (0).*
o   Working on campaigns
o   Being an aide to an elected official
o   Employment in several state agencies
o   Having held elected office
o   Age
o   Employment in different levels of government
o   Employment in different branches of government
o   Moves between public and private sector
o   Relationships with those in the public sphere

o Childbearing/child care
o Spouse's career

Q14. *Why did you run for elected office? Check all the reasons that apply.*
o Career advancement or other reason related to career
o Opportunity to work with others in government
o Support for my party's policies
o Interest in policy area or issues
o Interest in state government
o Opportunity for public service
o Opportunity for broadening experience
o Opportunity for future elected office
o Other; please specify

Q15. *On average, how satisfied are you with your current elected position in your state?*
o Very dissatisfied
o Dissatisfied
o Somewhat dissatisfied
o Neutral
o Somewhat satisfied
o Satisfied
o Very satisfied

Q16. *How satisfied are you with your compensation for the job you do with the state?*
o Very dissatisfied
o Dissatisfied
o Somewhat dissatisfied
o Neutral
o Somewhat satisfied
o Satisfied
o Very satisfied
o I do not receive compensation

Q17. *How satisfied are you with your influence over policies in your state assembly?*
o Very dissatisfied
o Dissatisfied
o Somewhat dissatisfied
o Neutral
o Somewhat satisfied

o Satisfied
o Very satisfied

Q18. *Generally speaking, how difficult is it to get elected to the office you cur-rently hold?*
o Very difficult
o Difficult
o Somewhat difficult
o Neutral
o Somewhat easy
o Easy
o Very easy

Q19. *There are a lot of challenges in being an elected official. How did you feel about . . . ? I was comfortable with it (1), It did not bother me (2), It was a seri-ous consideration (3), It almost deterred me from accepting the appointment (4), Not applicable (5).*
o Spending less time with family
o Loss of privacy
o Less time for personal interests
o Dealing with members of the press

Q20. *Did any of the following individuals ever suggest that you run for office and/or seek political appointment in the past? Check all that apply. Suggested running for elected office, suggested seeking appointment.*
o Political party member
o Coworker/business associate
o Elected official
o Political appointee
o Friend/acquaintance
o Spouse or partner
o Family member
o Nonelected political activist
o Someone from a women's organization
o Other; please specify

Q21. *Which of the following best describes your plans affecting your career in the next three to five years? Check all that apply.*
o No change planned
o Seek higher elected office in this state
o Seek higher elected office in the federal government
o Leave the elected office to work outside the state government

o   Retire from elected politics
o   Seek a position in the federal government
o   Take a leave of absence
o   Resign from my current job
o   It depends on future politics

Part III. I would now like to ask you about your opinions on what it means to be an elected official in your state.

Q22. *In your view, are men and women equally likely to be encouraged by your party to seek elected office?*
o   Strongly disagree
o   Disagree
o   Neither agree nor disagree
o   Agree
o   Strongly agree

Q23. *There are many different qualities that are sought after in an elected official; which of the following do you think are important qualities to look for in elected officials? Check all that apply.*
o   Having worked in a government department or agency before
o   Having held an appointed position before
o   Having held an elected position before
o   Public speaking skills
o   Having campaign experience
o   Having a law degree
o   Having policy experience

Part IV. Many people may not be interested in seeking higher office, but I'm interested in your impressions and experiences even if you are not interested in these things.

Q24. *Overall, how qualified do you feel you are to attain a higher level of political office, such as state senator or representative for the US House?*
o   Not at all qualified
o   Somewhat qualified
o   Qualified
o   Very qualified

Q25. *Which best characterizes your attitudes toward holding appointed office in the future?*
o   It is something I would not do.
o   I would not rule it out, but I currently have no interest.

o It is something I might undertake if the opportunity presents itself.
o It is something I definitely would like to undertake in the future.

Q26. *Overall, how interested are you in obtaining a higher office?*
o Not interested at all
o Somewhat interested
o Very interested

Q27. *I would now like to ask you about your interest in specific public offices. What offices might you be interested in seeking? Check all that apply.*
o City council member
o Mayor
o State representative
o State senator
o Member of the US House of Representatives
o US senator
o Governor
o Statewide office (e.g., attorney general)
o Appointment to a state board or commission
o Appointment to a state agency or department
o Appointment to a federal agency or department
o President
o I am not interested in any of these offices

Q28. *Regardless of whether you are interested in seeking political appointment or higher elected office, have any of the following individuals/groups ever recruited you to run or seek higher office since you obtained your current political appointment?*
o Someone from a women's organization
o A party official
o An elected official
o An appointed official
o Someone from the governor's staff

Part V. Finally, I would like to end by asking you a few questions about your background and family life.

Q29. *How would you describe your party affiliation?*
o Strong Democrat
o Democrat
o Independent, leaning Democrat
o Independent
o Independent, leaning Republican

o Republican
o Strong Republican

Q30. *Besides during your political career, have you ever . . . ? Check all that apply.*
o worked or volunteered for a candidate?
o attended a city council or school board meeting?
o attended a political party meeting, convention, or event?
o observed or attended a state legislative committee meeting or floor session?
o had an elected official as a family member or friend?
o served on the board of a nonprofit organization or foundation?

Q31. *How closely do you follow national politics?*
o Very closely
o Closely
o Somewhat closely
o Not closely

Q32. *What is your sex?*
o Male
o Female

Q33. *What is your age?*

Q34. *What is the highest level of education you have completed?*
o Some high school
o High school graduate
o Attended some college (no degree attained)
o Associate's degree
o Completed college (BA or BS degree)
o Attended some graduate school (no degree attained)
o Completed graduate school

Q35. *In what category does your family income fall?*
o Under $50,000
o $50,001–$75,000
o $75,001–$100,000
o $100,001–$200,000
o Over $200,000

Q36. *What is your race/ethnicity? Check all that apply.*
o White
o Black
o Asian
o Latino
o Native American
o Other; please specify:

Q37. *Do you consider yourself to be . . .*
o heterosexual or straight?
o gay?
o lesbian?
o bisexual?

Q38. *What is your marital status?*
o Single
o Long-term or committed relationship
o Married
o Widowed
o Divorced

Q38a. *If you are married or live with a partner, which statement best describes the division of labor on household tasks, such as doing laundry and cooking?*
o I am responsible for all household tasks.
o I am responsible for more of the household tasks than my spouse/partner.
o The division of labor in my household is evenly distributed.
o My spouse/partner takes care of more of the household tasks than I do.
o My spouse/partner is responsible for all of the household tasks.
o Other:

Q39. *Do you have any children? Check all that apply.*
o Yes, I have children over eighteen.
o Yes, I have young children still living at home.
o No, I do not have any children.

Q39a. *How many children under the age of eighteen do you have?*

Q39b. *If you have children, which statement best characterizes your child-care arrangements?*
o I am the primary caretaker of the children.
o I have more child-care responsibilities than my spouse/partner.
o My spouse/partner and I share child-care responsibilities.

o My spouse/partner is the primary caretaker of the children.
o Other:

Q40. *When you were growing up, how frequently, if at all, did your parents suggest that, someday, you should run for elected office?*
o Frequently
o Occasionally
o Seldom
o Never

Q41. *When you think about politics, how important are the following issues to you? Not important at all (1), Not very important (2), Neither important nor unimportant (3), Somewhat important (4), Very important (5).*
o Abortion
o Education
o Environment
o Health care
o Economy
o Guns
o Crime
o Gay rights
o Women's rights

Q42. *Please mark your level of agreement with the following statements. Strongly agree (1), Agree (2), Neither agree nor disagree (3), Disagree (4), Strongly disagree (5).*
o Taxes are too high.
o More gun control laws should be passed.
o Abortion should always be legal in the first trimester.
o The federal government should provide a pathway to citizenship for undocumented immigrants.
o The government pays attention to people when making decisions.
o It is just as easy for a woman to be elected to a high-level public office as a man.
o It is just as easy for a woman to be appointed to a high-level public office as a man.
o Most men are better suited emotionally for politics than are most women.
o Despite the election of an African American president, the United States still has a long way to go on the issue of race.

Q43. *Is there anything else you would like to share with me about your political history or experiences as a public official in your state?*

Q44. *Would you be willing to take part in a phone interview sometime in the near future to discuss your experiences as a public official at the state level?*

o Yes.
o No.

Appendix B: Appointed and Elected Official Interview Transcripts

1. How did you first get involved in politics?
2. Was there anyone specifically, a colleague, family member, or political actor, who contributed to your interest in politics?
3. Has anyone recruited you to run for office?
   a. If Yes: Whose support do you think was most important to your career?
   b. If No: Do you think your lack of recruitment had an effect on your interest in public office?
4. Did you ever consider seeking elected office instead of appointed office?
   a. If Yes: When was the most recent time you've thought about it?
      i. What makes you think you might want to do this? What's your motivation for wanting to get involved?
   b. If No: Why not?
      i. When you say you've never considered running, does that mean it's something you could never see yourself doing? Why not?

And now thinking about your current position:

5. How did you attain the position you are currently in?
6. What were some of the motivations for seeking your current position?
7. Can you outline your responsibilities in your current position?
8. Do you feel the board/commission/department you are in has a clearly defined role within your state?
9. For board/commission members: Do you feel your board/commission is political? If so, what is your definition of political?
10. What are the major challenges facing your board/commission/department?
11. Do you feel your position affords you the opportunity to make real changes in the area of [insert department area or board topic]?
12. I would like to understand the effects of your political career on family life. Has your political career ever affected your family life?
    Now thinking about the future:

13. What is your level of interest in seeking a higher elected or appointed office, and what major factors drive this interest/disinterest?

    a. If you are interested, what levels of offices are you interested in?

14. What do you think are the most important qualifications or credentials in public officials and candidates?

Thank you for your time. I'd like to ask a few more general questions.

15. As a woman, do you think running for elected office would pose greater challenges to you than it would if you were a man? What about seeking appointed office? How so or why not?

16. When it comes down to it, what would it take for you to throw your hat into the ring and seek a higher position in government?

ELECTED OFFICIAL INTERVIEW SCRIPT

1. How did you first get involved in politics?

2. Was there anyone specifically, a colleague, family member, or political actor, who contributed to your interest in politics?

3. Has anyone recruited you to run for office?

    a. If Yes: Whose support do you think was most important to your career?

    b. If No: Do you think your lack of recruitment had an effect on your interest in public office?

4. Did you ever consider seeking appointed office instead of elected office?

    a. If Yes: When was the most recent time you've thought about it?

       i. What makes you think you might want to do this? What's your motivation for wanting to get involved?

    b. If No: Why not?

       i. When you say you've never considered seeking appointed office, does that mean it's something you could never see yourself doing? Why not?

And now thinking about your current position:

5. How did you attain the position you are currently in?

6. What were some of the motivations for seeking your current position?

7. Can you outline your responsibilities in your current position?

8. What are the major challenges facing your state?

9. Do you feel your position affords you the opportunity to make real changes in your state?

10. I would like to understand the effects of your political career on family life. Has your political career ever affected your family life?

Now thinking about the future:

11. What is your level of interest in seeking a higher elected or appointed office, and what major factors drive this interest/disinterest?

   a. If you are interested, what levels of offices are you interested in?

12. What do you think are the most important qualifications or credentials in public officials and candidates?

Thank you for your time. I'd like to ask a few more general questions.

13. As a woman, do you think running for elected office would pose greater challenges to you than it would if you were a man? What about seeking appointed office? How so or why not?

14. When it comes down to it, what would it take for you to throw your hat into the ring and seek a higher position in government?

INTERVIEW SUBJECT POSITIONS AND DESCRIPTIVE CHARACTERISTICS

Characteristic	Number
Interviewees from the Northeast	5
Interviewees from the South	3
Interviewees from the Midwest	7
Interviewees from the West	6
State senators	4
State representatives	0
High appointees	7
Board and commission members	10
Interviewees from commerce departments	5
Interviewees from natural resource departments	4
Interviewees from environmental departments	2
Interviewees from health departments	6
Total Interviews	21

Positions of individuals interviewed:
- State senators: 4
- State representatives: 0
- Commissioner of department: 3
- Deputy commissioner of department: 1
- Director of department: 2

- Deputy director of department: 1
- Regulatory board appointees: 4
- Advisory board appointees: 2
- Policy-making board appointees: 4

Appendix C: Coding of Variables

Variable	Range	Coding	Chapter(s)
Age	21–85	Indicates respondent's age	2, 3, 5, 6, 7
Children over eighteen	0, 1	Indicates whether the respondent has no children, children under eighteen (0), or children over eighteen (1)	2, 5, 6, 7
Compensation salary (appointee only)	0, 1	Indicates whether the appointee was compensated for their appointment via salary: 0 if No, 1 if Yes	3
Current position value (appointed)	0.5–24.5	Indicates the value respondents place on their current positions via job satisfaction in general and satisfaction with policy influence. The higher the number, the more valuable the position is to the respondent. Cronbach's alpha: 0.7645	6
Current position value (elected)	1–7	Indicates the value respondents place on their positions via their feelings on their job satisfaction and policy influence. Ranges from Very dissatisfied (1) to Very satisfied (7)	7
Democrat	0, 1	Indicates whether the respondent identifies as Democrat (1), Republican, or Independent (0)	2, 3, 5, 6, 7
Difficulty of being appointed (appointee only)	0, 1	Indicates the appointed officials' opinion of how difficult the appointment process was based upon whether it was a serious consideration/almost deterred them from accepting the appointment (1) or not (0)	5, 6
Difficulty of being elected (elected only)	1, 7	Indicates the elected officials' opinion of how difficult it is, on average, to get elected to their current position. Ranges from Very difficult (1) to Very easy (7)	7
Education	1, 7	Measures the level of education of respondents ranging from Some high school (1) to Completed graduate school (7)	2, 3, 5, 6, 7
Family income	1, 6	Measures the respondent's family income ranging from Under $25,000 (1) to Over $200,000 (6)	2, 3, 5, 6, 7

Variable	Range	Coding	Chapter(s)
Female	0, 1	Indicates whether the respondent is male (0) or female (1)	2, 3, 4, 5, 6, 7
Governor congruence	0, 1	Respondents' party congruence with current governor in their state. 0 represents that the party of the appointee and the party of the governor did not match; 1 represents that the party of the appointee and the party of the governor did match, including Independents matching with either Democratic or Republican governors	5, 6, 7
Had sponsor or mentor	0, 1	Indicates whether respondents did not have a sponsor or mentor (0) or did have a sponsor or mentor who helped them in their political career (1)	3, 5, 6, 7
Held appointed office	0, 1	Indicates whether public officeholders had previously held appointed office (1) or had never held appointed office (0)	3, 7
Held elected office	0, 1	Indicates whether public officeholders had previously held elected office (1) or had never held elected office (0)	3
High appointee	0, 1	Indicates whether respondents are on a board and commission (0), or are high appointees (1)	3, 6
High appointee × female	0, 1	Indicates whether the respondent is male or female on a board and commission or a high-level male appointee (0), or a high-level female appointee (1)	3
Independent	0, 1	Indicates whether respondents identify as Independent (1) or Republican or Democrat (0)	7
Issue passion			
Appointees: Elected:	1, 5 0, 1	Appointees: Indicates the number of issues the respondents feel strongly about, including Abortion, Education, Environment, Health care, Economy, Guns, Crime, Gay rights, and Women's rights. Cronbach's alpha: 0.7291. Elected: average of answering "Very important" to the same issue areas. Cronbach's alpha: 0.7075	5, 6, 7

Variable	Range	Coding	Chapter(s)
Local political opportunity structure	74.08–2,699	Based on Lawless and Fox's measure (2010). Indicates the total number of seats in the US Census Bureau count of the total number of "government units" in the state, divided by the size of the congressional delegation	3, 5, 6, 7
Low level	0, 1	Indicates whether the respondent is in the House or is on a board and commission (1), or is in the Senate or a high-level appointee (0)	5
Low level × qualifications	0, 4	Interaction between level of office and self-assessed interactions	5
Low level × sex	0, 1	Interaction between level of office and sex	5
Married/long-term relationship	0, 1	Indicates whether the respondent is not married (0) or married/in a committed relationship (1)	5, 6, 7
Moralistic state culture	0, 1	Indicates whether the state culture is moralistic (1) or not (0)	3
Nonwhite	0, 1	Indicates whether the respondent is white (0) or nonwhite (1)	3
Number of elected offices held	1–6	Indicates the number of elected offices the public officeholder held	
Number of years in position	1, 25	Indicates the number of years respondents have held their current position; 25 represents twenty-five years or longer	3, 5, 6, 7
Parental suggestion	1, 4	Indicates whether respondents' parents had suggested when they were growing up that someday they should run for elected office. Ranges from Never (1) to Frequently (4)	5, 6, 7
Percent female appointees	21.4%–54.5%	From the Center for Women in Government and Civil Society (CWGCS) measure of the percentage of appointees in each state	3, 5, 6, 7
Percent female state legislators 2012	11.1%–38.9%	Indicates the percentage of women in the appointee's state legislature	3, 5, 6, 7
Percent Obama vote 2012	24.75%–66.57%	The 2012 Democratic presidential vote share for the state where the respondent resides	

Variable	Range	Coding	Chapter(s)
Personal encouragement for elected office	0, 1	Indicates whether a respondent had received encouragement from a spouse or family member to run for elected office (1) or had not received any encouragement from those sources (0)	6
Political efficacy	1, 5	Indicates respondent's agreement with "The government pays attention to people when making decisions." On a scale from Strongly disagree (1) to Strongly agree (5)	5, 6, 7
Political interest	1, 4	Indicates how closely respondents follow national politics from Not closely (1) to Very closely (4)	5, 6, 7
Political participation (appointee only)	0, 1	Indicates level of respondents' political involvement in the following: Volunteering for a candidate, Working for a candidate, Attending a city council or school board meeting, Attending a political party event, Attending a state legislature session, Serving on the board of a nonprofit. The closer respondent is to 1, the higher the political participation. Cronbach's alpha: 0.6433	3, 5, 6
Position value (appointee)	0.5–24.5	Indicates the value respondents place on their current positions as represented by job satisfaction in general and satisfaction with policy influence. The higher the number, the more valuable the position is to the respondent. Cronbach's alpha: 0.76	6
Position value (elected)	1, 7	Indicates the value respondents place on their positions as represented by their feelings on their job satisfaction and policy influence. Ranges from Very dissatisfied (1) to Very satisfied (7)	7
Professionalism	1–3	Indicates whether the state legislature is Professional (1), Semiprofessional (2), or Citizen (3)	6, 7
Qualifications for higher office	1, 4	A self-assessment by respondents measuring their qualifications for higher political office, from Not at all qualified (1) to Very qualified (4).	5, 6, 7

Variable	Range	Coding	Chapter(s)
Qualifications × sex	0, 4	Interaction between self-assessed qualifications and sex	5
Recruited since position	0, 1	Indicates whether respondent was recruited for elected or appointed office since their current position by a party official, elected official, appointed official, or women's organization (1) or was never recruited (0)	3, 5, 7
Republican	0, 1	Indicates whether the respondent identifies as Republican (1) or Democrat or Independent (0)	2, 3, 5, 6, 7
Responsible for majority of household tasks	0, 2	Indicates whether respondent is responsible for less than half of the household tasks (0), half (1), or the majority of household tasks (2); those not married or not in a long-term relationship were counted as 0	5, 6, 7
Senate	0, 1	Public official is a member of the Senate (1) or is not (0)	7
Sexism (appointee only)	1, 5	Measures amount of discrimination each respondent experienced according to the following questions: Men receive preferential treatment compared to women, Minority women face extra obstacles to advancement, The viewpoint of a woman is often not heard at a meeting until it is repeated by a man, once a woman assumes a top appointed position that position can or may lose much of its prestige and power, and The organization is reluctant to appoint women. Responses to each of those questions was on a 1 (Strongly disagree) to 5 (Strongly agree) scale; all responses were added up and divided by the total number of questions (5). Cronbach's alpha: 0.89	5, 6
Sex × children over eighteen	0, 1	Indicates whether the respondent is a mother (1) or is not (0)	5

Variable	Range	Coding	Chapter(s)
Sex × qualifi-cations × low level	0, 4	Interaction between sex, self-assessed qualifications, and level of office.	5
Sought appointment prior to position	0, 1	Indicates whether respondent sought appointed office in the past (1) or did not (0).	5
State legislature congruence	0, 1	Respondents' party congruence with current party in control of the state legislature in their state. 0 represents that the party of the appointee and the party of the state legislature did not match; 1 represents that the party of the appointee and the party of the state legislature did match, including Independents matching with either Democratic or Republican state legislatures	5, 6, 7
State political opportunity structure	9.83–190	Based on Lawless and Fox's (2010) measure; indicates the total number of seats in the state legislature divided by the size of the congressional delegation	3, 5, 6, 7
Term limits	0, 1	Indicates whether respondents have term limits (1) or not (0)	6, 7
Traditionalist state culture	0, 1	Indicates whether the state culture is traditionalist (1) or not (0)	6, 7
Volunteered for a candidate	0,1	Indicates whether respondents volunteered for candidates independent of their own political careers (1)	7
White	0, 1	Indicates whether the respondent is white (1) or nonwhite (0)	5, 6, 7

Appendix D: Supplemental Table for Chapter 5
Step-Wise Logistic Regression Interest in Higher Office for Political Appointees (Chapter 5)

	Model 1	Model 2	Model 3	Model 4	Model 5
Demographics					
Sex 1 = Female	-0.568* (0.227)	-0.952** (0.313)	-0.449 (0.600)	-0.566 (0.823)	2.905 (1.999)
Education	0.009 (0.075)	0.019 (0.075)	0.014 (0.075)	0.018 (0.075)	0.021 (0.075)
Family income	-0.262** (0.088)	-0.264** (0.088)	-0.263** (0.088)	-0.276** (0.088)	-0.284** (0.089)
White 1 = White	0.502 (0.333)	0.457 (0.331)	0.451 (0.330)	0.409 (0.332)	0.437 (0.331)
Age	-0.087** (0.011)	-0.087** (0.011)	-0.087** (0.011)	-0.088** (0.011)	-0.088** (0.011)
Family Dynamics					
Married or long-term relationship	-0.641* (0.293)	-0.644* (0.293)	-0.645* (0.295)	-0.615* (0.295)	-0.622* (0.295)
Majority household responsibilities	0.276+ (0.151)	0.273+ (0.150)	0.271+ (0.150)	0.265+ (0.150)	0.251 (0.151)
Children over eighteen	0.496* (0.215)	0.238 (0.256)	0.230 (0.258)	0.214 (0.259)	0.218 (0.261)
Parental suggestion	0.205+ (0.113)	0.199+ (0.112)	0.196+ (0.112)	0.188+ (0.113)	0.193+ (0.113)
Personal encouragement	0.806** (0.190)	0.813** (0.191)	0.814** (0.191)	0.832** (0.191)	0.833** (0.191)
Political Dynamics					
Recruited since position	0.366+ (0.196)	0.371+ (0.197)	0.377+ (0.197)	0.376+ (0.197)	0.364+ (0.196)
Republican	0.171 (0.234)	0.197 (0.235)	0.198 (0.256)	0.210 (0.236)	0.193 (0.238)
Democrat	-0.371 (0.256)	-0.361 (0.257)	-0.357 (0.256)	-0.370 (0.259)	-0.395 (0.260)
Percent Obama vote 2012	-0.679 (0.843)	-0.691 (0.846)	-0.721 (0.843)	-0.819 (0.857)	-0.792 (0.853)
Sexism	0.165 (0.115)	0.166 (0.116)	0.168 (0.115)	0.167 (0.115)	0.166 (0.116)
Issue passion	0.020 (0.188)	0.034 (0.188)	0.035 (0.189)	0.040 (0.189)	0.048 (0.190)
Political participation	1.324** (0.381)	1.311** (0.384)	1.311** (0.384)	1.295** (0.386)	1.309** (0.385)
Political interest	-0.009 (0.109)	-0.008 (0.110)	-0.012 (0.110)	-0.008 (0.110)	-0.006 (0.111)
Political efficacy	-0.073 (0.077)	-0.080 (0.077)	-0.083 (0.078)	-0.075 (0.078)	0.077 (0.078)

	Model 1	Model 2	Model 3	Model 4	Model 5
Personal Political Characteristics					
Number of years in position	−0.010 (0.011)	−0.009 (0.011)	−0.009 (0.010)	−0.008 (0.010)	−0.008 (0.011)
Sought appointment prior to position	0.522* (0.209)	0.526* (0.209)	0.509* (0.208)	0.513* (0.207)	0.504* (0.207)
Position value	0.009 (0.015)	0.008 (0.016)	0.009 (0.014)	0.009 (0.014)	0.009** (0.014)
Difficulty of attaining position	0.828** (0.280)	0.829** (0.278)	0.838** (0.256)	0.832** (0.276)	0.812** (0.271)
Qualifications	0.635 (0.452)	0.508** (0.147)	0.474** (0.144)	0.397** (0.109)	0.400** (0.109)
Low appointee	1.133 (1.687)	0.657 (0.297)	0.355 (0.253)	0.366 (0.252)	0.374 (0.252)
Had sponsor or mentor	0.033 (0.220)	0.036 (0.220)	0.070 (0.219)	0.076 (0.218)	0.074 (0.219)
State-Specific Variables					
Traditionalist	−0.240 (0.213)	−0.240 (0.214)	−0.239 (0.213)	−0.225 (0.212)	−0.210 (0.211)
Governor congruence	−0.265 (0.296)	−0.235 (0.294)	−0.254 (0.295)	−0.526 (0.296)	−0.232 (0.297)
State legislature congruence	−0.032 (0.311)	−0.054 (0.309)	−0.025 (0.306)	−0.013 (0.306)	−0.004 (0.307)
State political opportunity structure	0.004 (0.003)	0.004[+] (0.003)	0.005[+] (0.003)	0.005[+] (0.003)	0.005[+] (0.003)
Local political opportunity structure	−0.0003 (0.0002)	−0.0003 (0.0002)	−0.0003 (0.0002)	−0.0003 (0.0002)	−0.0003 (0.0002)
Interactions					
Sex × children over eighteen		0.725* (0.362)	0.729* (0.361)	0.657[+] (0.359)	0.642[+] (0.361)
Qualifications × sex			−0.939[+] (0.558)	−0.279 (0.193)	−0.173 (0.184)
Low level × sex				−3.473[+] (2.091)	−0.884[+] (0.490)
Low level × qualifications					−0.135 (0.462)
Sex × qualifications × low-level					0.755 (0.594)
constant	1.598 (1.953)	2.056 (1.269)	2.235[+] (1.265)	2.398[+] (1.260)	2.211[+] (1.243)
N	865	865	865	865	865
Pseudo-R²	0.2261	0.2243	0.2216	0.2209	0.2181

[+] $p < 0.10$, * $p < 0.05$, ** $p < 0.01$

SELECTED
BIBLIOGRAPHY

Arceneaux, Kevin. 2001. "The 'Gender Gap' in State Legislative Representation: New Data to Tackle an Old Question." *Political Research Quarterly* 54, no. 1: 143–160.

Bafumi, Joseph, and Robert Y. Shapiro. 2009. "A New Partisan Voter." *Journal of Politics* 71, no. 1: 1–24.

Baiocchi, Gianpaolo, Elizabeth A. Bennett, Alissa Cordner, Peter Taylor Klein, and Stephanie Savell. 2014. *The Civic Imagination: Making a Difference in American Political Life*. Boulder, CO: Paradigm.

Bellah, Robert, Richard Madsen, William Sullivan, Ann Swindler, and Steven Tipton. 2008. *Habits of the Heart: Individualism and Commitment in American Life*. Berkeley: University of California Press.

Bernstein, Robert A. 1986. "Why Are There So Few Women in the House?" *Western Political Quarterly* 39, no. 1: 155–164.

Black, Gordon S. 1972. "A Theory of Political Ambition: Career Choices and the Role of Structural Incentives." *American Political Science Review* 66, no. 1: 144–159.

Bledsoe, Timothy, and Mary Herring. 1990. "Victims of Circumstances: Women in Pursuit of Political Office." *American Political Science Review* 84, no. 1: 213–223.

Bok, Derek. 2003. "Government Personnel Policy in Comparative Perspective." Pp. 255–272 in *For the People: Can We Fix Public Service?* Edited by John D. Nye and Joseph S. Nye Jr. Washington, DC: Brookings Institution.

Borrelli, Maryanne. 2002. *The President's Cabinet: Gender, Power, and Representation*. Boulder, CO: Lynne Rienner.

Bowling, Cynthia J., Christine A. Kelleher, Jennifer Jones, and Deil S. Wright. 2006. "Cracked Ceilings, Firmer Floors, and Weakening Walls: Trends and Patterns in Gender Representation among Executives Leading American State Agencies, 1970–2000." *Public Administration Review* 66, no. 6: 823–836.

Brehm, John, and Scott Gates. 1999. *Working, Shirking, and Sabotage: Bureaucratic Response to a Democratic Public*. Ann Arbor: University of Michigan Press.

Brooks, Deborah Jordan. 2010. "A Negativity Gap? Voter Gender, Attack Politics, and Participation in American Elections." *Politics and Gender* 6, no. 3: 319–341.

Brooks, Deborah Jordan, and John G. Geer. 2007. "Beyond Negativity: The Effects of Incivility on the Electorate." *American Journal of Political Science* 51, no. 1: 1–16.

Bullard, Angela M., and Deil S. Wright. 1993. "Circumventing the Glass Ceiling: Women Executives in American State Governments." *Public Administration Review* 53, no. 3: 189–202.

Burrell, Barbara C. 1994. *A Woman's Place Is in the House: Campaigning for Congress in the Feminist Era*. Ann Arbor: University of Michigan Press.

Byrnes, James P., David C. Miller, and William D. Schafer. 1999. "Gender Differences in Risk-Taking: A Meta-Analysis." *Psychological Bulletin* 125, no. 3: 367–383.

Calhoun, Craig. 1998. "The Public Good as a Social and Cultural Project." Pp. 20–35 in *Private Action and the Public Good*. Edited by Walter W. Powell and Elisabeth S. Clemens. New Haven, CT: Yale University Press.

Carman, H. G. 1958. "The Historical Development of Licensing for the Professions." *Journal of Teacher Education* 11, no. 2: 136–146.

Carroll, Susan J. 1984. "The Recruitment of Women for Cabinet-Level Posts in State Government: A Social Control Perspective." *Social Science Journal* 21, no. 1: 91–107.

———. 1985a. "Political Elites and Sex Differences in Political Ambition: A Reconsideration." *Journal of Politics* 47, no. 4: 1231–1243.

———. 1985b. *Women as Candidates in American Politics*. Bloomington: Indiana University Press.

———. 1986. "Women Appointed to the Carter Administration: More or Less Qualified?" *Polity* 18, no. 4: 696–706.

———. 1989. "The Personal Is Political: The Intersection of Private Lives and Public Roles among Women and Men in Elective and Appointive Office." *Women and Politics* 9, no. 2: 51–67.

———. 1994. *Women as Candidates in American Politics*. Bloomington: Indiana University Press.

Carroll, Susan J., and Kira Sanbonmatsu. 2013. *More Women Can Run*. New York: Oxford University Press.

Cassese, Erin C., and Mirya R. Holman. 2017. "Party and Gender Stereotypes in Campaign Attacks." *Political Behavior* 40, no. 3 (September): 785–807.

Cayer, N. Joseph, and Lee Sigelman. 1980. "Minorities and Women in State and Local Government: 1973–1975." *Public Administration Review* 40 (September–October): 994–1015.

Center for American Women in Politics (CAWP). 1983. *Women Appointed to State Government: A Comparison with All State Appointees*. New Brunswick, NJ: Rutgers, The State University of New Jersey Press.

———. 2013. "Women in State Legislatures 2013." New Brunswick, NJ: Rutgers, The State University of New Jersey Press.

———. 2018a. "Results: Women Candidates in the 2018 Elections." New Brunswick, NJ: Rutgers, The State University of New Jersey Press.

———. 2018b. "Results: Record Number of Women Elected to State Legislatures Nationwide." New Brunswick, NJ: Rutgers, The State University of New Jersey Press.

Center for Women in Government and Civil Society (CWGCS). 2008. "Appointed Policy Makers in State Government: Glass Ceiling in Gubernatorial Appointments, 1997–2007." Albany, NY: State University of New York Press.

China Global Television Network America. 2017. "Elaine Chao on Her Decision to Return to Public Service." January 19, 2017.

Commission on Presidential Debates. 2012. General Election Presidential Debate.

Congressional Research Service. 2018. "Membership of the 115th Congress: A Profile." Washington, DC: Congressional Research Service Press.

Coontz, Stephanie. 2012. "The Myth of Male Decline." *New York Times*, September 29, 2012.

Costantini, Edmond. 1990. "Political Women and Political Ambition: Closing the Gender Gap." *American Journal of Political Science* 34, no. 3: 741–770.

Costantini, Edmond, and Kenneth H. Craik. 1972. "Women as Politicians: The Social Background, Personality, and Political Careers of Female Party Leaders." *Journal of Social Issues* 28, no. 2: 217–236.

Council of State Governments. 2014. *The Book of States*. Lexington, KY: American Legislators Association.

Craig, Stephen C. 1993. *Malevolent Leaders: Popular Discontent in America*. Boulder, CO: Westview.

Crowder-Meyer, Melody. 2010. *Local Parties, Local Candidates, and Women's Representation: How County Parties Affect Who Runs for and Wins Political Office*. PhD diss., Princeton University, Princeton, NJ.

———. 2013. "Gendered Recruitment without Trying: How Local Party Recruiters Affect Women's Representation." *Politics and Gender* 9, no. 4: 390–413.

Darcy, Robert, and Sarah Slavin Schramm. 1977. "When Women Run against Men." *Public Opinion Quarterly* 41, no. 1: 1–12.

Darcy, Robert, Susan Welch, and Janet Clark. 1994. *Women, Elections, and Representation*. New York: Longman.

Deckman, Melissa. 2016. *Tea Party Women: Mama Grizzlies, Grassroots Leaders, and the Changing Face of the American Right*. New York: New York University Press.

Diamond, Irene. 1977. *Sex Roles in the State House*. New Haven, CT: Yale University Press.

Dolan, Julie. 2000a. "The Senior Executive Service: Gender Attitudes and Representative Bureaucracy." *Journal of Public Administration Research and Theory* 10, no. 3: 513–529.

———. 2000b. "Influencing Policy at the Top of the Federal Bureaucracy: A Comparison of Career and Political Senior Executives." *Public Administration Review* 60, no. 6: 573–581.

———. 2004. "Gender Equity: Illusion of Reality for Women in the Federal Executive Service?" *Public Administration Review* 64, no. 3: 299–306.

Dolan, Kathleen. 2004. *Voting for Women*. Boulder, CO: Westview.

———. 2008. "Women as Candidates in American Politics." Pp. 110–127 in *Political Women and American Democracy*. Edited by Christina Wolbrecht, Karen Beckwith, and Lisa Baldez. New York: Cambridge University Press.

———. 2014. *When Does Gender Matter?* New York: Oxford University Press.

Dolan, Kathleen, and Lynne Ford. 1997. "Change and Continuity among Women State Legislators: Evidence from Three Decades." *Political Research Quarterly* 50, no. 1: 137–151.

Dubeck, Paula J. 1976. "Women and Access to Political Office: A Comparison of Female and Male State Legislators." *Sociological Quarterly* 17, no. 1: 42–52.

Ekstrand, Laurie E., and William A. Eckert. 1981. "The Impact of Candidate's Sex on Voter Choice." *Western Political Quarterly* 34, no. 1: 78–87.

Elazar, Daniel J. 1966. *American Federalism: A View from the States*. New York: Thomas Crowell.

Epstein, Michael, Richard G. Niemi, and Lynda W. Powell. 2005. "Do Women and Men State Legislators Differ?" Pp. 94–109 in *Women and Elective Office: Past, Present, and Future*. Edited by Sue Thomas and Clyde Wilcox. New York: Oxford University Press.

Fiorina, Morris P., and Samuel J. Abrams. 2008. "Political Polarization in the American Public." *Annual Review of Political Science* 11: 563–588.

Flammang, Janet A. 1985. "Female Officials in the Feminist Capital: The Case of Santa Clara County." *Western Political Science Quarterly* 38, no. 1: 94–118.

Fox, Richard L., and Jennifer L. Lawless. 2010. "If Only They'd Ask: Gender, Recruitment, and Political Ambition." *Journal of Politics* 72, no. 2: 310–326.

———. 2011. "Gaining and Losing Interest in Running for Public Office: The Concept of Dynamic Political Ambition." *Journal of Politics* 73, no. 2: 443–462.

———. 2014. "Uncovering the Origins of the Gender Gap in Political Ambition." *American Political Science Review* 108, no. 3: 499–519.

Fox, Richard L., and Zoe M. Oxley. 2003. "Gender Stereotyping in State Executive Elections: Candidate Selection and Success." *Journal of Politics* 65, no. 3: 833–850.

Frederick, Angela. 2013. "Bringing Narrative In: Race-Gender Storytelling, Political Ambition, and Women's Paths to Public Office." *Journal of Women, Politics, and Policy* 34, no. 2: 113–137.

Fridkin Kahn, Kim, and Patrick J. Kenney. 1999. "Do Negative Campaigns Mobilize or Suppress Turnout? Clarifying the Relationship between Negativity and Participation." *American Political Science Review* 93, no. 4: 877–889.

———. 2011. "Variability in Citizens' Reactions to Different Types of Negative Campaigns." *American Journal of Political Science* 55, no. 2: 307–325.

Fulton, Sarah A., Cherie D. Maestas, L. Sandy Maisel, and Walter J. Stone. 2006. "The Sense of a Woman: Gender, Ambition, and the Decision to Run for Congress." *Political Research Quarterly* 50, no. 2: 235–248.

Gilmour, John B., and David E. Lewis. 2006. "Political Appointees and the Competence of Federal Program Management." *American Politics Research* 34, no. 1: 22–50.

Gneezy, Uri, Muriel Niederle, and Aldo Rustichini. 2003. "Performance in Competitive Environments: Gender Differences." *Quarterly Journal of Economics* 118, no. 3: 1049–1074.

Gross, Stanley J. 1984. *Of Foxes and Hen Houses: Licensing and the Health Professions.* Westport, CT: Praeger.

Hartig, Hannah. 2018. "Few Americans See Nation's Political Debate as 'Respectful.'" Washington, DC: Pew Research Center.

Heclo, Hugh. 1977. *A Government of Strangers.* Washington, DC: Brookings Institution.

Hegewisch, A., J. Liepmann, J. Hayes, and H. Hartmann. 2010. *Separate and Not Equal? Gender Segregation in the Labor Market and the Gender Wage Gap.* Washington, DC: Institute for Women's Policy Research.

Herbert, Steve. 2005. "The Trapdoor of Community." *Annals of the Association of American Geographers* 95, no. 4: 850–865.

Herrick, Rebekah, and Michael K. Moore. 1993. "Political Ambition's Effect on Legislative Behavior: Schlesinger's Typology Reconsidered and Revisited." *Journal of Politics* 55, no. 3: 765–776.

Hill, David B. 1981. "Political Culture and Female Political Representation." *Journal of Politics* 43, no. 1: 159–168.

Hogan, Robert E. 2001. "The Influence of State and District Conditions on the Representation of Women in US State Legislatures." *American Politics Research* 29, no. 1: 4–24.

Illinois Advisory Board for Services for Persons Who Are Deaf-Blind (IABDB). 2014. "About IABDB." http://www.bemyvoice.com/about.html.

Illinois Department of Natural Resources. 2014. "Illinois Nature Preserves Commission: Defense Programs." http://dnr.state.il.us/INPC/defense.htm.

Illinois Office of Executive Appointments. 2014. "Real Estate Administration and Disciplinary Board." http://appointments.illinois.gov/appointmentsDetail.cfm?id=235.

Iowa Boards and Commissions. 2018. https://openup.iowa.gov/board.

Jensen, Jennifer M., and Wendy L. Martinek. 2009. "The Effects of Race and Gender on the Judicial Ambitions of State Trial Court Judges." *Political Research Quarterly* 62, no. 2: 379–392.

Kaid, Lynda Lee, and Christina Holtz-Bacha. 2000. "Gender Reactions to TV Political Broadcasts: A Multicountry Comparison." *Harvard International Journal of Press/Politics* 5, no. 2: 17–29.

Keane, John. 2009. *The Life and Death of Democracy*. New York: Norton.

Kelly, Rita Mae, Mary E. Guy, Jane Bayes, Georgia Duerst-Lahti, Lois L. Duke, Mary M. Hale, Cathy Johnson, Amal Kawar, and Jeanie R. Stanley. 1991. "Public Managers in the States: A Comparison of Career Advancement by Sex." *Public Administration Review* 51, no. 5: 402–412.

King, James D., and Jason B. McConnell. 2003. "The Effect of Negative Campaign Advertising on Vote Choice: The Mediating Influence of Gender." *Social Science Quarterly* 84, no. 4: 843–857.

Kirkpatrick, Jeane. 1974. *Political Woman*. New York: Basic Books.

Kling, Kristen C., Janet Hyde, Carolin Showers, and Brenda N. Buswell. 1999. "Gender Differences in Self-Esteem: A Meta-Analysis." *Psychological Bulletin* 125, no. 4: 470–500.

Lawless, Jennifer L. 2012. *Becoming a Candidate*. New York: Cambridge University Press.

Lawless, Jennifer L., and Richard L. Fox. 2005. *It Takes a Candidate: Why Women Don't Run for Office*. New York: Cambridge University Press.

———. 2010. *It Still Takes a Candidate*. New York: Cambridge University Press.

———. 2015. *Running from Office: Why Young Americans Are Turned Off to Politics*. New York: Oxford University Press.

Lee, Marcia Manning. 1976. "Why Few Women Hold Public Office: Democracy and Sexual Roles." *Political Science Quarterly* 91, no. 2: 297–314.

Levendusky, Matthew. 2009. *The Partisan Sort: How Liberals Became Democrats and Conservatives Became Republicans*. Chicago, IL: University of Chicago Press.

Lowi, Theodore J. 1972. "Four Systems of Policy, Politics, and Choice." *Public Administration Review* 32, no. 4: 298–310.

Macedo, Stephen. 2005. *Democracy at Risk: How Political Choices Undermine Citizen Participation, and What We Can Do about It*. Washington, DC: Brookings Institution.

MacManus, Susan, and Charles S. Bullock III. 1994. "Electing Women to Local Office." Pp. 155–177 in *Gender in Urban Research*. Edited by Judith A. Garber and Robyne S. Turner. Thousand Oaks, CA: Sage.

Maestas, Cherie. 2000. "Professional Legislatures and Ambitious Politicians: Policy Responsiveness of State Institutions." *Legislative Studies Quarterly* 25, no. 4: 663–690.

Mahoney, John. 2018. "2018 Legislator Compensation Information." Denver, CO: National Council of State Legislatures.

Martin, Janet M. 1989. "The Recruitment of Women to Cabinet and Subcabinet Posts." *Western Political Science Quarterly* 42, no. 1: 161–172.

Michaels, Judith. 1997. *The President's Call*. Pittsburgh, PA: University of Pittsburgh Press.

Mitchell, Jerry. 1997. "Representation in Government Boards and Commissions." *Public Administration Review* 57, no. 2: 160–167.

Moore, Perry, and Mary Ellen Mazey. 1980. "Minorities and Women in State and Local Government: 1973–1980." *Journal of Urban Affairs* 8, no. 3: 1–13.

Moore, Robert G. 2005. "Religion, Race, and Gender Differences in Political Ambition." *Politics and Gender* 1, no. 4: 577–596.

National Bankruptcy Review Commission. 1997. http://govinfo.library.unt.edu/nbrc/.

National Council of State Legislatures. 2014. "Full- and Part-Time Legislatures." http://www.ncsl.org/.

Nechemias, C. 1987. "Changes in the Election of Women to the U.S. State Legislative Seats." *Legislative Studies Quarterly* 12, no. 1: 125–142.

Newman, Jody. 1994. "Perception and Reality: A Study Comparing the Success of Men and Women Candidates." Report for the National Women's Political Caucus.

Newman, Meredith Ann. 1994. "Gender and Lowi's Thesis: Implications for Career Advancement." *Public Administration Review* 54, no. 3: 277–284.

Niederle, Muriel, and Lise Vesterlund. 2007. "Do Women Shy Away from Competition? Do Men Compete Too Much?" *Quarterly Journal of Economics* 122, no. 3: 1067–1101.

———. 2010. "Explaining the Gender Gap in Math Test Scores: The Role of Competition." *Journal of Economic Perspectives* 24, no. 2: 129–144.

———. 2011. "Gender and Competition." *Annual Review of Economics* 3, no. 1: 601–630.

Niven, David. 1998. "Party Elites and Women Candidates: The Shape of Bias." *Women and Politics* 19, no. 2: 57–80.

———. 2006. "Throwing Your Hat out of the Ring: Negative Recruitment and the Gender Imbalance in State Legislative Candidacy." *Politics and Gender* 2, no. 4: 473–489.

Norrander, Barbara, and Clyde Wilcox. 2005. "Change and Continuity in the Geography of Women State Legislators." Pp. 176–196 in *Women and Elective Office: Past, Present, and Future*. Edited by Sue Thomas and Clyde Wilcox. New York: Oxford University Press.

———. 2008. "The Gender Gap in Ideology." *Political Behavior* 30, no. 4: 503–523.

Norris, Pippa. 2011. *Democratic Deficit: Critical Citizens Revisited*. Cambridge, UK: Cambridge University Press.

Offe, Claus. 2006. "Political Disaffection as an Outcome of Institutional Practices? Some Post-Tocquevillian Speculations." Pp. 23–45 in *Political Disaffection in Contemporary Democracies*. Edited by Mariano Torcal and J. R. Montero. London: Routledge.

Ors, Evren, Frédéïric Palomino, and Eloïc Peyrache. 2013. "Performance Gender Gap: Does Competition Matter?" *Journal of Labor Economics* 31, no. 3: 443–499.

Oxley, Zoe, and Richard Fox. 2004. "Women in Executive Office: Variation across American States." *Political Research Quarterly* 57, no. 1: 113–120.

Palmer, Barbara, and Dennis Simon. 2003. "Political Ambition and Women in the U.S. House of Representatives, 1916–2000." *Political Research Quarterly* 56, no. 2: 127–138.

———. 2006. *Breaking the Political Glass Ceiling: Women and Congressional Elections*. 2nd ed. New York: Routledge.

Pfiffner, James P. 1987. "Nine Enemies and One Ingrate: Political Appointments during Presidential Transitions." Pp. 141–155 in *The In-and-Outers*. Edited by G. Calvin Mackenzie. Baltimore, MD: Johns Hopkins University Press.

———. 2001. "Presidential Appointments: Recruiting Executive Branch Leaders." Pp. 50–80 in *Innocent until Nominated*. Edited by G. Calvin Mackenzie. Washington, DC: Brookings Institution.

Pharr, Susan, and Robert Putnam, eds. 2000. *Disaffected Democracies: What's Troubling the Trilateral Countries?* Princeton, NJ: Princeton University Press.

Preece, Jessica Robinson, Olga Bogach Stoddard, and Rachel Fisher. 2016. "Run, Jane, Run! Gendered Responses to Political Party Recruitment." *Political Behavior* 38, no. 3: 561–577.

Pruysers, Scott, and Julie Blais. 2018a. "A Little Encouragement Goes a (Not So) Long Way: An Experiment to Increase Political Ambition." *Journal of Women, Politics, and Policy* 39, no. 3: 384–395.

———. 2018b. "Narcissistic Women and Cash-Strapped Men: Who Can Be Encouraged to Consider Running for Political Office, and Who Should Do the Encouraging?" *Political Research Quarterly* 69, no. 4 (July) 842–851..

Putnam, Robert. 1995. "Robert Putnam Responds." *American Prospect* 25: 26–28.

Reed, W. Robert, and D. Eric Schansberg. 1995. "The House under Term Limits: What Would It Look Like?" *Social Science Quarterly* 76, no. 4: 699–716.

Reid, Margaret, Will Miller, and Brinck Kerr. 2003. *Glass Walls and Glass Ceilings: Women's Representation in State and Municipal Bureaucracies.* Westport, CT: Praeger.

———. 2004. "Sex-Based Glass Ceilings in U.S. State-Level Bureaucracies, 1987–1997." *Administration and Society* 36, no. 4: 377–405.

Riccucci, Norma M. 2009. "The Pursuit of Social Equity in the Federal Government: A Road Less-Traveled?" *Public Administration Review* 69, no. 3: 373–382.

Riccucci, Norma M., and Judith R. Saidel. 2001. "The Demographics of Gubernatorial Appointees: Toward an Explanation of Variation." *Policy Studies Journal* 29, no. 1: 11–22.

Rohde, David W. 1979. "Risk-Bearing and Progressive Ambition: The Case of Members of the United States House of Representatives." *American Journal of Political Science* 23, no. 1: 1–26.

Rosenthal, Cindy Simon. 1995. "The Role of Gender in Descriptive Representation." *Political Research Quarterly* 48, no. 3: 599–611.

Rule, Wilma. 1981. "Why Women Don't Run: The Critical Contextual Factors in Women's Legislative Recruitment." *Western Political Quarterly* 34, no. 1: 60–77.

———. 1990. "Why More Women Are State Legislators. A Research Note." *Western Political Science Quarterly* 43, no. 2: 437–448.

Sanbonmatsu, Kira. 2002. "Gender Stereotypes and Vote Choice." *American Journal of Political Science* 46, no. 1: 20–34.

———. 2004. *Democrats, Republicans, and the Politics of Women's Place.* Ann Arbor: University of Michigan Press.

———. 2006. *Where Women Run: Gender and Party in the American States.* Ann Arbor: University of Michigan Press.

Sanbonmatsu, Kira, Susan J. Carroll, and Debbie Walsh. 2009. "Poised to Run: Women's Pathways to the State Legislature." Center for American Women and Politics, Rutgers, The State University of New Jersey Press.

Sapiro, Virginia. 1982. "Private Costs of Public Commitments or Public Costs of Private Commitments? Family Roles versus Political Ambition." *American Journal of Political Science* 26, no. 2: 265–279.

Schlesinger, Joseph. 1966. *Ambition and Politics.* Chicago, IL: Rand McNally.

Schneider, Saundra K. 1986. "The Policy Role of State Professional Licensing Agencies: Perceptions of Board Members." *Public Administration Quarterly* 9, no. 4: 414–433.

———. 1987. "Influences on State Professional Licensure Policy." *Public Administration Review* 47, no. 6: 479–484.

Shames, Shauna L. 2017. *Out of the Running: Why Millennials Reject Political Careers and Why It Matters.* New York: New York University Press.

Shimberg, Benjamin. 1982. *Occupational Licensing: A Public Perspective.* Princeton, NJ: Educational Testing Service.

Skocpol, Theda, and Vanessa Williams. 2016. *The Tea Party and the Remaking of Republican Conservatism.* New York: Oxford University Press.

Sneed, Bethany G. 2007. "Glass Walls in State Bureaucracies: Examining the Difference Departmental Function Can Make." *Public Administration Review* 67, no. 5: 880–891.

Squire, Peverill, and Gary Moncrief. 2015. *State Legislatures Today: Politics under the Domes.* Lanham, MD: Rowman and Littlefield.

Swinerton, E. Nelson. 1968. "Ambition and American State Executives." *Midwest Journal of Political Science* 12, no. 4: 538–549.

Thomas, Sue. 1994. *How Women Legislate.* New York: Oxford University Press.

Thompson, Joel A., and Gary F. Moncrief. 1993. "The Implications of Term Limits for Women and Minorities: Some Evidence from the States." *Social Science Quarterly* 74, no. 2: 300–309.

US Census Bureau. 2013. *U.S. Census Quick Facts.* Washington, DC: Government Printing Office.

Volgy, T. J., J. E. Schwartz, and H. Gottlieb. 1986. "Female Representation and the Quest for Resources: Feminist Activism and Electoral Success." *Social Science Quarterly* 67, no. 1: 156–168.

Warren, Elizabeth. 2014. *A Fighting Chance.* New York: Metropolitan.

Welch, Susan. 2008. "Commentary on 'Recruitment of Women to Public Office: A Discriminant Analysis 1978.'" *Political Research Quarterly* 61, no. 1: 29–31.

Werner, Emmy. 1966. "Women in Congress: 1917-1964." *Western Political Quarterly* 19, no. 1: 16–30.

Williams, Margaret S. 2008. "Ambition, Gender, and the Judiciary." *Political Research Quarterly* 61, no. 1: 68–78.

Windett, Jason Harold. 2011. "State Effects and the Emergence and Success of Female Gubernatorial Candidates." *State Politics and Policy Quarterly* 11, no. 4: 460–482.

Women's Campaign Forum (WCF). 2008. "Unlocking the Cabinet." www.wcfonline.org.

INDEX

Numbers in italics refer to pages with figures or tables.

Printed in the USA
CPSIA information can be obtained
at www.ICGtesting.com
LVHW050334041123
762996LV00003B/216